Drive to Five

How Lake Travis High School went from

football doormat to Texas dynasty

By Jay Plotkin and Max Thompson

Drive to Five

Please address inquiries to:
Plotkin Publishing
3301 Glen Rose Dr.
Austin, TX 78731
www.ltfootballbook.com

First Edition
August 2012

Cataloging-in-Publication Data

Plotkin, Jay/Thompson, Max
Drive to Five
ISBN: 978-0-9859311-0-0 Pbk
LOC Control number: 2012912969

Printed in the United States of America

Dedications

For my family and their selfless support, and the grandfather that's no longer here because he would have enjoyed it the most. - MT

For my wife. children and family with their constant support and encouragement, and you, Dad, taken much too soon, who only got the chance to see one game long ago. It got better. - JP

"Always be the best, my boy, the bravest, and hold your head up high above the others. Never disgrace the generation of your fathers."
Hippolochus to his son Glaucus
--The Iliad. Homer, translated by Fagles--Book 6, ln 247-249

Drive To Five:

How Lake Travis High School went

from football doormat to Texas dynasty

Contents

Appendices

Foreword

I admit that this entire surreal story snuck up on a lot of people, myself included, because it started out so innocently in such relative obscurity that positively no one would have dared dream as big as this became.

Who would ever have imagined that a school district with no buildings and no history and no real sense of itself and what it could become might take shape and evolve into one of the most impressive football programs in the high school history of the state of Texas?

That's what happened at Lake Travis, a 1980s offshoot from Austin's urban sprawl that had its origins in a breakoff from Dripping Springs and ultimately resulted in a heretofore undistinguished Cavaliers program that once lost 18 straight games but has now won an unprecedented five consecutive 4A state championships. And counting.

In their compelling book, "Drive to Five," Jay Plotkin and Max Thompson traced those roots back to their beginnings in the summer of 1981 and their meteoric climb into one of the state's most singular dynasties after a winless season as recently as 2002. They do a masterful job of story-telling of this magical run at the once-nondescript school on Ranch Road 620, recreating in depth the litany of coaching changes, extraordinary quarterbacks like three Big 12 products Todd Reesing, Garrett Gilbert and Michael Brewer and outstanding comebacks that emerged out of the hard work and inspired leadership of so many people.

In fact, the Cavaliers might have won even more games, had one resident Oliver Luck not left town for Houston with sixth-grade son Andrew in tow for a job with the Houston Dynamo soccer team. But Lake Travis more than made do with every other quarterback who went to Big 12 college campuses with Baker Mayfield set to duplicate those journeys.

Maybe now after this book, the tireless work and energy of athletic director Jack Moss and head coach Jeff Dicus in joining forces in 2003 and transforming a community that put a very low priority in football will be acknowledged in full. As Moss so simply put it to a skeptical school district, "We buy scoreboards for a reason."

We learn more of Dicus, who once dreamed of becoming the next Bobby Knight and who could be as polarizing as he was polished. We learn of Moss's unmatched focus and support and Dicus's offensive mind and how they took a program that had been 1-19 and had gone through five head coaches in 10 seasons and propped it up on the doorstep to history. They changed everything from fancier uniforms with the names sewn on the back to discipline and tougher practices that weren't for everyone. Dicus and Moss overcame near-disastrous turmoil at midseason when the coach may have come within days of handing in his resignation, combined with some extraordinary athletes to produce the school's first state championship in 2007 and forever changed a culture.

I don't think Dicus and Moss ever received the credit they're due. Not until now, did a balanced account of what transpired during the season when the coach considered quitting amidst concerns that the players might stage a walkout come to light. But winning – and new commitment to having fun – set Lake Travis on the right and irreversible path (even though Dicus would quit and head to Duncanville after hearing a sermon from my friend Randy Phillips at Promiseland West Church) with two more outstanding Cavalier head coaches in Chad Morris and Hank Carter and a whole lot of victories and championship rings to follow.

The two authors left no stone unturned and were not afraid to uncover any of the potentially divisive problems like meddling parents, lacking discipline and at times an illogical chain of command that threatened to undo a splintered vision.

They did countless interviews and research and did not gloss over the warts and infighting and delved into every facet of the rise of Lake Travis from the disappointing, initial year when the seniors were allowed to play every sport except football at Dripping Springs and many cynics, including a number on Lake Travis's own school board, weren't even interested in playing football.

In the spring of 1982, Lake Travis's first football coach, George Jackson, had gone before the board and made a request of 50 helmets. A female board member scoffed at the request and said, "There will never be 50 kids come out for football."

Three decades later, not only were scores more young Garrett Gilbert wannabes participating in football with the opening of a second middle school, but Lake Travis was trying to figure where to cram yet another state championship trophy.

At its beginnings, Lake Travis had no stadium and not even a practice field. In its earliest years, it even held its homecoming at nearby Leander. The school didn't even field an official varsity team until 1984, and Don Cowan figured to follow the success he had had at Thorndale and do the same at Lake Travis.

But there would be growing pains. At least two of Cowan's coaching assistants were custodians at the school. They had no athletic period at the school, and he would leave after three losing seasons and return to Thorndale where he would win a state championship.

Lake Travis is the new Westlake, and, in fact, copied the blueprint of the high school in the ultra-successful Eanes Independent School District just miles to the east. The population boom was moving further west, and Lake Travis would be there to capitalize on it.

Plotkin and Thompson team up to do a remarkable and comprehensive job of capturing Lake Travis' phenomenal story of how a number of dedicated coaches, players and administrators took a football program where kids had been more interested in how quickly they could get their boats off their trailers in the high school parking lot and into Lake Travis' cooling waters.

The lake kids from Lake Travis have become the state's latest link toward the champions of the past, and I think you will find it as mesmerizing a tale of dedication and commitment as I did. If you call yourself a fan of Texas high school football, this is a must-read for you this summer.

Kirk Bohls

Kirk Bohls is a long-time columnist for the *Austin American-Statesman*, where he's enjoyed a bird's-eye view of the best sporting events in Texas, the U.S. and the world. Many of us enjoy getting our sports week started each Monday with Bohls' weekly feature "Nine Things and One Crazy Prediction."

Prologue

Close your eyes and let your mind take you there. It's finally Friday. The final bell has rung, ending the school day. The final whistle has blown, ending the work day. It's time to go home. Another week has ended. Almost. For this is football season, and in the thousands of big cities and small towns across Texas, the real fun has yet to start.

Entire communities gather at the biggest place they can, the most majestic place they can: the local high school football stadium. There, they'll put differences aside and embrace the romantic notion of community pride (real or imagined), where every fan – whether they're at the game to watch the football, cheer the cheerleaders or dance along with the band – understands that this is life in Texas, and for four hours every Friday, the trials and tribulations of the local high school team will define each and every fan. They'll share it all: the glory and the heartbreak, the good and the bad, and sometimes even the ugly.

To reference Friday Night Lights (both generally and when specifically mentioning H.G. Bissinger's book) is to acknowledge a truth about football and its place as a vital organ in the body of Texas and its communities, alongside the Alamo and barbecue and oil and a few other things. If you get deep enough into a conversation about Texas high school football, the stories and opinions become less about the game and more about identity.

If you come from a football community in Texas, and where you're from represents the first window into who you are, then football has given you a branded identity for life. You came from East Texas? Ah yes, the land of the tall pines, the game's best athletes and some incredible tradition, as heartbreaking as some of it has been. You call West Texas home? Flat land, oil, endless drives and Midland and Odessa and MOJO. The kids from the valley? They're undersized, but they fight harder than anyone. The Coastal Bend? Calallen, Gregory Portland and Port Lavaca Calhoun will all be waiting for you in the playoffs. San Antonio has Converse Judson for old, gritty, jaw-rattling pride, and Cibolo Steele for new, gritty, jaw-rattling pride. Houston has Katy, the suburban boys who've cleaned up in the playoffs for two decades straight, and everyone trying to become the next Katy. Rich or poor, Dallas epitomizes the land of equal opportunity, where inner city teams such as Carter and Skyline have had powerhouse moments, and the suburbs are run by Southlake Carroll, Highland Park, a couple of schools from Denton and Aledo. And every once in a while, a school far from city lights has its moment under them in a big stadium in December. Celina, Sealy, Cuero, Stephenville, Brownwood: little towns immortalized in football lore, and remembered for little else. And that's fine by them. It's hard to imagine a community being more proud of any other accomplishment in this state than one tied to football.

Austin? It was the Reagan Raiders in the late '60s followed by a whole lot of nothing until Westlake emerged as a perennial power. The Chaparrals gave the city legitimacy for two decades, winning a title in 1996 behind Drew Brees, a quarterback who earned just one college scholarship offer before developing into a record-setting NFL MVP, and appearing in a few more championship games along the way. For the longest time, Westlake defined Austin football, Central Texas football. And then a funny thing happened. A team with its own lake further west of Austin went from doormat to king, changing the landscape in just a few short seasons.

The rest of this book illustrates how that happened. It's not a story about one season that changed everything, but the moments, drama and people that built the single greatest team accomplishment in the history of Texas – five straight football titles. It transformed what Lake Travis meant to the state, from an area known for hill country retreats to a hotbed of football power. Like all the places mentioned up above, the football identity now represents the greater currency.

That's because every community in Texas chases the dream. Every August, each of the 1,300 high schools across the state starts with one goal. In every interview with every player for this book, whether that player had suffered through a losing season or celebrated a state championship, the goal remained the same.

"Every year, you start with a goal of winning a state championship, even if you know you probably won't," former Lake Travis quarterback Michael Brewer said. "That's just how it is for schools in Texas."

Every team starts with the dream. The boys from Permian did. But this story isn't Bissinger's legendary tome and never could be. It took a bigger dream to get the team in a position to make its own dream a reality, especially at Lake Travis, where losing had been the norm, talent got lost in the wash, and a community lost all reason to believe. Now they believe they lived their own version of a movie, watching a Texas legend unfold in front of their eyes.

1: The Aftermath

The clock approaches midnight on an otherwise non-descript December Friday in Texas. But this isn't any ordinary Friday night. It is Texas State Football Championship Friday, and an entire community has happily endured the three-hour journey from the shores of Lake Travis, outside Austin, to Cowboys Stadium in Arlington. It is a spaceship of a football stadium erected in the spirit of the Colosseum of Rome, the true monument to the sport that matters most in this corner of the country. Thousands, from Lake Travis or otherwise, watch on TV sets at home.

The community stands as one under the glow of the bright lights and massive jumbotron and continue cheering as they have since kickoff occurred nearly four hours ago. Tears flow amongst prolonged victory shouts. They haven't just witnessed a state championship football game between their beloved Cavaliers and the Panthers from Midway High School, just outside Waco. They've witnessed Texas high school football history, and not just any Texas high school football history. With their hard-fought, well-earned 22-7 win, the Lake Travis Cavaliers – only nine seasons removed from a disastrous 0-10 campaign – become the first team in Texas history to win five consecutive state championships. Their 30 consecutive playoff wins also set a state record. This spaceship monument, with its storied ring of honor hovering above the field and vivid colors throughout, hadn't even been built when the drive to five titles began. The moment will live on for years to come, perhaps because there will never be another like it.

"No one can ever take what you accomplished tonight away from you," Lake Travis coach Hank Carter tells his players as they gather near the famous star marking the center of the Cowboys' field. "One day they will make a movie about what you've done."

Only two other schools that play 11-man football have managed to win four consecutive state titles. Sealy, a University Interscholastic League Conference 3A school that is little more than a dot on Interstate 10 on the way to Houston and home town of the legendary Eric Dickerson, won four straight titles from 1994-97. Celina, located north of Dallas, won four straight titles in Conference 2A from 1998-2001. Tiny Fort Hancock, which plays 6-man football, also won four straight titles from 1988-91 and reached the championship game in 1992 before falling. Storied Southlake Carroll, in suburban Dallas, also played in five consecutive title games, winning four between 2002 and 2006. The Dragons lost to Katy 16-15 in 2003 to miss out on a run of five straight Conference 5A titles. One unlucky break can derail years of progress toward the unimaginable.

There is a reason it hasn't been done before. This is the land of *Friday Night Lights,* and blasphemy aside, football is a religion in Texas. Town and tradition matter, and the greatest imprints left on the game are often as significant as any battle won fighting for the state's independence. The association of schools such as Permian and Celina with Texas is arguably as strong as legendary names Crockett and Bowie (both names of which adorn no less than six schools in Texas) with the state. Football matters to every town in Texas, more than 1,000 of them. The dream of a championship means everything to any team when it steps on the sweltering practice field in early August. Earning just one state title can be remarkably tough. The road to five consecutive titles is all but impossible, but here the Cavaliers stand.

The reasons for Lake Travis' historic accomplishment vary. Circumstances, attitude, resources, population growth and a few extremely talented players only scratch the surface. Football pundits long thought that the Lake Travis community could produce successful football, though it would take 30 years and a near-catastrophic two-year stretch that saw Lake Travis win just once in 20 games for the right people to put the right plan into place. No one in their wildest dreams, though, thought Lake Travis, which had only four winning seasons between 1984 and 2002, could become the school to summit the tallest mountain on this December night.

"It's just awesome what they're doing right now," said Jim Shewmake, who coached the Cavaliers from 1998-2000. "We felt when we first arrived there – we looked 10 years out and thought it would be an outstanding place. I never thought they'd win four or five state titles in a row, but I envisioned that within that window they would become perennial district champions and a perennial playoff team. Things have to go your way to win it all, but we really thought they'd be in the hunt for championships. With the growth that was coming and people who wanted to be there and do the right things, it really panned out. I'm pleased for the community."

Through the years, as success came to Lake Travis, the bar measuring that success rose. From simply winning games to winning district titles and now winning state titles, Lake Travis' most recent coaching staff began working on meeting that bar each day at practice. One difference between Lake Travis and other schools can be seen in a regular practice week. The

Cavaliers no longer spend a great deal of practice time game-planning for the opponent. While there remains some of that, identifying key tendencies and devising schemes to stop them, much of the focus remains on the Cavaliers themselves. Lake Travis improbably now plays to its own standard, and regardless of who takes the field opposite the Cavaliers any particular Friday, those wearing red and black believe that simply executing their plan, meeting their own standards, will result in a convincing victory. What's happened has been nothing short of remarkable. The standards that the coaches and players set and accepted, and the unwavering desire to meet and exceed those expectations at all costs, combined to drive a recently-lowly program to heights never previously achieved.

"We talk about the only team that can beat us we feel is Lake Travis," said Carter, who in 2011 had just finished his second year as the Cavaliers' head coach after spending two years coordinating the defense, where with his broad shoulders and strong chin he looks as if he could lead a goal-line stand as a linebacker. "As long as we go out and play our game and we don't make mistakes, then regardless of who we're playing, we're going to be fine."

Such was the case as the Cavaliers neared the pinnacle of their penultimate victory. As they prepared to take on Midway at the beginning of championship week, it became clear to any observer that the Cavaliers' success has not jaded the team; that the important moments remain worth working toward. Opportunity rose again, and the Cavaliers focused on making the most of it.

"That being said, the things we talk about the most, too, are we have an opportunity to win a state championship this year, and you can't say that every year," Carter said the Monday prior to the title game. "We've been able to say that lately, but that doesn't last forever. And so when we have an opportunity, let's make sure that we make the most of it. It's kind of cliché, but we don't want to have any regrets."

Standing with another championship trophy near the Cowboys' bright blue and silver star midfield, there are no regrets. A dream three decades in the making has come true five times over. Go back to the beginning, though, and it's hard to imagine the story winding up here.

2: From Drip with no love lost

The Lake Travis Independent School District celebrated its 30th anniversary in the fall of 2011. Growth and development have made Lake Travis a much different community than when school opened, even a much different place than a decade ago. Lake Travis opened its doors in 1981, but the district's origins stretch back even further, to the birth of its longest standing rivalry.

What later became Lake Travis ISD started out as part of a much larger Dripping Springs ISD, and by the 1970s, residents adjacent to Lake Travis' south shore had grown tired of the long commutes their children made each day to school. The major roads, including Ranch Road 620 through Lakeway, Texas 71 through Bee Cave and to a degree Ranch Road 12 from the Hamilton Pool area into Dripping Springs, weren't as stable as they are today. As Lake Travis' main road today, RR 620 didn't become a four-lane highway until the mid-1990s. It existed as a two-lane path crossing the Colorado River atop Mansfield Dam. The bridge, which moved traffic from atop the dam to alongside it, didn't open until 1995, and when it did, travel to and from Lake Travis became much easier.

Around 1980, urban sprawl had yet to find Lakeway and its surrounding communities. The area's older students, depending where along Lake Travis they lived, spent two hours on a school bus getting to school in what has become Dripping Springs proper. Growth has given Dripping Springs more of a small-town feel with Highway 290 as a main street featuring modern new commercial developments. In the 1970s, though, Dripping Springs existed a country town with no identifiable town center or easy way to access school campuses. Parents living close to the lake had seen enough, and in the early 1970s a group filed suit in district court to form their own school district closer to home, wishing to split from Dripping Springs ISD. The suit sat in district court, and Lake Travis residents continued to send their kids to Dripping Springs as they waited for word they feared would never come.

Word finally came, though, in the spring of 1981. Lake Travis' formation as a school district would happen quickly, changing many lives and all but ruining what had been a symbiotic relationship between communities. When George W. Jackson, a high school principal in the north Texas community of Clarksville, wanted to get back into coaching, he applied for and got a job at Dripping Springs. His wife planned on coming with him, and he had arranged for his new school to hold a teaching position for her. But when the courts approved Lake Travis residents' request to effectively secede from DSISD, things changed quickly.

Other than an old school room and a tax office where the odd administrator hung his hat, the newly-formed Lake Travis ISD had no school facilities. Jackson remembered that Lake Travis parents agreed that their students would continue to attend Dripping Springs schools until the new district could get facilities in place, but that idea didn't sit well with the Dripping Springs folks.

"The Lake Travis people wanted to give their seniors a chance to finish at Drip," Jackson said. "Well, the Dripping Springs people wanted the Lake Travis students to pay a fee to keep attending the school, and that created a lot of bad feelings back then for all the people involved. So, the Lake Travis people just decided to build their own schools."

Lake Travis' decision to open its doors for the 1981-82 school year forced change upon Dripping Springs, and the DSISD officials met almost nightly to deal with the change. Facing a drastically reduced student enrollment for the coming year, officials implemented a reduction in force. Jackson, who had taken a coaching job, still had a position, but the teaching job promised to his wife vanished.

Where one door closes, another opens. Jackson figured that if Lake Travis planned to open immediately and teach students in the 1981-82 school year, it needed teachers.

"I called over to the lake to see if they would interview my wife, and the person I spoke to, 'Aggie' was going to be a principal at LT starting the next school year," Jackson recalled. Dr. Ann "Aggie" Hall was set to be the principal at Lake Travis Elementary when the district opened, but her advice and guidance proved fruitful for the Jacksons. "She had come from Drip and knew the situation, and she wanted me to talk to the new superintendent – Dr. Frank Jennings."

Jennings, like Jackson, came to Austin for a job other than Lake Travis. Jennings had moved to Austin to pursue his doctorate at the University of Texas, and he had signed on as principal at a middle school in the South Austin community of Oak Hill, Jackson recalled. When the split occurred, Jennings applied for and got Lake Travis' new superintendent position.

That meant he had to accomplish a great deal, and quickly, since the district needed facilities and a staff to start the school year.

"They had two choices: pay per student to go to Dripping or get some buildings built and get the kids set up at the lake, so that's what they did," Jackson recalled.

Jennings went about beginning construction of classrooms, and others jumped in to their roles as well. In getting the district set up, Hall let Jackson know that Lake Travis would also need an athletic director and football coach, and she advised him to talk to Jennings about that upcoming opening.

"She told me that LT was going to need a coach/athletic director, and Dr. Jennings had a plan," Jackson recalled. "I went to talk to him, and he wanted to hire me but said I would have to cut all ties to DSISD due to the hard feelings. So I went back over there and sold them my contract back."

Once a part of the newly created Lake Travis ISD, Jackson's task became to get the athletics program off the ground. Because the district formed so late in the calendar, summer of 1981, there was no time to get football up and running for that first fall. The new Lake Travis students who had played football at Dripping Springs as juniors had nowhere to play as seniors. That became just one of the frustrations facing the new district. Before football could be considered, the district needed classrooms. That became the obvious priority.

"That first year, we started school late because the buildings weren't ready," Jackson recalled. "Dr. Jennings had decided to have people come in and build portables on site so they would be a little nicer. It was pretty hectic for a few years."

And despite the fact this is Texas where football is king, only a precious few people cared that Lake Travis wouldn't field a football team that first year. In fact, some in positions of power didn't care if Lake Travis ever fielded a football team.

"That whole mindset was new," Jackson said. "I had made football my dream. I had no idea why people didn't want football. You would think the way it is now that people always cared for football, but that wasn't the case. Back then it was just the opposite. Everybody thought their kids were going to go graduate from college, and they didn't want them to play football. We offered every sport but football that first year, and we were competitive in most sports, especially golf and tennis."

In future Lake Travis football coach Don Cowan's words, football didn't yet have the heart of the Lake Travis community.

"Football has been important to people at Lake Travis for a long time, but maybe it wasn't important to the right people," Cowan said.

At least one football skeptic got elected to the initial Lake Travis school board. Jackson recalled making his official presentation and budget request for football and being told in no uncertain terms that his plan was off-base.

"In the spring of 1982, a lot of people and most of them on the school board didn't want us to play football," Jackson said. "When I made my presentation to the school board about what we needed to do to get football started, I said I needed to order 50 helmets. One school board member, the only woman on the board at the time, stood up and said that, 'There will never be 50 kids come out for football.' I wonder where she is today and if anyone's taken her to see a game today."

Jackson laughed as he recalled a conversation with current Lake Travis coach Hank Carter at the district's 30th anniversary celebration in October 2011.

"When we came back for the 30th reunion, I couldn't believe what we saw," he said. "I think the current staff did a great job taking care of us. I got to speak at the team breakfast on Friday, and they didn't have to do that. I told the story about the school board member and the 50 helmets we needed, and everyone laughed. Then [Coach Carter] told me that morning he'd turned in an order for 93 replacement helmets."

Back in 1982, Jackson continued to lobby for football. He came to realize that if he didn't have the board's support, he had the parents' support, and even in 1982 it became clear that parents had the last, or at least the most influential, word when it came to district priorities.

"Anyway, one parent stood up and raised a fuss," Jackson said. "She said, 'We were told that if we went with the split that we'd have everything we had at Drip, and now you're going back on that.'"

The board eventually approved Jackson's football plan, and in 1982 Lake Travis finally joined the football culture. New schools don't play varsity football right away, at least not in the eyes of the University Interscholastic League, which oversees Texas' public high school sports. Until a new school has had time to accumulate enough student population to match up with schools with similar enrollments, new teams compete against other schools on the junior varsity level. And so that's how Lake Travis took the field in those early days. Despite not having a field to call home and an early environment that viewed football with disdain, the Cavaliers found success. Jackson's first team posted a 9-1 record. His second team went 7-3.

"We played anybody who would play us those first years," Jackson said. "Mostly we played 4A and 5A junior varsity teams. We didn't have our own practice or game field, so we had our homecoming at Leander. It turned out pretty good. It was amazing how those kids adapted to everything, especially for football. Our only loss was to Westwood's JV, and they had a quarterback who would go on to play at the University of Texas [Mark Murdock] and he was outstanding. I think we started a lot of freshmen that season. There were lots of good athletes and several good seniors. We just needed to fill in some voids with sophomores and juniors."

Lake Travis became an official varsity team in 1984. The Cavaliers went 5-5 playing Conference 2A opponents, and that became Jackson's final year as the team's coach. He saw the future and surmised that the school faced a potential rough patch on the gridiron. The school district had begun to grow, and the biannual UIL realignment meant stepping up in class to Conference 3A. With his concentration split between coach and athletic director, he decided it would be better for the district if someone else took over the football program.

"We needed somebody who could help us go up in classification [to 3A] and it looked like we were going to have a few lean years," Jackson said. "We had been scrimmaging Don Cowan's teams when he was up in Thorndale, and in 1985 in the spring he had decided to move up and coach Groveton, which was a strong 2A team."

"That was a strange deal," Cowan explained. "I had been at Thorndale and had been successful there. Then I took a job at Groveton, which had just won the 2A title. I took the job and spent a few weeks up there, and it just didn't feel right. I resigned. I didn't have a job, and I had gotten to be friends with George Jackson. He told me he was hiring a coach."

Cowan liked Lake Travis' potential. The school district appeared prime for a population boom, and officials and parents alike had taken note of the successful Eanes ISD, which sat just off Lake Travis' eastern border. EISD, with its Westlake High School, had found both academic and athletic excellence, and Lake Travis officials viewed that as a blueprint to their own success. Cowan agreed, though he'd find that Lake Travis struggled in its infancy to duplicate Eanes' success.

"Everyone then felt Lake Travis was going to become another Westlake, and I guess it finally has," Cowan said later. "I was excited."

But Lake Travis in 1985 didn't compare to Eanes, and wouldn't for quite some time. Where Westlake High School forged ahead and became the premier athletic and academic high school in Central Texas, Lake Travis still needed to grow into itself. On the gridiron, Cowan inherited a small group of players who would make the leap from 2A to 3A. He also inherited a program that had yet to take steps to put itself on par with other school districts in terms of supporting athletics alongside academics.

18

"I had two coaches on the staff who were custodians and maintenance people," Cowan said. "We had no athletic period at the high school or junior high level. It was very similar to being at a private school. There was no priority placed on being good at football. The parents of players wanted us to be good, but that was about it."

Thanks to an unexpected influx of newcomers, Lake Travis posted a 7-3 mark in 1985, which stood as the school's high-water mark through the 1990s and into the mid-2000s.

"We had some success," he said. "That first year we went 7-3 with lots of kids who had moved in. We had 12 kids show up in 1985 who we'd never seen before. We had someone move from Arizona, another from Round Rock, another from Westwood, some really good players. We only had them that one year. We were fairly competitive the last few years, too. We weren't getting blown out. I remember us playing a pretty good Copperas Cove team and they beat us 38-13 or something…that may have been the worst beating."

Worse beatings would come as Lake Travis continued to concentrate on its academic development, often at the expense of its athletic development. Off the field, the students shined. Academics became the priority, and no one says a school district shouldn't concentrate on making its academic programs the best they can be, even in football-loving Texas. Jack Moss, who would become the school's athletic director in 2003, believes athletics should also be a significant part of what school districts offer their students.

"Philosophically, everything in school that is provided [for the students] should have a direct tie to the educational process," Moss explained. "If not, then it doesn't serve a purpose."

In the 1980s and 1990s, Lake Travis offered athletics and found success in certain sports, but if school officials didn't lack a purpose for athletics, they never seemed to give it the same attention or chance to succeed as other districts did. Lake Travis still had plenty of facilities to build, ranging from classrooms to an administration building. Today, Lake Travis' administration building remains one of the district's most iconic structures: a two-story complex adjacent to the high school with views that reach downtown Austin.

When district officials did turn their attention to athletics, and football in particular, they didn't like what they saw. After three losing seasons, Cowan took the blame, and the ax. Guy Clayton earned all-state honors as a basketball player at the school, graduating in the early 1990s. Today he's a member of the Lake Travis community as a businessman, parent and member of the Lake Travis ISD Board of Trustees. He recalled Cowan's ouster and said the coach bore the blame for a problem no one could fix.

"People wanted to put all the blame on him, they thought he couldn't coach because we didn't win enough," Clayton said. "But he went up the road to Thorndale and won two state titles. I guess it wasn't him."

Cowan harbors no hard feelings about his exit. In fact, the big picture at the time told him that he should have gotten out on his own earlier.

"The priority was always on academics," he said. "At the good schools – Westlake, Southlake Carroll – they excel at everything they do, football, One Act Play, everything, and Lake Travis is doing that now. We just weren't in a position to do those things. It wasn't my choice to leave Lake Travis, but I needed to leave when I did. It worked out well. Seeing how everything was going there, I needed to leave after that first year. We were moving up [in classification] and we had no foundation to make the program better, and I couldn't see where we would have that in the near future. Down the road it was going to be tough. I don't regret having been there for four years. I enjoyed it and it made me a better coach. I feel good about the time I spent there."

Cowan returned to Thorndale and won a state championship. Lake Travis continued to struggle. While the occasional season proved promising, only three managed to bring Lake Travis to the cusp of success: a spot in the Texas high school football playoffs.

During Clayton's high school tenure, the team won 10 out of 40 games despite sending quarterback Rob Walker to UCLA. Despite playing in an offense that coach Roy Farmer once told the *Los Angeles Times* "dropped 35-40 passes when he was a senior," Walker became Lake Travis' first major college recruit. He'd start seven games for UCLA over three seasons before getting into coaching. He spent 2011 as the offensive coordinator at Jersey Village High School outside of Houston.

Part of the problem Walker faced, Clayton said, stemmed from some of the school's best athletes never stepping foot on the high school field.

"I played football in middle school, but when we got to high school I didn't and that was partly because we weren't good," he said. "I know at least five or six guys who were the best athletes at the school, but we didn't play football. We just played basketball."

Clayton's basketball teams found success. A 6-foot-2 guard gifted with a deft shooting touch and quick hands honed on the tennis courts, he became an all-state performer who'd earn a scholarship to Texas Tech after leading the Cavaliers on a playoff run that showed him fans would come out to support a winner. Clayton also stood out on the tennis courts, winning a Conference 3A state doubles championship at Lake Travis.

"The community didn't really think about football," he recalled. "It takes a winner, but nobody was talking about football. I remember when I was playing basketball, we started winning and people started packing the house. And those people travelled with us. All you have to do is win and people start coming out of the woodwork. It was pretty cool for us."

Football, though, remained on everyone's periphery. Farmer's teams struggled, posting a 10-30 record from 1989-92. Mark Ball got the next crack at coaching, and after two seasons that produced a 5-14-1 mark, the district again changed coaches, promoting defensive coordinator Keith Tuck into the head spot. Tuck had come to Lake Travis from the much larger Humble High School, and he personified the image of a Texas high school football coach. A massive man whose ever-present goatee only enhanced his intensity on the field, Tuck inherited a program, and a community, still needing an identity as well as modern amenities. The school's antiquated facilities hardly reflected the beauty in the surrounding countryside.

"Obviously, even back then, when you drove up to the campus, it was just gorgeous," Tuck recalled. "The setting was very picturesque as it is now. The facilities were lacking at the time. Our weight room that we inherited was very small and had some obsolete equipment. That was one of our first main goals, to expand the weight room and get up to date, nice equipment. We started holding lift-a-thons to accomplish that, and we raised every penny that went into that weight room."

The lift-a-thons became the football program's first community outreach efforts, and they worked. The fundraisers helped step the program along toward stability, and a core group of leaders helped the team emerge from years of struggle. Tuck's first year enjoyed quite the reversal of fortune. Led by seniors John Gurasich, Adam Van Ackeren, Travis McAshan and Darren Ferris and junior Ben Reid, the Cavaliers packed a punch. Gurasich would earn a scholarship to the University of Hawaii. McAshan became an all-American runner at Texas A&M, and Reid would eventually become Lake Travis' first all-state football selection before moving on to play at Angelo State. They formed the nucleus of a team that coaches felt had the best chance of making the playoffs for the first time, and it showed on the field.

That group also made an impression on a middle schooler who would later follow in their footsteps. Young Greg Wiggins, then an athletic eighth grader, fancied himself a high school quarterback, and he spent as much time as he could around the high school players on game days, travelling on the bus and serving as a ball boy on the sidelines.

"I idolized John Gurasich, Adam Van Ackeren, Ben Reid, all those guys," Wiggins said. "I can remember riding on the bus to and from away games. To me, those 17, 18-year old guys were grown men. Seeing the way that Tuck and [assistant coach Phil Pettey] dealt with them, I thought that was just a whole other world from [Ryan] Ledford and Brian Taylor at the middle school. I think I was in 7th grade then. Frank Pugsley. I just remember thinking those guys were giant. Strongest guys, fastest guys you'd ever seen. And they were good. Gurasich's senior year, Ben's junior year, they were good."

Those Cavaliers got out to a fast start, beating Wimberely 28-6, marking the first time Lake Travis had won its season-opener as a varsity program. Wins over Del Valle, San Antonio Cole, San Saba and Ingram Moore followed, and just like that the Cavaliers entered district play undefeated. When running back Seth Breazeale scored a late touchdown to give the Cavaliers a come-from-behind win over Brady to open District 25-3A play, Lake Travis faced the most significant game in its 13-year existence. The Cavaliers travelled to face Dripping Springs, the school from whence it came where feelings still ran plenty hard. The schools had become bitter rivals.

The Cavaliers entered the game expecting big things. In the 11 years the teams had played, the Tigers dominated the series, 9-2. The Cavaliers had won in 1993 by a 34-0 score to end a six-game skid, but in 1994 the Tigers restored order with a 43-0 blanking. As the 1995 meeting – both teams entered the game unbeaten – approached, the Tigers wanted nothing more than to keep on beating little Lake Travis. Tuck's Cavaliers saw the game as the chance to make a statement. A win would surely send them on the path to the school's first playoff berth. A loss wouldn't be devastating, but it would make the road to the playoffs a bit longer, without any margin for error.

The game started promisingly for Lake Travis, but by halftime the Tigers had edged ahead. Trailing 18-9, the Cavaliers began their comeback. Gurasich, with his strong arm and active feet, drove his offense across midfield, and Reid did the damage with a 30-yard touchdown run, closing the gap to 18-16. Midway through the final quarter, Lake Travis had a chance to take the lead, having driven from its own three-yard line out to the 30 before disaster struck. The Tigers blitzed Gurasich, sacking him, forcing and recovering a fumble. They added a late touchdown for the final margin, handing the Cavaliers a heartbreaking 24-16 loss.

Lake Travis never fully recovered. Llano blanked the Cavaliers 32-0 the following week, and though the Cavaliers bounced back to defeat Liberty Hill 35-7 and even their district record at 2-2, their fate had been sealed heading into the season's final week when Burnet came calling. Even a win wouldn't put the Cavaliers in the playoffs. Burnet got off to a fast start and never looked back, clinching the district title with a 36-23 win.

Despite the season-ending loss and the bitter pill of the continued post-season break, the team had finished with its best 3A record, 7-3, its first winning season at that level. With Reid coming back to anchor the offense along with some standout linemen, Tuck had reason to believe that 1996

22

would be the year the Cavaliers finally broke through and reached the playoffs. But injuries defined that season, and Lake Travis struggled to gain momentum early.

"[In 1995], we went 7-3 but all of our losses came in district so we didn't make the playoffs," assistant coach Kevin Halfmann said. "But that was a great group of seniors. It was John Gurasich, Darren Ferris, Adam Van Ackeren. They were a good group of kids, but there wasn't that many of them, so we had some success but whenever they left, the leadership fell off and we were right back where we were. We were awful the next year."

Awful might be too harsh an adjective, but then again Halfmann speaks with recent history as a backdrop, and these days anything short of a long playoff run constitutes awful. Given its history to that point, knocking on the door to the playoff party qualified as a good season.

The 1996 season started slowly. Lake Travis stood 1-3-1 after five games, and Tuck felt he needed to make a change at quarterback. Wiggins, then a freshman, had made his way to the high school and found success as the junior varsity quarterback. What he lacked in experience he more than made up for in the tangibles coaches look for in quarterbacks. Approaching 6-foot-3 on his sturdy, athletic frame, Wiggins had displayed a strong, accurate right arm and plenty of athletic ability. He'd also start on Lake Travis' basketball team for three years and also played baseball as a freshman. But he didn't think he'd play on the varsity that year. Midway through the season, though, Tuck had other ideas and wanted to make sure the freshman could handle the jump.

"Tuck called my dad before he even told me to ask my dad whether or not he'd be good with it," Wiggins said in 2012. "Pop said, yeah, sure, so Tuck calls me in."

Even as a freshman, Wiggins recognized the atmosphere surrounding the athletic department at the time. Opinionated parents hadn't been shy about sharing their thoughts, and while he couldn't know at the time the extent of the parental involvement, looking back, Wiggins saw how Tuck's decision to insert him at quarterback extended beyond the white lines.

"Tuck's replacing the booster club president's son, who's a senior, with a freshman," Wiggins recalled. "He knew immediately he wasn't going to make any friends with that decision. But you've got a kid who can't drive and doesn't shave with 18-year-olds and it's a totally different world."

Tuck had plenty of friends. He wanted to win games, and he felt Wiggins, age aside, gave the team its best chance. So into the lineup he went. While Wiggins would develop into an all-district quarterback later in his career and played well in spots that year, he remained a freshman making the quick adjustment to varsity football, and it showed.

"First game was Dripping Springs at Drip," the quarterback said. "I threw an interception on my first pass. I can still remember Rhett Eickenloff. He was a linebacker for Dripping Springs. Some guy hit me low and he hit me high and I did a back flip. I look over and all I see is Tuck screaming , 'Get up, get up.' I was thinking damn, this is varsity football, huh?"

Another slow start to district play haunted the Cavaliers. Only two teams qualified for the playoffs then, and teams could ill afford to play without room for error, especially teams with a freshman quarterback. With Reid nursing a sprained ankle, the Cavaliers couldn't keep up with Dripping Springs and dropped a 45-3 decision. A second loss followed against Burnet, putting the Cavaliers in the all-too-familiar position of having to win their final three games to earn the school's first playoff berth.

The Cavaliers gave it a run. Protected by mammoths such as Jake Stoetzner and Dustin Wuest, Wiggins figured out how to pass effectively enough to keep the running lanes clear for Reid. The Cavaliers downed Wimberley and then used a nifty lineup tweak to win against a pass-first Liberty Hill team. For certain plays in the game, Tuck had Reid switch places in the team's I-formation with fullback Travis Mayo. With the Panthers keying on the tailback, Reid rushed for 180 yards and three touchdowns from the fullback spot, keeping the Cavaliers' playoff hopes alive.

To make that first playoff dream become a reality, all the Cavaliers had to do was upset upbeaten Llano, which featured future NFL linebacker Bradley Kassell at quarterback and safety.

"[Kasssell] was one of those guys who was a grown man at 18 years old," Wiggins remembers.

Needing a near-perfect performance, the Cavaliers came up short.

"I remember never having a chance in that game," Wiggins said. "It was 11 of the most pissed off country boys you'd ever seen on every snap. We tried to run Ben on first and second down, and then it's third-and-eight. I drop back to pass and there's only so much you can do."

Llano pounded out a 42-7 win, ending Lake Travis' season at 3-6-1. For Wiggins, the season became his ultimate learning experience.

"I learned a lot about leadership, being that young and being around guys who it was their friend too that got replaced, and the sacrifices that everyone makes for a team and that it's not necessarily the most fiery guy who gets in peoples' faces that leads," he said. "It's all the preparation that goes in during the week, that you start to earn the respect of senior linemen or guys like Ben, and they realize that he's going to put in the work and make the effort , that he's not just some freshman who's been given the chance."

Wiggins, with the valuable experience gained as a freshman playing varsity football, looked forward to better things in 1997. His freshman class had several talented performers who figured to join the varsity, and despite losing Reid, the school's all-time leading rusher, they figured to take another step forward, to compete again for the elusive first playoff berth. That step, however, wouldn't come.

The 1996-97 school year proved tumultuous for the Lake Travis athletic program, something that still puzzled Tuck 15 years later. From his Dripping Springs High School office in February of 2012, he remembered the mid-1990s as, to that point in the school's athletic history, one of the more successful stretches across all sports. Parents, who he noticed back in 1994 as highly opinionated and very vocal to the district administration, began flexing their considerable muscle. Feeling some teams should have more success, they met as a group and mobilized, calling principals, school board members, the superintendent and the athletic director demanding changes, much to the dismay of the man in that position, Bill Wakefield, a patient, easy-going coach who felt things had been going well. The parent unrest weighed heavily on Wakefield, who did all he could to act as buffer between parents and coaches. In the end, though, the pressure became too much and he stepped down. Tuck remembered it vividly.

"Bill Wakefield, still to this day, is the best leader I've ever worked for, but he got frustrated with the fact that one year removed of our volleyball team playing for the state championship, a group of parents organized a 'lynch mob' at a local restaurant to get rid of that very same volleyball coach [Pam (Glaser) Scippa, who left and then returned to Lake Travis High School as a teacher]," Tuck said. "And then it happened again in basketball with the only girls' basketball coach [Kelly Jo Sexton] to win 20 games up until that point, and they were wanting to get rid of her. Bill fought it and he fought it and he fought it and finally threw his hands up and basically said 'if you want my job I'll get out of the way.'"

Wakefield resigned and left the district. Others followed.

"Both the volleyball coach and basketball coach left after that season," Tuck said. "That was right after we had gone 7-3 in football [in 1995], volleyball had gone to the state playoffs, and the basketball team had beaten Dripping Springs for the first time maybe in school history in girls basketball. That was right after arguably, up until that point, the most successful athletic year in Lake Travis history."

The players soon noticed that the environment at Lake Travis didn't exactly foster coaching stability.

25

"We heard it," Wiggins said of his teammates. "We weren't mature enough to understand how serious some of that stuff was. You had parents threatening people's jobs. It was always, 'If you've done nothing wrong you don't have to worry about it.' There was a naiveté there that we didn't understand the power and influence there, that the coaching staff doesn't get the support. If you don't have the support of your administration, your athletic director and your superintendent, and they are listening to Mr. and Mrs. Smith and backing them more than the coaches, then you cut their legs out and they never stand a chance, ever. An unnamed coach sat down and told me, 'You know the reason I left, with the way the administration was, there was no way we could ever do what we wanted to do because it was the word of the parent over ours.' A coach doesn't deserve that, and if I was a coach I wouldn't want to coach in a system [like that]."

Tuck said he also had heard rumors at the time that the superintendent, Gloria Berry, E.D., had planned to step aside, though she remained at her post until the early 2000s. When Wakefield resigned, Tuck approached Berry to inquire about assuming that role in addition to his football duties. Berry declined, telling the coach that she would hire a new athletic director. At that point, Tuck began to question his future at the high school.

"I tried to explain to her at that point, if you bring in a new athletic director they're going to want to bring in their own people. That's just natural," he said.

Berry heard Tuck's concern and followed her own path. In the early summer of 1997, she hired Jim Taylor as athletic director. While Taylor, a quiet, somewhat reserved administrator, had been a football coach and athletic director at Bellville, Berry made it clear to Tuck that he'd maintain control of the football program.

"[Taylor] said all the right things, basically stated that the football program was still going to be my program, he wouldn't interfere and he was just here to help, everybody in the community really liked what I was doing with the football program, blah, blah, blah," Tuck said. "So I felt, okay, maybe this will work."

However, Tuck's concern that Taylor would want to come in and bring his own people with him played out. One summer day, Tuck had come to the field house to open the weight room. He sat in his tiny office talking football with Jim Hooten, the coach of Lake Travis 1997 3A state champion boys golf team. and a former football coach himself.

"The first week of summer, I'm sitting in my office," Tuck said. "I had the weight room open. At that time you couldn't actually be in there with the kids. I'm sitting in my office with Coach Hooten, and we're actually talking Xs and Os because he's a man I really respect. I see a young couple walk by the door. So I walk out and basically said, 'Excuse me, can I help ya'll?' And the young man, all of about 26 years old, introduces himself as the new offensive line coach at Lake Travis High School."

A flurry of emotion ran through the coach, but he thinks he did well to keep his composure.

"And I said, 'Oh really, I'm the head football coach. My name is Keith Tuck.' And I could feel my face just catch on fire."

After exchanging some polite pleasantries, Tuck went back into his office, closed the door, told Hooten what had happened, picked up the phone and called Berry.

"I called Dr. Berry and basically said, 'I've been lied to. Either make me middle school coordinator and I'll take the softball program, or you'll have my resignation by five o'clock.' She immediately came up the hill and tried to talk me out of it. She sent Jim Taylor up the hill to try to talk me out of it. What I told Jim was, 'Had you come to me and said I've got a young coach who coached with me in Bellville, he's a good kid, a hard worker, I'd have hired him on the spot. But for you to have hired him without consulting me, I can't look myself in the mirror and say truthfully that I can work for you.' That's how my tenure as head coach ended."

Tuck walked away from the high school football program, opting instead to coach the varsity softball team – his daughter Brittany had entered the high school as a softball standout, joining a team that Tuck and Wakefield had coached to the brink of the state tournament – in addition to overseeing athletics at Lake Travis Middle School, where he also coached the football teams. Tuck became one of a handful of head coaches who stepped down or otherwise did not return for the 1997-98 school year. In all, that 1996-97 school year saw six varsity head coaches and several assistants step down following their seasons. Many cited parental involvement. Tuck thought back to what he had heard when he joined the district three years earlier.

"The community itself was very supportive, but they were also …they were also very involved," he recalled. "For instance, they could make a phone call to the superintendent or any board member and would get their ear. That was different from any place I'd ever worked. It made for some interesting events, shall I say. A lot of the cases were a kid would go home and he or she would be upset with the coach and their parent would immediately call a school board member or superintendent. So before the coach even knew there was a problem, it had already been to the top of the food chain. I personally didn't ever really have any of these problems, but I witnessed it with coaches that I coached with."

Later, a school board president would ask Tuck why Lake Travis suffered so much turnover and what the administration might do to fix it. The coach said he'd be happy to offer suggestions, but only if the school board could handle him speaking exactly what he felt.

"I said, 'Are you sure you want me to do that, because if I do I'm probably going to step on some toes of the school board and probably the superintendent, because if you're going to ask me, I'm going to tell the truth?' He said, 'By all means, I think all of us need to hear it.'"

So Tuck made his way over to the board room and found a packed house, not necessarily to hear him but a packed house none-the-less. He kept his opening remarks simple and eloquent and immediately talked about the issues as the coaching staff saw them.

"The way I opened it was," he recalled nearly 14 years later, "if your son is a senior, he will have played for three head football coaches, three head basketball coaches, two head baseball coaches and two track coaches. If your daughter is a senior, she will have played for three head volleyball coaches, three head basketball coaches, three head softball coaches, and two track coaches. When you look at successful athletic programs throughout the state, the biggest key is continuity. And so, what we need to look at [here] is why there is no continuity."

For coaches to want to stay at a school, several things need to fall into place. They should be successful, both as coaches and as educators. They should feel like the administration supports them. And lastly, they should feel that the parents, the community and the fan base in general support the plan and direction the coach wants to take the program. For many of the coaches who left Lake Travis in the 1990s, none of those three criteria existed, at least in their minds if not in reality.

Parents, whose children are the lifeblood of any team, had become too close, too involved, Tuck said. When the parents called with concerns, administrators, board members and even the superintendent not only took the call but often times acted on it before the coach even knew an issue existed. Tuck advised the board to direct callers to the appropriate person.

"So I explained to them how a parent has an open line to any of the seven you and the superintendent, and ya'll will hear their complaint. I realize that you are public, elected officials, and you feel like it's your job to listen, but what you don't understand is that if you set up a chain of command that things will run so much smoother."

Tuck's chain of command included six matter-of-fact levels he felt would let the board and superintendent attend to more pressing needs, which at that time included opening new elementary schools and planning for growth, and let the coaching staff settle into positions that could be pretty desirable. Tuck based his plan partly on common sense, partly on professional courtesy.

"For instance, if a parent has a problem with a coach, this is the chain that should happen," Tuck explained to the board. "Number one needs to go to the coach that they have the problem with. Actually, the kid should first, and then the parent. If that doesn't work, they go to the head coach of that sport. If that doesn't work, they go to the athletic director. If that doesn't work they go to the principal on that campus. If that doesn't work, then they go to the superintendent, and last is the board. That's six steps before it gets to ya'll, and 99.9 percent of the problems will be solved in either step one or step two."

When he finished, the board thanked him for what he had to say. Later, Tuck said the district, that board in particular, took steps to implement the plan he had outlined. Whether they made it official district policy or not he didn't know, but when he returned to Lake Travis in 2004 as Dripping Springs' softball coach, he could tell things had changed.

"I don't know for sure that it was adopted as school board policy, but I know that particular board did do that," Tuck recalled. "When I came back in 2004 to Dripping, and we were playing LT at LT, one of the members who was still on the board sought me out and thanked me for what I said that night. He basically said that one of the reasons they'd been able to keep their coaches in tact was what they'd heard that night."

The Cavalier football program hasn't exactly been the model of stability since Tuck delivered that message in 1998. Following his two years, the school has had six different head coaches, none of whom held the position longer than five years. Had any stayed, Tuck included, could the Cavaliers' have found success sooner? Tuck said yes.

"We knew even then that the potential was. You had the model right down the road from you in Westlake. And Southlake Carroll. And Highland Park," Tuck said. "We knew you could be very successful with these types of kids, and by these types of kids, I mean very affluent, smart, hard working. You have parents that are willing to get the program to where it needs to be."

The parents again. Motivated and hungry for success, the school still lacked important pieces crucial to the success the parents' desperately desired. Part of the problem might be traced to the reputation they had developed as over-involved. Halfmann used to be the assistant coach who would drive head coaching candidates around the campus in a golf cart. He said candidates have been asking him about parental involvement since 1998.

Following Tuck, the Cavaliers landed a coach with a college background, Jim Bob Helduser. A former assistant to Dennis Franchione, Helduser had succeeded his mentor as head coach at Southwest Texas State University. After five years and an overall record of 20-30-1, the school decided to make a change. Helduser saw the Lake Travis opening and wanted the work.

"The next hire was one of those big-name hires but he had no intent of staying," Halfmann said. "Looking back at it, he got hired mid-July and he was gone in December. He didn't do anything during that time to put himself out there as building a program."

Players recall Helduser's offensive proficiency, but they say he did little to instill discipline or excitement. The lack of discipline proved troubling, and a complete 180 degree shift from the way Tuck and his staff ran things.

"In a weird way, they were complete opposites, going from Tuck to Helduser," Wiggins said. "Helduser was a college guy, came in with a pretty hands-off, laid back approach to coaching whereas Tuck and Pettey were the complete opposite. Some of the hardest workouts I've ever done to this day were with Pettey in the weight room Saturdays after a football game where guys are throwing up in trash cans and Pettey's screaming, yelling. That's the way they were going to build it. They were going to build tough guys, hard-working guys."

Players have no recollection of an intense workout program under Helduser. They simply remember a sense of excitement about a more open offense than the base I-formation set that the Cavaliers had employed the previous few seasons. Offense was Helduser's strength, and Wiggins felt that would be how the team would grow, more from scheme than fundamental work.

"It seemed like Helduser, he was going to try and do it through a system," Wiggins said. "It was going to be an Xs and Os kind of deal. With Helduser it was a totally different approach."

While the 1997 Cavaliers featured some athletic players to build around, none emerged with more promise than a freshman who would develop into the unquestioned star of the defense. Quiet and already more of a physical presence than many of his older teammates, Mark Kuenstler didn't think he'd figure into the varsity plans when he arrived at the high school after two stellar years at Lake Travis Middle School. He'd played running back at middle school, and with a trio of more experienced players ahead of him, he figured he'd bide his time on either the freshman or junior varsity teams so he'd be ready when his time came. Little did he expect, his time came quickly.

"Mark was benching 225 as a freshman," Wiggins recalled. "He shows up and Mark was the most tenacious, physically gifted athlete, more so than [Frank] Pugsley because he had such great instincts. But he was the quietest, calmest person you ever played with."

Kuenstler said he learned about two weeks prior to the season opener against Caldwell that he'd dress with the varsity. He knew freshmen rarely made varsity rosters, and he braced himself for the realty of a learning year. If transitioning from middle school to high school didn't represent enough of a challenge, he'd been assigned a new position.

"I was playing defensive end, and I'd never played it before," he recalled.

As the team travelled east to Caldwell for the season opener, Kuenstler didn't expect to play much, but he watched the game intently, trying to figure out what he'd do if he got a chance. By the time the team headed off to the locker room at halftime, Kuenstler hadn't seen the field and had resigned himself to the fact he wouldn't play much. He told Brian Taylor he might just want to go back to the junior varsity team where he could get some playing experience at running back.

"Brian Taylor was the defensive ends coach, and he was a great, great guy," Kuenstler said. "He was always very supportive. In the first game, I didn't play in the first half. I thought I wanted to go back down to the junior varsity and play running back so I'd at least get some playing time. But he told me not to worry, that I'd get some snaps."

Taylor proved correct. Kuenstler started the second half. Once he got on the field, he never came off again.

"I got in the game in the second half and didn't come out for three years," Kuenstler recalled. "Coach Taylor was a good coach and a good friend."

In that second half, the freshman made a dozen tackles and recovered two fumbles. Things happened quickly, but Kuenstler met each new challenge.

"I was six feet, maybe 170 pounds, and [I found out quickly] this wasn't middle school football anymore," he remembers. "There were some big boys out there. It was an interesting year, lots of fun. The seniors were good guys. It was a learning year."

Halfmann said the coaches knew about Kuenstler prior to that performance. They saw his talent and knew he would become a key contributor. They just didn't think it would happen immediately.

"He was working when he was a little kid," Halfmann said. "He had physical skills that were unbelievable. He was fast. He was the first freshman to start on the varsity that I knew of. He started at defensive end as a true freshman and made plays. So that's what started his legend. He was just a hard-nosed kid who worked hard and did everything you asked, and he had some talent to go with it. We'd had kids who were coachable and did what we asked, but they didn't have that level of talent, and he was just very humble. Very humble."

Kuenstler developed into the team's consistent bright spot. On a team that would finish 3-7, Kuenstler dominated games from his defensive end spot, surpassing 100 tackles for the season and becoming the anchor for Lake Travis' defense. Through it all, he kept his head down, his mouth shut.

"I think Mark was leading the district in tackles as a freshman from the defensive end position, and he never said a word about it," Wiggins said. "It's just what he did."

Following the season Helduser took Franchoine's offer to rejoin him when the former moved from New Mexico to Texas Christian. Wiggins said things never really clicked between the coach and team. Some players never fully dedicated themselves to the task of football, nor did the coaches ever come out and demand that dedication.

"When we were in high school, I bet a good portion of our halftimes were devoted to guys figuring out where they were going to party after the game," Wiggins recalled. "It's a totally different world. I can remember a game at Dripping Springs. We're sitting out in the portables my sophomore year. Literally guys are making party plans at halftime. I'm not saying anything about the coaching staff, but…"

Kuenstler echoed his teammate's view.

"Most of the coaches were just there to be there," he said. "They just went through the motions. And everybody was okay with that, the athletic director and others. We just weren't a football school. They just wanted to beat Dripping Springs. Coach Tuck had been there before. He was a fiery guy and I never got to play for him. He was an old school, ground and pound coach. The new coaches were getting away from that, but they just lacked the discipline to do it."

The season proved frustrating for most everyone.

"We had upperclassmen – Dustin Wuest was one – who were good guys and were possible Division I athletes," Kuenstler said. "Some even went on to play. That team had no discipline whatsoever. The seniors were the leaders, not so much the coaches. [Some of them,] they collected their checks. Those of us who took it serious were pretty good players, but there just weren't enough of us."

Helduser's decision neither surprised nor disappointed anyone. He also followed Franchione to Alabama and then back to Texas A&M, where he worked mainly as the offensive line coach. He would go on to work at Bryan

High School and finished his coaching career in 2009. He passed away Feb. 26, 2010 after a courageous battle with cancer.

If Helduser and his staff lacked discipline, his successor returned it, and quickly. Jim Shewmake had been coaching at Mansfield in the DFW Metroplex when he took the challenge at Lake Travis. No nonsense on the field and relaxed off of it, Shewmake arrived at Lake Travis with a sports car and golf clubs before graduating to the more coach-preferred pick-up truck. He worked long and hard from the beginning, taking only the occasional break to keep his golf swing in shape by pitching balls through the goalposts while his colleagues broke for lunch. His first task became putting an off-season program in place that would benefit every sport, not just football.

Mansfield's football program featured an off-season program that didn't exist at any level at Lake Travis, from what Shewmake could tell. Mansfield's program stood out, he told Berry and Taylor when he interviewed, because it worked with and alongside other seasonal sports to maximize the overall training athletes received. That would be important, he stressed, as Lake Travis made the pending jump in classification from Conference 3A to 4A. He drew from his experience as a high school athlete. He played baseball, not football.

"At that time, Lake Travis was a 3A school with a 3A mentality, but if it was going to go up to 4A, it needed a strong strength and conditioning program to make better athletes," Shewmake explained. "At Mansfield, we did it like this: if you were a basketball player, we released you from strength and conditioning because you were going to stay in shape, and after basketball season all we'd have to do is work on strength. We kept the baseball players in our program because if we increased their speed, we could make them faster going from first to third base. I was a baseball player growing up and went to college on a baseball scholarship, so I understood what it took. If the baseball team didn't have a game, they worked out with us before practice. If there was a game, or if the baseball coach asked us to rest a kid the day before a game, those kids just didn't work out that day. And it worked. Through the program, baseball got better. There was some cooperation between coaches that went on."

As he evaluated his new program, Shewmake found that with years of coaching changeover, the football program had struggled to form an identity, either at the school or in the community.

"I have never wanted to criticize those who came before me because they were doing the best with what they had, but at a time when we were making the move from 3A to 4A, things just weren't where they needed to be," Shewmake said. "The off-season wasn't where it needed to be and the facilities weren't where they needed to be. It didn't matter that it was me; whoever was coming in was going to have to make changes. We got things that we needed in order to compete. We were moving from a 3A mentality to a 4A mentality. It was different for me. I was bringing a 5A mentality to a place that had moved to 4A. It was difficult, but the kids understood and bought into it. It was fine."

So the new coach started putting his program into place. He knew the job would be challenging: not only were the Cavaliers not used to winning, they were about to step up into a new realm of football, where schools worked hard at being good and had the necessary support from administration and community alike. Shewmake understood the formula: win and support would come, later if not sooner but hopefully sooner. The Cavaliers went back to work and transitioned from the half-year of Helduser into Shewmake's program.

The players, who had just gone through a coaching transition, did it all over again. From the outset, they much preferred Shewmake's approach, which featured a renewed sense of discipline.

"To the minute when Shewmake walked in you could tell that there was a new sheriff in town," Kuenstler said. "You could tell things would be different. The playoffs were his main goal. He brought in discipline and a new trainer so people just didn't go hide in the training room and goof off. He wanted discipline in the locker room and he wanted to get the kids to respect the coaches."

Wiggins agreed. He also liked the offense Shewmake brought with him. Shewmake preferred a fast-paced attack that included a no-huddle aspect. When the coach wanted to eschew a huddle, he and the offensive assistants would shout "Bang, Bang" over and over from the sidelines, and Wiggins and the rest of the offense scrambled to get to the line and run the next play.

"Then Shewmake comes in, and it goes back to very structured, hard work, build it from the ground up kind of system, and that was really the first time that we had tried to implement a true spread," Wiggins said, referring for the first time to Shewmake's offensive philosophy, music to a strong-armed quarterback's ears. "There were elements of it with Tuck and with Helduser, but Shewmake and Coach [Matt] Jones, they came in and that was their system. Let's get in the shotgun and spread it. We kind of rode the same wave with the rest of high school football at that time."

Finding success after a history without it takes time, and Shewmake's first year proved full of close calls and frustrating learning experiences. Depth, raw numbers, continued to be a challenge, but the varsity team featured some quality players. Wiggins and Marcus Franki both had experience at quarterback, and Franki had proven too athletic to keep off the field, earning significant time at running back in 1997. Matt Lewis and Dustin Wernecke gave the quarterbacks a capable duo at receiver, and Paul Pugsley emerged as a big-bodied running back who would just as soon run over tacklers as run around them. Defensively, the Cavaliers proved feisty though undersized. Kuenstler anchored everything despite learning another new position – middle linebacker. He had gotten used to defensive end and had success there.

"My sophomore year they moved me to middle linebacker," he said later. "I didn't have a say in it. But it was enjoyable. It was fun to be able to fly around. Now, the game has changed so much I would have to be much faster [to play today]."

In 1998, Kuenstler had plenty of speed to make any and every play. He justified the move by dominating play throughout the season. In a memorable game against Burnet's option attack (before the record setting, NFL-bound, passing duo of Steven McGee and Jordan Shipley came along), Kuenstler made the tackle on 26 of the Bulldogs' 34 rushing attempts. But his play (more than 170 tackles) couldn't turn Lake Travis' recent fortunes. The offense remained a work in progress, adjusting to Shewmake's pass-first system. And the season had marked the team's first foray into the 4A ranks following realignment. By the time the Cavaliers dropped an overtime decision to district champion Marble Falls in the finale, they'd managed just two wins in Shewmake's first season. The coach didn't enjoy the 2-8 record and he wouldn't let the players accept or forget it either.

"That first year we were 2-8, and he pounded that into our heads," Kuenstler recalled.

Through the team's hard work in the offseason, Kuenstler could see the change starting to take hold. Though it would be another spring and summer before the results would show on the field, things had begun to come together.

"His strength and conditioning program worked us hard," Kuenstler recalled. "We were developing quicker, stronger, faster athletes, and that allowed us to move to a 4-3 defense where our safeties could fly around too. That worked to our advantage."

In addition to implementing the offseason program, Shewmake also began working with his players on improving leadership, getting the key players to embrace that role.

"Shew did a lot just as far as … he brought the kids in and did a leadership class, trying to develop the kids,"Halfmann said. "Senior leadership was big with him, and it wasn't just a select few. He tried to make it the kids' program, their responsibility."

3: Heartbreaking Success

Things began to change for Lake Travis with the 1999 season. Jim Shewmake's second year at the helm saw the Cavaliers line up with an experienced offense, a talented defense and promise that hadn't existed in a handful of years.

Three-year starter Greg Wiggins stood ready to lead the offense in senior season. His cadre of weapons included running back Paul Pugsley and a talented, speedy if undersized receiving corps of Matt Lewis, Dustin Wernecke and pre-season all-district pick Reggie Stephey. Defensively, the Cavaliers had put some hard-working pieces around the harder-working Mark Kuenstler, who brought two years of starting experience with him into his junior year. The Cavaliers had morphed from an I-formation running team to a spread team that used a mix of huddle and no-huddle to keep opposing defenses from settling into any rhythm.

The difference showed immediately. Where the younger 1998 team struggled to get on top in tight games, the season-opener at Wimberley saw the Cavaliers convert a late strike from Wiggins to Stephey for a last-minute comeback win. By the time the Cavaliers beat Burnet on Sept. 17, they stood 3-0 for the first time in years five years. Kuenstler had secured the win with an interception return for a touchdown. The three wins equaled the most the team had achieved in a full season since 1995.

But tragedy struck the Lake Travis community following that Burnet game. And to be clear, the tragedy lies not in the impact to a high school football team but in the magnitude of the accident caused by one of its members — a team captain and one of its most respected players.

According to police reports and court records, late Saturday night or early Sunday morning Sept. 19, 1999, Stephey was driving his black Bronco up Tumbleweed Hill on Ranch Road 2222 after attending a party in Austin at the University of Texas, and he had been drinking. Near the crest of the hill, he crossed the center line and collided with an oncoming car. In the ensuing accident and fire, two women lost their lives and a third, Jacqueline Saburido, suffered horribly disfiguring injuries. Her recovery and ordeal became an international story.

Stephey was convicted of vehicular homicide and was paroled after serving a seven-year sentence in the Texas State Penitentiary at Huntsville. Saburido, a Venezuelan native in Austin to study English, lost her nose, eyelids, ears and parts of her fingers to the fire, as reported in an *Austin American-Statesman* story detailing Stephey's 2008 release from prison.

Everyone attached to the Lake Travis school district and football program had been devastated by what had happened, none any more than Shewmake, who still tears up when talking about Stephey.

"I think about Reggie all the time," Shewmake said in December, 2011. "My wife went to court during the trial every day and sat with or right behind his mom. I had been subpoenaed so I didn't attend until I was called, which was after the trial and during sentencing. I still love Reggie. Everyone knows I called him Reginald Vanclief Stephanopolis the third."

On the field, Stephey epitomized what Shewmake, or any coach for that matter, wanted in a player. A clean-cut, respectful player, he worked hard, he led by example on the field, and, best of all, he made plays. Shewmake once recalled having to warn the entire team about leaving a locker room messy. He wouldn't find it messy again, and he later learned that Stephey had taken it upon himself to organize a clean-up schedule and then make sure those responsible did their part. If he thought more highly of another Lake Travis player, Shewmake never said so.

Even as Lake Travis struggled through a 2-8 season in 1998, Stephey's play caught the attention of opposing coaches. As the motion receiver in Shewmake's set, Stephey's movement before the snap forced coverages to adjust, creating mismatches. Though he didn't lead the Cavaliers in receiving, district coaches put him on the all-district team because he adeptly forced defenses to account for him on every play. When the local Rotary Club invited to Shewmake preview the 1999 season, he made sure Stephey went with him, an honor the coach bestowed only on players he considered team leaders and quality people.

While he felt for Stephey, a player with whom he had become exceptionally close, he had to support the other 30 or so varsity players, as well as the subvarsity players impacted because of Stephey's status as a football player. While he'd never hide from the accident and didn't shy away from the fact that Stephey had been a key part of the football team, Shewmake tried to make sure the media didn't paint all of Lake Travis' players with one broad brush.

"It was a bad time," Shewmake recalled. "[From a football standpoint] I think the thing about the whole time was that any time you looked in the papers or on the news, it was 'Lake Travis football player Reggie Stephey...' and I thought that was unfair to the rest of the team. I talked to the editor of the [*Austin American-Statesman*] and told him that I had no problem using his name and that he was a part of the football team, but using it in headlines the way they did was unfair to the entire team."

Shewmake and his staff worked feverishly to encourage the team to focus on the season that remained. While they suffered for their friend and teammate, their opponents surely wouldn't.

"When it happened, we met with the team," Shewmake said. "We had always told the kids that there were things you can't control or get worried about, that we just had to overcome. That was what we were trying to instill, that we can control how we react to things. When the accident happened, we told the kids that there isn't anyone here who isn't affected by this, and this will sound cruel, but we still have a game to play. No matter what, we have to overcome and go play. 'It will be hard, but we will pray for Reggie...we love Reggie, but they want to kick our ass. They don't care, so we have to be ready. The worst thing we can do is play terrible, and the best we can do is play hard and represent ourselves.' It was a tough time for all of us."

To their credit, the Cavaliers did not shy away from their relationship with Stephey, but they did close ranks and concentrate on the season's task at hand. Wiggins said how Shewmake handled that time remains one of the fondest memories he has of his Lake Travis career.

"And then that senior year was tough because that deal with Reggie happened at the end of the summer, but seeing how Coach Shewmake really stepped in and tried to shelter us and isolate us from all that stuff, I've got a lot of respect for him as a man, not only as a coach but more as a man, for the way he handled that," he said.

The Cavaliers met the challenge. They defeated Elgin the following week before suffering their first loss during an implosion against a Manor team guided by former Cavalier coach Don Cowan. Still, entering district play at 4-1, the Cavaliers felt this might be the season that the team earned its first playoff berth. The Cavaliers dropped their district opener to Belton 35-7, regrouped to beat Lampasas 33-14 but dropped a 29-7 decision to up-and-coming Pflugerville Connally. Sitting at 1-2, knowing that only the top three teams reached the playoffs, the Cavaliers knew they would need to win out, and even that might not be enough to make the dream a reality.

But win out they did. In a memorable, back-and-forth game with arch-rival Dripping Springs, the Cavaliers ended a multi-year skid against the Tigers and kept their hopes alive in thrilling fashion.

The game began just like any recent Lake Travis-Dripping Springs game. The Tigers jumped all over the Cavaliers and led 21-0 before Shewmake and staff knew what hit them. But these Cavaliers proved a resilient bunch, reinforced by all they had already been through that year, and began plugging away, though by halftime they still trailed 28-7. Needing a huge second half, the Cavaliers got just that. Kuenstler, who played a little offense during the 1999 season but seldom returned kicks, fielded the second half kickoff and battered his way around, over and through the Tigers' coverage team for an 80-yard touchdown, breathing new life into his team.

"I remember we got in the starburst return," Kuenstler later said of Shewmake's preferred return formation that tried to factor in some misdirection and sleight of hand. "It was a pretty deep kick, and Jared Quick let it go over his head. It bounced to me and I picked it up and just started trucking. I remember that play like it was yesterday. Those were good times."

The defense closed ranks and kept the Tigers out of the end zone, and the offense finally got untracked, thanks to Quick's coming-out party. Quick, a lanky, sure-handed junior receiver, kept finding ways to get open against the Tiger secondary, and Wiggins, the seasoned veteran in his fourth Dripping Springs battle, found him time and again.

"We were down 21-0 in the first quarter," Wiggins recalled. "I think Kuenstler ran back a kickoff. Defense actually started making stops. All I did...it seems like I'd throw it up and guys would just come down with it."

The duo connected 10 times for 180 yards and two second half-scores, including one that tied the game at 31 in the closing seconds.

In overtime, the Tigers won the toss and sent their battered defense on the field, as overtime's strategy dictates. Wiggins and Quick wasted little time, connecting for a touchdown on the Cavs' first play. Jeff Lynn's extra point gave the Cavaliers a 38-31 lead. The Tigers answered by driving 25 yards for a touchdown to get within 38-37. Faced with the decision to kick a tying extra point and extend the game, which would have forced their defense back on the field, or trying for two and the quick win, the Tigers went for the win. They ran their bread-and-butter power sweep, but Lake Travis saw it coming. Undersized safety Josh Jahner crashed the end and met running back Brian Hendrickson in the backfield. Jahner held on until the cavalry arrived, and when it did the Cavaliers celebrated a 38-37 win and rode that momentum into the regular season finale against Marble Falls.

"In overtime they go for two to try and win it," Wiggins remembered with a smile. "Every once in a while I'll see [then-Dripping Springs coach] Howard Ballard at the Tucks' benefits [in honor of their daughter Brittany, who was killed in an auto accident outside of Dayton, Texas in 2003], I'll always ask him if he'd go for two again, and he says, 'Every time.'"

Wiggins would come to have one more memory involving his only win over Dripping Springs. It came much later in the school year, months removed from the season, in fact.

"We were going to prom senior year," Wiggins recalled. "We may or may not have been enjoying ourselves before. We get to the door and Mr. Claypool [high school Principal James Claypool] says to me, 'Greg, a sheriff wants to speak with you.' My only thought was, 'Uh, oh.' Sheriff looks at me and says, 'Are you Greg Wiggins?' I said, 'Yes sir.' He says, 'I just want to tell you, I was a referee in that Dripping Springs game and to this day that was the best high school football game I've ever seen.' And he shook my hand. I'm sweating as I thank him and walk off. That was a fun, fun game."

Having beaten Dripping Springs, Lake Travis found itself staring at the possibility of ending the season in a three-way tie for the district's final playoff spot. Texas football tiebreakers are unique to begin with. Stories are legendary, none more famous than the 1987 tiebreaker that decided the outcome of the "Little Southwest Conference" results. As immortalized in Buzz Bissinger's *Friday Night Lights,* Odessa Permian, Midland Lee and Midland High all finished the regular season with 5-1 district records. But only two teams made the playoffs. So the coaches from the three schools met at a supposedly secret location to flip coins to break the tie. Only they couldn't keep the location a secret. Fans from the schools found out about it, and a local radio station broadcast live updates from the midnight meeting. The process would be simple: the three coaches would flip coins, the odd coin out would lose and that team wouldn't make the playoffs. In a spectacle befitting the passion and cruelty of high stakes Texas high school football, the coaches stood in the center of a diner, tossed their coins and learned their fate. Midland Lee and Permian's coins came up heads, Midland's came up tails, and the regular season officially ended. Three teams season's worth of hard work decided by the flip of a coin.

But multi-team tiebreakers aren't always that cut and dry. Each district can set its own standards. Belton ran the table and finished 5-0 to win the district. Connally, Lake Travis and Dripping Springs were locked in a three-way race for second. Two teams would advance and the third, if things remained tied, would be left on the outside looking in. The three-way tiebreaker was based on an aggregate score formula. So at 2-2 in district play heading into the final week, not only would Lake Travis need to beat Marble Falls to stay tied, it would need to win by a certain number of points. A dozen years later, few from Lake Travis remember exactly what needed to happen, including the quarterback.

"They told us before the Marble Falls game that if we did x, x, and x that we would make it," Wiggins said. "If we won by a certain amount, we'd have gone to the playoffs. I guess we didn't get close enough."

Lake Travis won the game, but only by 28-21. Connally and Drip advanced, and despite its best season in five years and highest win total in school history, Lake Travis could only think about what might have been. Shewmake still takes pride in that 1999 season, even though the Cavaliers came up short.

"To go 7-3 and sit at home was frustrating, but that was when we could really tell that the kids had bought in to what we wanted to do," he said. "We went into the last game that year at Marble Falls, and really Marble Falls was a better team than we were. But we lined up and won the game and took it to them. That group for us was a talented group."

Wiggins graduated, as did top rusher Pugsley, earning a scholarship to Duke University as a hard-hitting safety. Promising wide receiver Wernecke, a standout pitcher who went on to earn a baseball scholarship to Rice University, gave up football following the 1999 season to concentrate on baseball. But talent remained. Do-everything linebacker Kuenstler, fresh off a season in which he made 190 tackles and scored touchdowns four different ways (rushing, receiving, interception return and kick return), eagerly awaited his senior year. Defensive end Luke Adkins continued to progress, adding strength to speed that made him difficult to handle coming off the edge and eventually earned him a scholarship to Colorado State University. Quick returned after his breakout performance against Dripping Springs. And some new faces emerged, including a senior linebacker and a sophomore offensive lineman. The linebacker, Ryan White, would play a huge role in the 2000 season and went on to play tight end at Texas A&M. The lineman, Robert Turner, went on to New Mexico and became the first Lake Travis player to make an NFL team when he signed and stuck with the New York Jets.

Shewmake's 2000 Cavaliers had to break in a new quarterback. Senior Travis Williams assumed the starter's position after a solid junior varsity career. He, along with a stable of running backs and what shaped up to be a defense that would bend but not break, couldn't wait to kick of the season against Hays Consolidated and storied coach Bob Shelton.

Going into the season, Shewmake had been encouraged by the turn the program had taken. He knew the 2000 team wouldn't be as talented as the 1999 team, but they had moxie.

"Then the group that followed them...they weren't as talented but they made up for it in work ethic and desire and heart," Shewmake recalled. "They had the intangibles. Just look at the quarterback. Cody Skaggs was maybe 5-foot-7, 145 pounds, soaking wet, in his uniform, and all he did was move the ball and score points."

That season opener turned into a defensive struggle. The Rebels, bigger, more experienced, and deeper, struck quickly and took a 7-0 lead. But Williams remained undaunted and led the Cavaliers back down the field for the tying touchdown on his first drive as the field general. The teams played to a stalemate for the rest of the first half, with Kuenstler leading Lake Travis as his dominating self, making tackles in the Rebels' backfield and from sideline to sideline. But on a play late in the second quarter, Kuenstler chased down a Hays ballcarrier on the far side of the field, dragged him down and didn't get up.

41

True to his personality, Kuenstler doesn't blame anyone but himself for the injury. Looking back on things in 2012, he offered a description of his playing style, then described the play as it unfolded.

"My motor was always running about 100 miles an hour," he said. "I also liked to wear longer spikes than I should have, but they gave me better traction.

"[The injury] was my fault. I overran the play, went to cut back and I blew everything in my left knee. I remember I had rolled my ankle in walk-through on Thursday. I never, ever taped my ankles, but I had them tape it. And when I overran it, my ankle was taped so instead of just rolling my ankle I blew out my knee. It was a bummer. The ACL and MCL were gone, and I couldn't move laterally. I wanted to go back in the game and play, but in the end we decided to get it taken care of and call it a year."

The injury shocked everyone on the Lake Travis side of Bob Shelton Stadium.

"When he got hurt, the team was visibly shaken," Shewmake said. "He planted to make a cut and the knee just exploded. He had been the team's leader since he was a freshman, and it was an ugly injury. I headed back over to the team and gathered them up and told them that we needed someone to step up. Ryan White did, and as he went out there to play middle linebacker for us, I told him that he can't play like Mark, so just play like himself. Just don't try and be Mark and go play. When something is thrown at you, how do you react? That night we played Hays to 14-7, and I think that was a heck of an effort. And to do that without your leader was even more of a credit to those guys."

The diagnosis proved heartbreaking for Kuenstler and the team. That Hays added a second half touchdown and held on for the 14-7 win paled with the realization that Kuenstler tore both knee ligaments and would miss the rest of the season. The linebacker who had begun to draw attention from across Texas saw his season end before it essentially began. What he would have accomplished we'll never know, but in that first half against Hays, he had already made 11 tackles before the injury.

"It was hard for everyone, knowing what was at stake for Mark," assistant coach Kevin Halfmann said. "Knowing what colleges were after him and what that meant. We knew the injury was going to hurt the team, but at the same time it helped us because he became a rallying point. Kids stepped up, not wanting to let him down. He was THE guy who would get things done for us on offense or on defense. That's what people expected of him, and they didn't want to let him down."

Hallmark couldn't have written Kuenstler's story any better, save maybe for a happy football ending. A hard-working, humble, respectful kid whose family worked extra hard for everything it had with a special talent, one that could potentially take him to new heights, into a world of untapped potential. And it came crashing down on a warm Friday night in front of thousands.

Shewmake, like many others who played with or coached Kuenstler, raved about the young man's football ability. After his junior year, major college coaches had come calling, wishing his senior year would wrap up so he could join their programs and make them better.

"Mark was the best natural football player I have ever been around, from the time I started in coaching and as I sit here today," Shewmake said later. "He could do things you did not coach. He saw things instantly and would go and make a play. He just saw natural alleys where he could go depending on what the offense was doing. It killed me when he blew that knee out. At that time, TCU really wanted him. Dennis Franchione was the coach. The recruiter, he practically lived at Lake Travis, watching Mark practice in the spring. There were others courting him – Oklahoma, Baylor – but no one as hot as TCU. They told me they'd love it if he could forgo his senior year and go to TCU so he could start right then and there [as a high school senior]. That's what they thought of him."

Kuenstler had spent the spring and summer talking to different college recruiters. He saw himself playing on Saturdays in the large stadiums of the Big XII.

"Tulsa had offered me a scholarship," he said. "Looking back, I should have just committed to them and gone there. Colorado was another main one. And there was Texas, Nebraska, USC when they started to turn their program around. But I really wanted to stay in the state. I felt like I had some choices. You never know how things work out. I had a good handful of schools I had visited, and I think at the time A&M was probably the front runner."

Wiggins, who would go on to play quarterback at Abilene Christian University, where he came across talented players both daily at practice and against him in games, said Kuenstler remains one of the two best players he ever played with.

"To this day, save for Danieal Manning, who's playing the [NFL], Mark Kuesntler is still the most physically gifted, best football player I've ever played with," Wiggins said. "If he hadn't hurt his knee, I still contend – and [Keith] Tuck can back me up – he'd have been an all-Big XII guy at A&M. It would have been a completely different story if he hadn't gotten hurt."

Kuenstler's knee became just the tip of an injury iceberg. The Cavaliers battled injuries all season, and they dealt with it admirably. White stepped in to Kuenstler's middle linebacker role and shone, beginning in the second week against McCallum at Austin's Nelson Field. White led a defense that held McCallum to just a single touchdown, recovering a fumble along the way and generally playing Kuenstler's role of monster in the middle.

While the Lake Travis defense kept the Knights contained, the offense suffered its own loss. After a promising start in the opener at Hays, Williams went down awkwardly on a quarterback keeper against McCallum and broke his leg. Like Kuenstler the week before, the injury would sideline him for the season. In his place scampered Skaggs, who as the junior varsity quarterback the prior year had impessed Shewmake with his intangibles. Which proved fortunate, because at 5-foot-7 and 150 or so pounds, Skaggs' tangibles didn't strike fear in opposing defenses. He more closely resembled a water boy than a quarterback. What he lacked in physical presence, though, Skaggs more than made up for with pluck, and he wasted no time getting going. Adept on the move, Skaggs led the Lake Travis offense to 35 points against McCallum and the season's first win.

"That was a gritty, scrappy team," Kuenstler recalled. "Boy I sure wish I would have been able to play because we had a good shot. I feel like I could have been a big help in the middle. Travis got hurt too and Cody Skaggs came in and did some quarterbacking. It was upsetting at the time because I couldn't play."

Though they couldn't play, both Kuenstler and Williams stayed involved with the program.

"To Mark's credit, once he had surgery he never missed practice from start to finish," Shewmake said. "He was there, doing whatever he could every day. And then Travis [Williams] gets hurt and he does the same thing, shows up every day. What they showed the entire school by doing that was that they were part of the team, and while it sucks that they were hurt and couldn't play, they were going to be there with their team every day. It would have been easy to go home and feel sorry for themselves, but neither did."

"For the most part, I tried to help the linebackers," Kuenstler said. "I could read tendencies and break down film, let them know that if [the offense] lined up a certain way they could expect a type of play. That was the positive part of it. It was good to still be with the guys."

Far from great and riddled by injuries, the Cavaliers persevered and played their way firmly into the playoff hunt when district play began.

"The injuries never stopped," Shewmake said. "I remember playing at Lockhart in the fifth week. We were drawing things up in the dirt trying to figure stuff out. We had people playing receiver who'd never played receiver before and the same thing at defensive back. We just got hammered injury-wise. Even during that game. I remember we started that game with 27 kids, and after halftime you turn around and see about eight of them with their uniforms off because they got hurt during the game. But we end up taking them to overtime before we lose, and I was very proud of that.

That's the kind of heart we had. They just never had any quit in them. I've never been much more proud of a group than I was at Lockhart."

Lake Travis' health would begin to improve, and with a solid work ethic the Cavaliers began putting the pieces together. The defense dominated in a 30-2 win over Del Valle. At Dripping Springs the Cavaliers, without starting running back Rhett Bowen, got more than 100 yards from diminutive Ryan Englehart and held on for a 13-7 win. The wins lacked flash, but the Cavaliers couldn't care less. Wins were wins, and that's all that mattered. A 48-0 setback on a rain-soaked night to district champion San Marcos did little to shake the Cavaliers' confidence, and they needed every bit of self-confidence heading into the regular season finale at Bastrop. The Cavaliers and Bears stood tied for third place, and the district's final playoff berth hinged on the outcome. Heading into the game, Shewmake and his staff took advantage of a scheduling quirk to find inspiration and motivation.

"This was totally by accident," the coach recalled a dozen years later. "I think the game fell on Veteran's Day weekend, and I remember in pregame we talked about how we were just going to keep coming at Bastrop, like the U.S. troops storming the beach at Normandy on D-Day. It didn't matter how many machine guns the Germans had on that beach, they just kept coming in waves. And that's what we wanted to do. We talked about wanting to keep coming all night long, and we were able to do exactly that. And on the sidelines throughout the game, you could hear that's what the kids were saying to each other."

The teams spent the first half locked in a physical battle, and the outcome remained very much unsettled as the teams broke for halftime. Faced with another interesting scenario, the Cavaliers decided to remain on the field at halftime rather than trek back across Bastrop's campus to their dressing room.

"They had given us a little dressing room that seemed like it was a mile away," Shewmake recalled. "We would have wasted half of halftime going back over there, so we just decided that we'd go down to the end zone. It was just like a junior varsity game. We went to the end zone, and I told the kids that when Bastrop came back, they'd see us waiting there for them."

It's highly doubtful the Bears got intimidated, because Lake Travis didn't intimidate anyone in 2000. But the Cavaliers kept taking the fight to the bigger Bears, and when James Duncan scored a late touchdown, the Cavaliers earned a 21-13 win, setting off a wild celebration for a team that had just earned its school's first playoff berth after 16 years of varsity football.

"It was a mixture of bedlam and relief, and there was almost a sense of exhaustion," Shewmake said of the post-game feeling. Parents joined their players on the field and they took picture after picture to freeze the moment in time.

"Thousands of pictures were taken," Shewmake said. "Moms and dads came out on the field. Players were hugging each other, patting each other on the back. We had accomplished the goal we set, to get the program into the playoffs. It was an emotional time. I remember Matt Jones and I were crying because we were seeing a dream come true again [the duo had coached Mansfield into the playoffs for the first time before coming to Lake Travis].

"For a coach to see a group of young men believe in something and then see it come true....it was really neat to watch them celebrate together. It really was something. The kids ran the whole show. They wanted pictures of each position group, and they wanted their position coaches with them in the photos. That made us feel good, to know that they had bought in and worked hard. I still get goosebumps talking about it, and it's 12 years later."

The Cavaliers' prize in the playoffs: a deeper, more talented, more athletic Connally team that had beaten them the only two times they had met. Shewmake knew the challenge that faced his team. He also knew the Cavaliers (5-5 following the regular season) would face it head-on.

"They had more talent and athletes than you could shake a stick at," Shewmake recalled of the Cougars. "We were honest with the kids. They were a deeper team than we were, and we knew a four-quarter struggle would not be in our favor. But we thought if we could score early and make them play catch-up, it would get them out of their comfort zone. They hadn't had to play from behind all year. The kids believed in what we could do, and we had told them that we needed to strike early and first."

When Connally and Lake Travis officials met prior to the game to establish location, referee choices, and the like, they did so by a series of coin flips, all of which the Cavaliers famously lost. Athletic Coordinator Lisa Spain, also the school's girls basketball coach, went with Shewmake and did all of the calling. They flipped a coin eight times that day, and she lost them all. Connally hosted the game on Friday night instead of Saturday afternoon, and so on.

Not that any of it mattered to the Cavaliers. Of course, following suit, they lost the coin flip before the game. Connally deferred their option to the second half, and the Cavaliers took the ball. The Cavaliers had their plan, and the time had come to hatch it.

"We'd played them the two years before and played them tough," Shewmake said. "This is what you live for. So we're preparing for the game, watching them on tape. [Offensive coordinator] Matt [Jones] noticed that their safety really liked to crash the line on running plays, so we practiced what we were going to do for our first play all week."

After Colin Matheny returned the opening kickoff to the 37-yard line,

Skaggs brought the offense straight to the line of scrimmage.

"So, we got in our two-back set with a tight end, and we faked the ball to the running back," Shewmake recalled. "I told the kids it didn't matter where we were on the field, if we were at midfield or if we were at our one-yard line. We were going to run that post."

Skaggs put the ball in the burly Bowen's belly and pulled it out. Quick, the Cavaliers' star receiver, split out to the left and ran a perfect post pattern.

"Sure enough, that safety came up and we threw it over his head and score on the first play," Shewmake said with a smile. "When you work like we had worked that week, and then you throw it for 80 and a touch on the first play, then you know it's going to be fun."

Eleven years afterwards, coaches and players still remembered the first play, and the game, as if it were yesterday.

"Jared was back on campus this fall [2011] and he was looking around the facility, amazed at where we are now," Halfmann said of the big receiver who went on to play college football at New Mexico State. "We walked past the trophy case and saw that first Bi-District trophy. I told him every time I look at that I see that post. It was an amazing time. Whatever was to come after that, to know that we had started it. That was a crazy night."

Offensively, the Cavaliers had the Cougars' number. Whatever Shewmake and Jones called worked. Connally couldn't cover Quick, and by the time that Skaggs found Atkins alone in the end zone for another score, Lake Travis led 21-0, and favored Connally wondered how it could be behind little Lake Travis. Looking back, Shewmake realized that his pregame plan worked to perfection. Lake Travis' early success had stunned the bigger, deeper Cougars, and they went away from their usual playing style.

"They started to throw the ball more than they ever had before," Shewmake noticed. "It was almost like they panicked. That kind of fell into our hands and gave us the opportunities we needed. We made them do something they weren't accustomed to."

Connally's change in strategy away from a power-based running game leveled the playing field. Lake Travis, which dressed just 24 players for the game, could compete with Connally's 60 players.

"Our defense was outstanding," Shewmake said. "Our kids really believed, and we hung on to win. I was, and we all were, thrilled to the gills."

Halfmann served as the defensive coordinator in 2000, and the Cougars made him sweat. He wasn't thrilled about watching his defense allow Connally to close the gap, but he could breathe easy when Skaggs took a knee to kill the clock in a 21-14 win.

"As defensive coordinator I wasn't very happy at the end, but we held on," he said.

The next week the Cavaliers lost all the flips again and ended up playing at New Braunfels on Thanksgiving Friday. Shewmake recalled the game, but he said the experience of practicing the week of Thanksgiving and seeing families come together for the experience still sticks with him.

"The fun that week was getting the kids to practice during the Thanksgiving holiday," Shewmake said. "We didn't have classes so we could practice when we wanted to, and it just felt special. We had our walk-through early on Thanksgiving so the kids could have dinner with their families. What was really cool about that week was the number of families who came to Austin for Thanksgiving so they could watch the game Friday night. We had a lot of players who had family members see them play for the first time."

Not that the family members would be disappointed, but the Cavaliers put on a good show just in case. The Cavaliers and Unicorns played a neck-and-neck, down-to-the-wire game. Lake Travis led late, and when each team needed to make a play to decide things, it just happened that the Unicorns made the play, and they won 28-25, scoring on a long, fourth down pass with less than a minute to play.

"We played them tooth and nail," Shewmake said. "They played good defense, we played good defense. They throw a long pass, and they catch it and we don't and that's the game. We had some opportunities early. It just comes down to this: they made one more play than we did."

For a program that had never gotten that far, the 2000 season turned into one for the ages, at least in a growing community that had gotten attached to a little team that did. Still, those close to the program couldn't help but wonder what would have happened if the Cavaliers had knocked down that late touchdown pass.

"It was disappointing, but we had nothing to be ashamed of, and that's exactly what we told the kids," Shewmake said. "I really wish we'd won, though, because the next game would have been against a team from South Texas, and they didn't look like they were anything special, at least on paper. We felt like we could win that game, and if we do, we're in the semifinals. But you have to have things go your way, and it didn't go our way that night. We played really well against some really tough teams. I couldn't have been any more pleased with our kids."

Halfmann agreed.

"If we had beaten New Braunfels, we would have won the next game too," Halfmann said. "Who knew what that could have been?"

Kuenstler, for one, had an idea. He'd spent the bulk of his senior season

48

rehabbing his knee, and by Thanksgiving had made enough progress that doctors said he'd be able to play again.

"It was bittersweet," he said. "I had put in all that work and effort. If we had made it one more round, I would have been cleared to come back and play."

Years later, though, they only remember the accomplishment, not the what-might-have-been.

"That year was just incredible," Shewmake said. "We ended up with 24 kids who could dress out for games. For both of our playoff games, the team went on one bus. What you have to remember at the time was that when we moved up to 4A [in 1998], we were the smallest 4A school by a long shot, and we were in the same district with Belton, which had moved down from 5A and was the biggest 4A in the state. And we had not been winning, so our numbers weren't great. When you aren't winning, kids don't come out for football. As we started to win, our numbers started to rise."

For Kuenstler, following the injury the major scholarship offers vanished, but coaches from several Division II schools gave him a look, including Abilene Christian, where Wiggins had been battling for the quarterback position. He recalled seeing Kuenstler enroll and go through preseason practice. The old passion, perhaps dampened by the year off and the work it took to get his knee put back together, wasn't there.

"I went up to Abilene," Kuenstler recalled. "I was still having some soreness and swelling in the knees. I just couldn't quite get it all worked out. And when you grow up at Lake Travis and then you go to Abilene, well there it's either 109 degrees or nine degrees, there's nothing in between. I didn't particularly care for it. I was ready to hang it up. I had this crazy idea to get into the portable toilet business and that's what I did. I moved back, started that, met my loving wife and I think it worked out pretty well."

ACU defensive coordinator Jerry Wilson tried to convince him to return, something Wiggins said he never saw the coach do. There was just something about Kuenstler and his untapped talent that Wilson thought could help his defense.

"Mark decides college isn't for him and he leaves," Wiggins recalled. "Wilson's calling him every day, twice a day to try and get him back. Wilson told me he'd never done that and wouldn't ever do it again, but Mark was that special."

The 2000 season turned out to be a special one for everyone around Lake Travis, but the euphoria would be short-lived. Few were prepared to witness and take part in what happened next.

4: Rock Bottom

That Lake Travis stands alone atop the dynastic programs in Texas history, above the likes of Amarillo, Katy, Permian and others, comes as a complete shock to those who stopped following the program just a decade ago. In fact, the only people who followed the program in the early 2000s were the parents and family members of players and coaches, and they admit that they only went to games because they had to.

Players graduate every year, and the Cavaliers expected that following the 2000 season. But the coaching carousel proved a different story. The program underwent a near-complete turnover. After the season, offensive coordinator Matt Jones applied for and got the head coaching job at Del Valle, which had moved into a new facility east of Austin Bergstrom International Airport. Head coach Jim Shewmake moved on as well.

Shewmake's decision to leave had nothing to do with football, or even Lake Travis really. He had tied Don Cowan's mark as the winningest coach in Lake Travis' brief history with 15 wins, but he had reached a personal crossroads: family or job. Faced with a difficult decision, he made it. He later admitted he didn't know if the change had been a good career move.

"Hindsight being what it is, my decision to leave was a double-edged sword," he said. "I had decided to leave for Haltom. I [had been] divorced and my daughter was in high school in Arlington. Before that I saw her when I could but almost never during the football season. When I left Lake Travis, I got to be there for everything: the first date to scare the boy, the driver's education, the prom, all of my daughter's big things. That was the right decision for me to make. Professionally, I have some regrets, but personally, it was the right decision."

Shewmake had no way of knowing what would soon become of the program he had started to build. Returning players, including those who planned on getting their first taste of varsity action, had been looking forward to working with Shewmake and his staff. The team appeared to have a strong nucleus coming back, the playoff appearance had generated excitement, and enthusiasm had never been better.

"Coach Shewmake and that whole group ran a pretty strict program and really enforced discipline," recalled Justin Pollard, an undersized sophomore eager to make the varsity as a running back/receiver heading into the 2001 season having moved to Lake Travis years earlier from football-loving Aledo. "I loved it. It was everything I was hoping it was going to be. I loved it, loved everyone that he had in place. That whole coaching staff was really good."

Pollard recalled the disappointment he felt when Shewmake and his staff went different directions, but he still couldn't wait for the season to start.

"I was a little disappointed that I didn't get to actually play for him, especially coming off of that good year," Pollard said. "We had a ton of returning players. Quarterback was coming back which was Cody Skaggs. Robert Turner was coming back. Jake Stabeno. Neil Abraham. Most of the skill positions and the best lineman [Turner, who left the New York Jets for the St. Louis Rams for the 2012 NFL season] ever to go through the program all coming back. The next year had just a ton of upside. And for them to leave, it was disappointing not to have them around for that."

To replace Shewmake, the Lake Travis administration didn't look far. Charlie Sadler lived in Lakeway when the job came open, and he applied for it, having just spent the 2000 season as the defensive coordinator at Stony Point High School in the Round Rock ISD. Sadler, like Jim Bob Helduser before Shewmake, had been a college head coach, posting an 18-37 mark from 1991-1995 at Northern Illinois University. He'd also been a part of Barry Switzer's coaching staff at Oklahoma when the Sooners had won national championships in the 1980s. Sadler knew Lake Travis. His daughter Dustin played tennis at the high school.

One of the incoming players liked Sadler's background and thought the coach would do well.

"When Sadler was first hired it was our opinion that it was a good hire," said Kyle Reesing, a sophomore and one of the more athletic players at Lake Travis heading into 2001. "He had lots of experience, had won a national title as an assistant at Oklahoma or whatever."

While other members of Shewmake's coaching staff went different directions, defensive coordinator Kevin Halfmann hadn't followed suit. Jones had offered him a spot running the defense at Del Valle, but Halfmann liked his job, and his wife Bertha also taught and coached at the high school. Entering his seventh year on the football staff, Halfmann wanted to hear what Sadler had planned for Lake Travis before making any decisions.

"I still wasn't sure what I wanted to do," Halfmann said. "[Matt Jones] had talked to me about coming over there. Then when Sadler came in and we had our first meeting, he basically said he was going to be the defensive coordinator, so I thought there was no place for me. So that's when I went and talked to Matt and decided to go over there."

The changeover didn't bother Lake Travis' fans. Many felt Sadler, with his college experience, would pick up where Shewmake had left off. Sadler came in, met with players and generated a new excitement.

"During that time, we were excited as parents because we finally saw a spark of hope that the kids saw in this new coach and new enthusiasm coming in," said Leigh Ann Pollard, Justin's mother.

Though he'd never worked directly with Shewmake while on the freshman team, Justin Pollard realized early on that Sadler's approach didn't fit, at least not with what had worked for Lake Travis in the immediate past. More reserved that his predecessor and at times down right relaxed at practice, Sadler never became a demanding figure in the eyes of the players.

"He came in and it was very relaxed," he said. "It was a complete 180 from Coach Shewmake and how [his] workouts were, where you felt almost like a drill sergeant was in charge. Having Sadler come in, it was too laid back. Football is not supposed to be like that."

Sadler meshed with the players and most enjoyed him as a person. But the enthusiasm parents felt didn't transfer to the players.

"Sadler and the coaches he brought in were very lax," Reesing said. "They ran the program like it was a college program, and that wasn't the right thing to do with high school kids. The workouts fell off in terms of intensity, dedication. The strength program fell off, and that's not good for a football team. That was huge."

"I loved him as a person," Justin Pollard recalled. "He was a great person and a really good coach as far as Xs and Os. He knew his stuff. There was a lack of motivation and a lack of inspiration that he didn't bring to the program. That is what I think went wrong the most."

It soon became clear that Lake Travis' second leap at a coach with college experience wouldn't fare well. Parents, some of the same ones who lauded Sadler's hire, saw the struggles of a coach accustomed to dealing with players of a certain, more fundamentally sound, background. Glenn Pollard, Justin's father, thought that Sadler had been too long removed from the high school game when he returned to Austin, and as the coach at Lake Travis he never adjusted.

"Here he had to teach the kids," he said. "In college they had already been taught. I don't think he could go back to the fundamentals. I'm not cutting him down, I just think that…when you're coaching college and you're in college, you have a scholarship and you're expected to do this, this, this and this. Well, these young kids didn't have the fundamentals."

To say that Sadler's Lake Travis teams struggled doesn't do struggling justice.

Todd Reesing, who would later quarterback Lake Travis' varsity team, remembered what he saw as a middle schooler getting ready to make the jump to high school. His older brother Kyle eventually became the varsity quarterback under Sadler.

"We actually had a pretty good team in middle school and did pretty well," he said. "But I remember watching the high school games. There was no one at the games. It was kind of …you hoped the games were competitive and maybe they'll win a couple of games. There wasn't really any excitement surrounding it. Mostly it was the parents and close friends of the guys playing. For all the rest of the students, if you didn't have a connection to the team, then you probably weren't at the game."

That, sadly, became a mixed blessing. The Cavaliers stunk, but at least not many people turned out to witness it. Sadler had made several puzzling decisions, from the way he handled practice to the type of offense he installed. He moved Lake Travis away from the spread that Skaggs and company had taken to the playoffs, and practices lacked focus, intensity and competition, at least compared to what players who had been through Shewmake's practices expected.

"I didn't get to see exactly how Shewmake ran his practices….we were always separate doing our own thing," Justin Pollard recalled. "But getting to practice with the varsity and going through everything [the next year], it wasn't what I had ever imagined high school football would have been like. It wasn't the intense environment with the competitiveness in everybody coming out. I think that's when it started become almost lazy. There was a lack of focus."

It showed quickly on the field. With a team that included Skaggs and the future NFL offensive lineman Turner, the Cavaliers lost their first five games under Sadler, beat Lockhart to open district play and didn't win again.

"We ran a little different style of offense which obviously didn't work the best," Pollard, who joined the varsity after two games, said. "They took a playoff team the year before with a lot of returning talent to a 1-9 football program. I don't know. I think that lack of intensity and the lack of someone being there to enforce the discipline and motivation and everything just made the whole season, made everything...there was no desire and I think that's a direct result of why we were 1-9 that year."

Pollard said later that the losses didn't seem to bother the coaches. He thought the disastrous season would have signaled the coaches – anyone – that the approach didn't work and changes would come. After the 1-9 season in 2001, things got worse.

"It went downhill from there," Pollard said. "Absolutely nothing changed from sophomore year to junior year. The same coaches, the same workouts, same level of ... You would think that after the 1-9 season, something would have triggered somewhere that, whoa, we're not doing something right. But nothing changed at all. They had the same mentality going into the next year. And at that point in time, losing was just expected. We weren't expected to go out and win. They didn't set the bar high. They didn't expect us to win. We didn't expect ourselves to win. The crowd and the community didn't expect us to win. The bar wasn't set very high for us, and so we went out there and we met the expectations. Whenever no one expects you to do good, that kind of attitude and mentality rubs off on everybody."

Todd Reesing had a rough time watching his older brother's team endure the struggles.

"When I first got into high school as a freshman, my brother was the quarterback as a junior and that's the year they went 0-10," he said. "It was a pretty disappointing year. I was really bummed for my brother. Going 0-10 and having no one at the games was pretty frustrating. The football program was a laughing-stock. I mean, we had a pretty good freshman team, and we knew we had a pretty good class with Fred [Robinson] and Luke [Lagera] and some of the other guys, but we were freshmen. It sucked to think that we had a pretty good team, but our varsity is 0-10 and basically the whole school thinks we're a joke."

With Kyle Reesing as quarterback, Brett Chapman as running back and a small group of undersized players, Sadler and offensive coordinator Roland Murray thought it best to get away from a pass-first offense and move to a more technical, option-style attack. If the service academies could use the triple-option and find success at the college level against teams with larger, more athletic, more talented players, then why not them as well?

"The coach at the time, I never felt like he looked at the type of kids he had and came up with a plan to sort of adjust to what they were," said Tom Manning, who covered the Cavaliers for the *Lake Travis View* from 2001 until early 2003. "The option offense they ran clearly never worked."

Kyle Reesing said the team never understood why the coaches changed the offense. As the quarterback, Reesing's primary responsibility becam\ executing the offense.

"In my junior year, when we went to the triple option, in my opinion that was monumentally stupid," he said. "We didn't have the ability to run over people. The offense didn't fit and we didn't buy why they told us that's what we'd be doing. Really, they just felt like we weren't good enough to run a spread, but we had people who could do it."

The coaches' lack of faith in the players' athletic ability rubbed everyone the wrong way, and that lack of faith translated into the core of the program. Because of the coaches' attitude toward the players, Kyle Reesing said, the players lost the desire to work hard, and in turn many left the program.

"A lot of our really good athletes quit playing football because they just didn't care," he said. "There was no sense of team pride. A lot of good athletes said, 'Screw it,' because the coaches weren't enthusiastic about football."

Whatever the issues, things never came together for those Cavaliers. During games the Cavaliers would fall behind early and coaches would struggle to change the momentum. Many a time, despite holding an index card containing the few plays the Cavaliers would run on offense, Murray struggled to get plays in to the quarterback and either burned time outs or suffered delay of game penalties when he'd exhausted the time outs.

Manning said the Cavaliers had some athletic players, but they never had a chance.

"I remember the players," he said. "Kyle Reesing was pretty athletic, a good baseball player. These kids weren't stiffs. Brett Chapman was the running back who ran track. They were pretty good athletes, hard-working kids. At practice you could see them working as hard as they could. But they were fighting such an uphill battle that it would be hard not to be discouraged."

Some players did become discouraged, and it showed several ways, which bothered other players.

"It was miserable," Justin Pollard remembered. "The part that was so miserable was that it seemed most people didn't think it was miserable. They didn't care. They were just going through the motions, like, 'This is what we're supposed to do. I don't care. I just want to get out of here. What are we going to do after the game? What are we going to do this weekend?' They just didn't care about it. And for someone like me, I take everything I do to another level. If I'm playing a board game with my wife, I want to beat her. I don't want to lose, so going through that was awful."

The losses took their toll on the players, but the damage done spread well past the players. Looking back, Todd Reesing could see people losing interest in the program, in the sport.

"The football players, they played because the liked football but they don't really care was the feeling you got," he said. "It was kind of guys thought they were giving up almost. There were guys who wanted to do well and played hard and fought, but at the end of the day, you just kind of got that feeling that no one really cared about football anymore."

Manning agreed.

"Friday nights weren't situated around, 'As a community let's go support the football team,' and as a realist I can understand that," Manning said. "Why go watch those kids get beat? Other than when they played Dripping Springs, that stadium wasn't full. The Americana view of [Texas] high school football as a community organizer, there was none of that."

While the team had some followers, for the most part the community had grown indifferent toward the high school football team.

"I think there was a core group of people in the community who felt it was important and were enthusiastic and supportive in the face of adversity and what any realist would say wouldn't be successful," Manning said. "The general community, though, had a degree of apathy. Beyond the core boosters, there were no rallies, no businesses having 'LT' spray-painted on its windows, no community events centered around football other than the Meet the Cavs deal. They were dark days."

It's one thing to lose games. It's quite another to lose without ever having a chance. On many a Friday night the Cavaliers took the field with an air of gloom.

"The games were so demoralizing," Manning said. "There was never a doubt that the kids were trying as hard as they could, but you almost feel like they were put in a position to fail. They weren't equipped, and it was as if [Sadler] just threw up his hands. There were a handful of games where it was clear that not only were they going to lose, they weren't going to score. And when you think about Friday night excitement, beyond the usual go to see and be seen crowd, there wasn't very much excitement about the team."

For the longest time, Lake Travis students had a reputation as privileged, undisciplined kids who could not be motivated, forced or encouraged to put in the hard work necessary to be good at football. In his career from 1996-99, Greg Wiggins understood that some players thought there was more to life than what they accomplished on the football field.

"We were told what we'd have to sacrifice, and some guys, not all but a lot of them, were more interested in girls and life after the game than they ever were in football," Wiggins recalled. "That was just the culture of Lake Travis at that time."

If that culture existed following Wiggins' years at the school, it didn't manifest itself on the practice field, even in 2001 and 2002. Lake Travis' players, most of them anyway, gave it their all.

"One of the things you heard back then was that these are wealthy class kids and they won't work hard," Manning said. "I never saw that with the kids or felt it with the kids. They would and did work hard and would work harder if they had someone there pushing them to do great things. I never ever felt the issue of kids who didn't care. These kids, in my mind, were put in a position to fail."

That 2002 team failed spectacularly. And the coach, it seemed to the reporter, wasn't terribly bothered by the losing or creative in looking for solutions. His interviews covered the gamut of coach-speak, all except one. That interview, possibly more so the paper's decision to include a colorful quote in its story that week, drew ire from parents.

"I would meet with Sadler every Monday afternoon for about an hour. He never gave me anything of substance – it was all coach-speak," Manning said. "One time, he says, 'We've just got to get better play out of our quarterback.' When he told me that, I felt it was actual, and I put it in the story, and sure enough the dad calls and laid into me about it, and then he tore into the coach about the system, which essentially set the quarterback up to fail, and how dare he say it's the quarterback when the entire offense isn't designed for the quarterback to do anything?"

The losses often became extreme. One in particular stands out, Manning recalled.

"They played a game at New Braunfels or New Braunfels Canyon," he recalled. "It was certainly the last road game of the season, it could have been the last game before Sadler was let go. Canyon kept driving down the field and stopping at the five-yard line and taking knees. They did it on first, second, third, and fourth down. I thought they could have scored 100 if they wanted to. After the game, Sadler gave me the, 'It was classy not to run up the score,' but I thought [what they did] was worse. It was beyond Xs and Os. The kids weren't seeing it as classy. They thought the other team was taking pity on them, and nobody wants to be pitied."

Kyle Reesing said he didn't quite recall a game like that, but he conceded that since he didn't play defense as a junior, he wouldn't necessarily remember something like that happening. He didn't doubt that it happened, either.

"I've really blocked out the 2001 and 2002 seasons," he said. "My junior year we went 0-10 and it seemed like we'd never get a break. No matter what we tried we could never put it together. It was really frustrating. It felt like the coaches had given up too. We all played hard because we had individual pride, but we didn't have any team excitement. As soon as something bad happened, guys would check out mentally and then you're getting blown out."

Manning summed up the two years simply. Sports writing in general should be fun.

"It was hard to write stories about games without hurting the feelings of 16 and 17 year old kids," he recalled. "As much as sports-writing can be difficult, that was difficult. Those were not fun games to cover at all."

Halfmann, who spent four years at Del Valle including one as head coach in 2004 when the Cardinals reached the playoffs, found it difficult to see Lake Travis struggling.

"I can't believe I was [at Del Valle] for four years," he said. "It went by fast but it was a good chance to get away. At that time the parents were still busy wanting to provide that input, telling everybody what to do. It was good over there, but it was hard to see what was going on here, having spent as much time as I did, seeing those kids growing up. It was hard to see them go through what they went through, especially those first two seasons."

After two seasons that produced a 1-19 record, 14 consecutive losses and a boat load of apathy, the district needed to evaluate its football program. Changes appeared imminent, because while the school hadn't put much energy into being good at football, being horrible didn't seem like a direction to go either.

At that time, Rockwell D. Kirk, E.D., had just become the Lake Travis school district superintendent. Kirk succeeded Gloria Berry at the district's helm in 2001, and as the son of a Hall of Fame football coach, it bothered him deeply that the high school team in his district, in a word, stunk.

5: Stepping in the Right Direction

Coming off the two worst years in school history, Lake Travis' administration realized change needed to take place. New superintendent Rocky Kirk, the son of Texas High School Hall of Fame football coach George Kirk, couldn't stand to watch his district's football team flounder any longer. He decided he needed a new athletic director to help guide the overall athletic program while making the top priority fixing football.

Kirk didn't have to look far to find an athletic director he trusted. His father's best friend, Jack Moss, had been a successful football coach in his own right and a better athletic director after starting his coaching career on the senior Kirk's staff in the 1960s. Moss hadn't been surprised when the younger Kirk called in late 2002 for help. He had a mess, and he wanted Moss to clean it up.

"I was athletic director in Waco, and we had just built the top high school stadium in the state [Waco ISD]," Moss explained. "It is still the most used high school facility in the state. I was close to retirement age, and I had just lost my wife to cancer and decided to keep working. Dr. [Rocky] Kirk called me around Christmas of 2002, his first year in the district. I met with him [the next] January."

Moss did some homework about Lake Travis and came to the conclusion that under the right conditions the job could be a good one.

"[Kirk] knew how I wanted to work, and we came to the conclusion that if I came, all athletic decisions would be made in the AD's office," Moss said. "I would always work with principals but the final call on athletics was made with me. And then they could hold us accountable to those decisions. I resigned and came. I had already built a ranch in Llano."

Moss, who'd also developed into an accomplished artist when he wasn't tending to the horses on his Llano farm, hit the ground running and assessed the situation. How bad had it gotten, not just for football but for the other sports as well? Moss jumped in with both feet, meeting with coaches, parents, students and anyone else who'd talk to him about Lake Travis athletics.

"I spent the first few weeks visiting with coaches and parents who had unbiased opinions about what the general issues were," Moss said.

More than looking at personnel, he looked at the overall environment. How did athletics fit with the district's philosophy on education? Did the district value winning? Did the administration provide an environment conducive to success on the fields as well as in the classrooms? That meant not only putting in his foundation for a football program, but as Moss relates, working to overhaul the entire athletic program, starting with the level of importance the administration placed on success.

Moss maintains athletics plays an important role in a student's education. If it didn't, he said, schools shouldn't offer it. It starts with teachers, and Moss believes that coaches can be integral in that process. If you look at each sport as an extension of education, the coaches become the teachers for that class, working with each student or group of students to make sure they learn what they need to learn to find success.

"Athletics can, without a doubt, be used in that process and be successful, because I've never seen a good coach who was a bad teacher," he said. "All coaching is, is teaching kids. I think teachers can take lessons from coaches because of the re-teaching process and the way coaches break things down to make sure the kids learn it."

In evaluating Lake Travis' athletics, Moss found something fundamentally amiss with the way the administration, both staff and elected board members, viewed and oversaw the athletic program. Athletics held no priority, and over the years decisions had been made and policies enacted that made it inherently difficult for the program as a whole to find success.

Greg Wiggins, who graduated Lake Travis in 2000 and lettered in both football and basketball, said the district's focus had unwaveringly been on academics.

"Lake Travis was an academic, theater powerhouse at that time," Wiggins recalled. "There was no sports. Maybe tennis and golf but that's it."

Wiggins' view meshed with what Moss learned after assessing the situation.

"Athletics in general, and football in particular, was not important at Lake Travis," Moss said. "Why? I don't know. It was just something that you did. There were no major expectations on the kids that could be enforced by internal or external people. There are lots of examples where kids were given too much freedom and it showed up on the field. There were not many kids playing and there was very little parent involvement."

From a student-athlete perspective, one key player from the 2002 football team said the program had no vision.

"I feel like the program lost its way," said Kyle Reesing, who quarterbacked the team in 2002 and graduated in 2004 after playing both football and baseball. "The kids, because the discipline wasn't there, they stopped caring deeply."

Moss also questioned the way the athletic department made decisions.

"People in athletic leadership were secondary in the decision-making process," he said. "Administrators made decisions that were roadblocks [to athletic success] and then held coaches responsible for the outcome of those decisions. No one can work like that."

Moss believed that creating a strong athletic program had a domino effect throughout not only the school, but the community. Success breeds success, and it should start from the day school opens for the year. Football provides a springboard for success at everything throughout the school year. Right or wrong, his philosophy makes sense, especially in Texas.

"You can ask any school administrator, anyone in the central office, and they always say the first few weeks are very important because how the school year starts has a major effect on the whole year," Moss said. "It's true in athletics, too. If you are successful, there is carryover because the same kids play different sports. Football is at the beginning of the year, and it's very important that it becomes successful. Everything else will follow suit. That advice stuck with me and I used it while coaching. School pride is built on extra-curricular events. You want strong academics, but you never see people line the streets for academics. Because of the success of the football team, school pride increased greatly, and now each team is feeding on the other's success."

Moss put the focus on the students playing the games and decided that the coaches in his department would make it their priority to put those student-athletes in position to succeed.

"Programs are built with kids. You add quality staff — you have to pay them and make the jobs so good that they don't want to leave — and an administration that understands priorities based on time of year," Moss said. "When I came on board, I told every coach that the scoreboard counts. I used to tell people we buy expensive scoreboards for a reason. My job is to help you get what you need to be successful with each kid. That's how it should be: remove hurdles, get what you need and then hold you accountable for success. Take football. Ninety-nine percent of the players don't play past their last high school game. It is then up to us to make sure they can succeed. If we don't, then we have sinned against these kids."

Seemingly overnight, winning became important, and the administration would get used to expecting it, no matter the sport. As Moss worked on changing the culture, he also faced some personnel decisions.

"We decided which coaches we needed to change," he said. "They weren't all bad but they were connections to things that weren't good."

Charlie Sadler topped the list. After releasing the football coach, Moss went about finding his replacement. The search proved challenging. In the end, he found only a few qualified candidates.

"When we opened up the position, we had very few quality applicants," Moss said. "Most were from small schools, not successful in the programs they were coming from. The good coaches just weren't going to come to Lake Travis. Then Dicus got on the scene."

Jeff Dicus had just finished his second year as head coach at Mission High School, where he'd guided the team into the regional semifinals and earned Rio Grande Valley coach of the year honors. He'd taken a team that finished 4-6 his first season and dramatically reversed its fortune, going 11-2 in 2002. His application, and background as an assistant on Texas City's 1997 4A state championship team, definitely grabbed the attention of both Moss and new Lake Travis High School Principal Charlie Little.

"The school had been 1-19 over two years when I got there," Little, who worked with Moss during the hiring process, said. "I worked with Jack Moss, got to interview coaches at the time the job was posted. Dicus seemed like the kind of guy who would relate to the kids."

Moss took the lead in the interview process and, like Little, came to the quick conclusion that, given the pool of applicants, Dicus stood out as the only choice.

"The process was that I would take the applicants and call and visit with people to get information on them," Moss said. "Jeff was highly successful at two places as head coach. He was one of the best things that ever happened [to Lake Travis]. At that time and that place, in that moment, he was what we needed. His discipline and his rules were key because we had good kids for whom the marks to get to play were never set high. Few kids wanted to be part of it. In 2002, the varsity and junior varsity had barely enough to finish the season."

**

A decorated athlete at Bishop Heelan Catholic High School in Iowa, Jeff Dicus figured his athletic career would take him into coaching once he graduated from the University of South Dakota. He just didn't figure it would take him to football.

"When I went to the University of South Dakota, I went there thinking I would be a basketball coach," Dicus recalled. "I dreamt of being the next Bobby Knight. Back then he was at the top of the game. Then, halfway through my sophomore year, I started thinking that I'd become a football coach. I was heavily influenced by coaches who were interested in me and inspired me to become a football coach."

When he finished his football playing career, earning a trio of all-conference honors as a tight end, Dicus returned to his high school as a teacher and assistant coach, helping guide his alma mater to the Iowa 4A state championship. When the 1983 school year ended, Dicus applied for and got a job in Mission, where he began to develop into the coach he is today.

"There were a group of us from that South Dakota, Iowa corridor that interviewed for a job in Mission, Texas, home of Tom Landry, and we went there and turned that program around," Dicus said.

Having helped rebuild the program at Mission High School, Dicus began to understand something about his life. He felt a calling to help turn the fortunes of struggling football programs, and as he worked his way up the coaching ranks from assistant to coordinator to head coach, that calling became even clearer to him. Through the years, Dicus has been the head coach at Boerne, Mission, Lake Travis and now Duncanville, opting to move from place to place to help new teams and new communities rediscover success.

"It hasn't been by design," he said in 2012. "It has been a calling from the good Lord. Coach Moss used to call me missionary coach, and that always meant a lot to me when he said that. I feel I was put on Earth to help communities, high schools and kids."

He coached at Boerne for three years and two years at Mission before taking over the Lake Travis program. At both Boerne and Mission, Dicus inherited teams that hadn't made the playoffs, and by the second year he had reversed that trend. He'd stay five years at Lake Travis before moving to Duncanville, where he entered his fifth season in 2012.

"I just take it year by year," he explained. "Sometimes things happen quickly, sometimes they happen more slowly. Sometimes I'm at places two or three years. Sometimes it's more like five years. You evaluate everything as it happens. It's just a calling from the Lord that moves me to another place."

***

Fast forward to Dec. 16, 2011. Lake Travis plays for its fifth straight state championship at Cowboys Stadium later that night. Jeff and Karen Dicus walk in to an Applebee's between Duncanville and Arlington to talk about his time at Lake Travis. It's clear that both the coach and his wife still relish what his teams accomplished between 2003 and 2007. They enter wearing Duncanville shirts and jackets, but amidst their Duncanville gear are two not-so-subtle souvenirs of Lake Travis' first state title. You can't miss Jeff's state championship ring, proudly displayed on his right hand. Karen wears diamond pendant necklace in the shape of the Lake Travis insignia. The Dicuses may have left Lake Travis years ago, but they both still carry the school with them.

Back in 2003, Dicus himself didn't think he'd land at Lake Travis. Off his success at Mission, he had also interviewed for the job at 5A Cedar Hill, a marquee program outside of Dallas.

"I had actually interviewed at Cedar Hill, and what was it, two weeks later I got the interview at Lake Travis?" Dicus recalled with a glance at his wife. "I didn't know anything about Lake Travis. We looked at it because it was closer to our folks, mine in Georgetown and hers in San Antonio."

The coach came to interview in early 2003, and the night before his interview he attended a Lake Travis soccer game. That evening proved memorable for him, and it set the tone for his interview the next day.

"I'm just in there, sitting there, watching a soccer game and someone comes over," Dicus said. "I don't remember their names. They start talking to me, and they know I'm interviewing tomorrow. They end up offering their little lake house to me if I got the job, I guess when I got the job was what they were saying. So, we hit it off during the game. I end up interviewing the next day with Coach Moss and fell in love with him then. [He was] real relaxed, down to earth."

Dicus learned of Moss' relationship with Kirk and took that as a sign of the district's commitment to developing a successful football program. The more he learned about Lake Travis, its football situation and the student body, the more intrigued he grew with the opportunity.

"So everything went well," Dicus recounted. "Good interview. Loved it. Good opportunity. Big challenge, I thought it was going to be. All I heard was that you can't get wealthy kids to buy into discipline and organization and working hard. So that was a tremendous challenge, to say okay, let's give it a shot. So they offered it to me and I moved up in February."

With new coaches, first impressions can be crucial, and by all accounts the impression Dicus made upon his arrival couldn't have been better.

"When you meet him, he's a motivating person," Little said. "He was a proven program builder and what we needed at the time. LT back then wasn't a place anyone wanted to be a head coach. It had promise, but it hadn't been successful. We wanted someone who would pay their dues to move it forward. He had everything we were looking for, and I felt we worked well together during that time."

Tom Manning covered sports for the *Lake Travis View* newspaper when Dicus arrived. Though Manning would leave the paper prior to the 2003 season, he has vivid memories of meeting Dicus.

"I remember the first time I sat with him," Manning said. "I came away thinking that this guy's going to do what he says he's going to do. It wasn't bravado. He just had faith that he was going to do this. When I told him I was moving on, he told me that I was picking the wrong time to leave because they were going to be good. I believed him, even though I never got to see him or his staff work with anyone on the field."

Dan Kleiner joined the *Lake Travis View* in 2004 and covered sports for three years. He came to work with Dicus regularly during that time, covering the Cavaliers as they began their climb.

"My first impression of Dicus was that he was a massive man," Kleiner recalled. "He looked the part [of a football coach], like he was born for that role: big, muscular and he had the mentality. He was a dominant figure. He was born to do nothing else but coach football."

Dicus quickly won the players over as well. Kyle Reesing, a senior on the 2003 team, recalls the impression that most everyone got.

"When Dicus came in, that was the biggest influx of enthusiasm I'd seen," he said. "Dicus and [Jim] Shewmake were identical in personality. They both were fair disciplinarians."

Justin Pollard, who'd also labored through a frustrating two years under Sadler, said the team's first meeting with Dicus proved exactly what the players had hoped for.

"One, there were a lot of us who were wanting to make a change, so that was exactly what we were hoping and looking for," Pollard recalled. "The other thing was, when he first came in, the first time we met him I think we were in the cafeteria and had a big player-parent type of deal. He introduced himself and told stories about his previous career with Texas City and Mission, where he had built these programs and this is what he wanted to do. He basically sat there and told us his plan and how he wanted to change not our football team but he wanted to change the community. That was pretty exciting because it wasn't just about us. He wanted to change the way people viewed it. He wanted to get the community involved and excited about it."

Both Reesing and Pollard noticed Dicus' intensity and enthusiasm immediately.

"The enthusiasm Dicus had was beyond belief, firing up everyone in the program," Reesing said. "He was overly passionate, and it was infectious. From day one, he was all smiles and pumped about being here. You could feel the energy and it translated into guys wanting to work hard for him."

Looking back, Pollard said Dicus and his staff's arrival had the same effect on the team that Sadler and his staff did. But where Sadler brought a more relaxed attitude that permeated the players, Dicus' style couldn't have been more different.

"When Coach Dicus came in, that attitude rubbed off on us the same way," Pollard said. "Seeing his intensity and his passion for it just kind of sparked everybody. You could tell that he was serious."

Dicus became the new sheriff in town, and everyone and everything football answered to him.

"The last thing was probably fear," Pollard said. "We didn't want to screw up and let him down. Because we had that fear, you didn't want to be late for a meeting, loafing at practice. You didn't want to get in trouble in class because we had that fear of being disciplined for it. We didn't have that in years past. We were held to a higher standard than we had been, so it elevated everybody."

Impressions work both ways, and Dicus recalled being pleasantly surprised at the first impression the community made on him. As expected after two dreadful years, excitement about Lake Travis football had waned, both in the community and inside the school from the students up to the administration. But change can be good, or at least interesting even to those who had stopped attending games. At the first meeting where Moss and Little introduced the new coach, Dicus didn't believe that his new community had grown apathetic toward football.

"What we were told was that the administration didn't support athletics," Dicus said. "It wasn't a football atmosphere at all. Our first meeting, I'll never forget, was in the cafeteria when they introduced me, and the place was pretty full, which I thought was pretty cool. I think it was a community that was looking for structure, looking for discipline, just looking for organization to help take their program to the next level."

And so he set about trying to do that.

While the actual coaching became Dicus' primary responsibility, there's more to being the head football coach than practices and games. Lake Travis had a long road to hoe, and Dicus needed plenty of support. He asked for it and he got it.

While Moss worked on things from the administrative level, Dicus went to work building a football program. While previous coaches had eyes toward program-building, none had stayed long enough to see anything through. Prior to Dicus' arrival, only four coaches had stayed more than two years, and when Dicus took the job in 2003, the school had seen five different head coaches in the 10 previous seasons.

Part of the issue, coaches recalled, had been overzealous parent involvement. Too often their interaction with the coach centered on strategy, playing time for their child or other football-specific things. Parents spent valuable energy questioning the program, not supporting it. Dicus created a structure where the parents became involved with the program through a reinvigorated booster club, and essentially didn't have time to come to him with football-specific questions.

"He was highly organized and had a tremendous ability to come up with things like the Cow Patty Drop to get people involved," Moss said. "I can't tell you how many parents were involved in different ways."

The players noticed the difference immediately.

"With Sadler, there wasn't any excitement," Reesing said. "Parents weren't involved. My senior year – with Dicus – the parents were stepping up and getting involved."

It hadn't taken Dicus long to get parents involved, and something about the way they mobilized at one of his first requests for help told him he had a parent group that could become a huge ally for him. His first office had been in the tiny field house atop the campus.

"It was a beautiful place, up there on the hill," Dicus said. "We loved it up there. We had that view up there on that game field and at the field house. I don't know when it was, maybe a month into it, we came in on a Saturday and painted it with the parents and gave the field house a new look. That was when things started to come together because we had parents working together and involvement and I think that kind of kicked off things."

Glenn and Leigh Ann Pollard had been among the first parents who chipped in with the painting project. They both saw Dicus as a much-needed breath of fresh air for the program.

"Then the heart came in, and the heart was Jeff," Leigh Ann said. "He had an organization, ability and he had a fire that he lit with excitement for the parents. He brought us in…we were up there painting posters, supporting midnight madness. Giving us excitement toward something, a hand in it."

"We painted the locker rooms for the kids," Glenn said. "The kids weren't allowed in there [while we were painting]. Only the parents were allowed in there. That was the old [facility] up on top of the hill. Jeff is a very good organizer. If you're going to start something new like that, you want him in there."

While the parents worked, Dicus and Moss rebuilt the booster club's structure. Prior to 2003, Lake Travis had operated with one large booster club that supported all sports. It had its strengths, but it also had weaknesses, and the pair of coaches went about implementing a structure that ended up benefiting every sport.

"There used to be one booster club for all the sports," Moss said. "We split the sports out and gave each of them their own club. That helped because people got to support each other and do their own thing. [Before, money the football parents raised went to basketball or baseball, and they didn't like that.]"

"To each their own with the booster clubs," Dicus said. "I think everybody was receptive to it. The biggest thing with that was the parents allowed me to make decisions for the program where as in the past the parents were making decisions for the program. What we did was supported through Coach Moss, Dr. Kirk and the administration."

With excitement growing even before the team gathered for its first practices, the football booster club took off. By the time Kevin Halfmann returned to Lake Travis as an assistant coach in 2005, he noticed a world of difference between the parents of the 1990s and the parents in Dicus' football program. Halfmann recalled that one of the biggest challenges to success in his previous stint as an assistant, from 1994-2000, had been an over-engaged parent base that wanted to insert themselves into football decisions. As Halfmann attended a booster club meeting with the head coach, he sat back and watched in awe as Dicus took over the room.

"The first parent meeting I went to, he starts throwing up all of these things [on a board] and then says we have all these volunteer opportunities," Halfmann said. "There were 16 opportunities, 16 heads with three, four, five people to help them out. I remember thinking you're taking up a lot of people, but really he was making it so their conversations with him were going to be about their particular job and not the football end of it. It was kind of brilliant. It got the community involved, and they saw the football program from a different perspective."

Booster club members started working on their projects, and the coaches concentrated on building the program. The coach, though, always kept an eye on those projects. Two parents new to the program found that out quickly.

"No matter what we did, Coach Dicus was always on top of things," Laurie Lagasse, whose sons Bryant and Colin would become varsity standouts, recalled. "He was the organizer. When the [2007] spring game came, we had volunteered for a little job, and when the game came I couldn't find our name on the list. So I called him, and he told me I was looking in the wrong spot. He had added Dave and I, who's never even been to the cow patty drop or whatever it was called back then, as the chairpeople. I said, 'Coach Dicus, I've never even been to one.' And he said, 'Don't worry, I've got this.' He knew the direction he wanted everything to go in, even in meetings with parents he was very good as a leader. He really was."

While the parents enjoyed their jobs, the coaches began implementing Dicus' program. They worked long hours, longer than many were accustomed.

"Jeff came in and he changed everybody's expectations," Halfmann said. "It wasn't just the kids. He changed the coaches' expectations of the parents and the parents' expectations of the coaches."

With the infrastructure taking shape, Dicus turned his attention to the football itself. The first culture change involved the players themselves. In the previous two years, players faced very little in the way of expectations or discipline, and they acted accordingly. No one voluntarily took part in off-season weight training or stayed after school to run or lift. They lived at Lake Travis, after all, and the water beckoned. Dicus recalled his first few weeks, seeing boats on trailers in the student parking lot.

"The boats were in the parking lot. After school, the bell would ring, kids would run up the hill, get in the cars and take the boats to the lake. That was the mentality."

Parents of players who came later heard this as well. They also heard that Dicus handled it perfectly.

"Everybody had said that before Dicus it was just a bunch of lake kids," said Dave Lagasse, whose family came to Lake Travis in 2006 from Louisiana, where he'd been a football coach. "They'd rather party out at the lake and go skiing than show up for football practice. There was not a big commitment to the program, so he was the right guy to implement the discipline, the structure and get this thing going in the right direction."

Dicus changed that mentality. He set different expectations and then held the students who wanted to play football accountable to those expectations.

"So our whole approach was that we wanted to invest some of our free time in what we're doing, in what we want to do. And this is what we have to do: we have to spend an hour, an hour and a half, two hours in the weight room, throwing after the workout, doing these type of things."

The players couldn't wait to get started. They saw a new coach excited about them, excited about football and excited about building a program with them.

"He changed the environment," Reesing said. "Workouts were 10 times more strenuous. Even as a baseball player, I still had to do my off-season football workouts. I had to get up at 6 a.m. and do them before school because I had baseball after school. It was a very big change."

And while the players couldn't know it in the spring, that change would have a profound effect on their play in the fall. Reesing realized that looking back on the 2003 season.

"Before, there was no sense of pride, culture, camaraderie. And that translates on the field. If we know they don't care, you play like that. It translates to the field."

As the traditional spring practice period drew near, Dicus and his staff faced a choice: get started in the spring or postpone practice until August, thus gaining a week of two-a-day practices. Justin Pollard recalled that all of Dicus' assistant coaches hadn't come to Lake Travis yet.

"The whole coaching staff wouldn't have been in place for spring, so they opted not to have spring ball so we could have an extra week of two-a-days," Pollard recalled. "He chose to have that extra week to get everyone more prepared before the season."

That the Cavaliers didn't hold formal practices in the spring doesn't mean the players didn't work, or work out. The coaches could implement the conditioning program and weight lifting, but as soon as footballs came out, they had to step away. But the Cavaliers still got to start learning the offense. Dicus brought his coordinators with him from Mission, including offensive coordinator Jerry Bird, who brought more than his playbook with him. Bird's son Nick had been an all-district quarterback at Mission as a junior in 2002, and he gave Lake Travis an experienced quarterback who served as a player-coach that summer.

"Nick Bird, he was able to take Chase Fickessen, [Justin] Pollard, some of the other kids and work out after school," Dicus said. "That group was the catalyst of getting us going offensively and getting our program going. Because Nick understood the offense it was easy for him to tell the others, 'We're gonna go work these routes.' Because as coaches we couldn't go out there."

Justin Pollard said a group of players worked out with the new quarterback as often as they could, both during the spring semester and throughout the summer once school ended.

"Since Nick had run their offense for so long, he already knew it all. He was able to teach us all the plays, all the route trees, all the stuff that we'd be running that year throughout the spring and summer of working out on our own."

Learning the offense became one priority. Forming relationships and bonds between players and their new quarterback became the other. As Bird entrenched himself, the shackles of the recent past began to loosen.

"We had that special handful who stuck with it and made it through all those tough losses and stretch of going 1-19 and made it through to senior year," Pollard said. "We could tell it was different in the offseason when the new coaches came in. One of the minor things that changed was there was a pretty small group of us who stayed through the summer to throw with

Nick. Obviously we didn't know him, so building a relationship with him was important, getting to know him. Getting our timing down with him was important. So there were a lot of us who threw with him, went and ran routes, worked out with him all summer, played 7-on-7 that summer and I think that helped us build a core group of leaders for that next year."

While some players got a leg up on the fall practice season by working throughout the summer, other players had a tougher time adjusting to Dicus and the new expectations. The Cavaliers didn't convene for formal football workouts until just before school started in 2003. To create excitement, Dicus decided that the first practice would take place at midnight the very first day the University Interscholastic League allowed teams to practice. Midnight madness was exciting. It was different. And it didn't go off without a hitch.

Moss attended almost every meeting the football team had. He recalled that, in meetings with the players prior to that very first midnight practice, Dicus set the expectation that in addition to the midnight workout, there would also be a workout the following afternoon with mandatory attendance – no exceptions. Not every player took the coach at his word, and a trio did not attend the subsequent afternoon practice. Dicus responded quickly, dismissing them from the team.

"The first year, after that midnight practice, there were kids who didn't show up for the afternoon practice," Moss said. "Jeff had set the expectation that it was mandatory, and these kids, who were starters in 2002, he removed them from the team."

They weren't the only 2002 players who left the program, Pollard said.

"I think every Friday night [of the 2002 season] I went home mad, and the frustrating thing was that there were only a handful of people on the team who cared," he said. "And that showed the next year when Dicus came in and completely flipped everything and enforced all the discipline that we'd been lacking for so long and drove probably eight to 10 seniors out of the program. Those are the ones I'm talking about who didn't care about it. Whenever we had a coach in there who enforced something, it was more than they were willing to put in so they just quit."

The midnight madness incident became a watershed moment. First, it gave Dicus the opportunity to put his foot down early, to let everyone know how much he valued and demanded discipline. Second, it cast him as a strong leader, showing the parents that he ruled his program with an iron fist.

"We had to remove three kids," he said. "They just wouldn't buy into it, wouldn't buy into the discipline and the expectations we had for them. I think from that point forward the parents understood that I can run this program and that we weren't going to be told how to run the program because that wasn't the job of a parent. Your job as a parent was to get him here on time, dressed, fed, rested, clean shaven."

Reesing said Dicus' attitude and demands were well-founded, and that the core group of players didn't want any distractions from classmates who hadn't bought into the new coach's plan.

"He didn't tolerate any bullshit nonsense," Reesing recalled. "He ran off kids who didn't want to put in the time. Some of them were really good athletes, but we didn't need negative cancers within the program. We needed everyone to be on board, and it was a good thing those guys left."

The three dismissed players appealed to the school board for reinstatement, and for possibly the first time, the board deferred to Dicus' decision. Moss points to that decision as another key moment in the program's development.

"Some of them went to the school board, and that was the first time we had that back-up from them," he said.

The result didn't get lost on the players, young or old.

"I think after that, after kind of everyone realized that this guy isn't joking around and everyone kind of knew his back history, that he had success in turning programs around, I think everyone kind of realized, 'Well, hey, let's get on board and let's go with this thing,'" said Todd Reesing.

Dicus' focus, drive and determination hit home with younger players. Three sophomores, Todd Reesing among them, hoped to make a varsity splash in 2003. As part of the freshman team in 2002, he saw what had happened to the program, to his older brother Kyle and his friends. He knew change needed to happen, and he quickly saw Dicus as the answer.

"I think with Coach Dicus, when he came in and brought that disciplinary, real stern, 'I'm not going to cut any corners, you're going to do things the right way and work hard and we're going to earn our way,' there were some guys that didn't quite fit that mold," Todd Reesing said. "He was quick to say, 'Hey, this is how things are going to be, if you don't want to comply and be a part of the team in turning this thing around, then you're welcome to walk out the door.'"

Dicus also changed the program's appearance. As trivial as it sounds, Dicus wanted people thinking big. That meant flash. He had the grounds crew paint the team's logo, an interlocking LT awash with flames, at the 50-yard line. He ordered new uniforms and had the players' names sewn onto their jerseys. The Cavaliers became dead ringers, at least in looks if not in playing style, to Mike Leach's wide open Texas Tech Red Raiders. Lake Travis may have been a high school program, but everything about the way Dicus looked at it, and wanted it viewed from the outside, screamed college or professional.

"I don't remember Texas Tech being in consideration as an example to look at, but we just wanted a complete change from the uniform, helmet and sticker that they'd had before," Dicus recalled. "Everyone – the players, the community — loved it."

He also began an outreach program where he and several other coaches and players would have lunch every Friday with booster club members and interested fans at Mulligan's, then an area restaurant/billiards bar about two miles from campus.

Dicus' first preseason progressed nicely. Players had adjusted to much tougher, more rigid practices. Justin Pollard quickly became impressed with Dicus' attention to detail and ability to plan.

"He was extremely intense, very into everything he was doing and very, very detail oriented," he said. "With the coaches before, we could go out and run through drills, then go do something else and try to get to some teamwork. When he came in, we didn't go out to a single practice not knowing exactly what we were going to be doing, knowing what was expected. He only had a certain amount of time to work us out, and he was going to get every possible thing out of that little bit of time. He had every practice detailed out too. Two minutes for this, seven minutes for this, and so on. As soon as the buzzer went off for the end of that time period, you moved to the next drill without missing a beat. It was organization like we'd never experienced."

The players liked it, and as the season approached they began to thrive, some in familiar spots, others in new roles. Nick Bird locked up the quarterback spot, which meant Kyle Reesing needed to find a new position, so he moved from offense to defense. He'd become a standout safety while also rotating in at receiver. While other key upperclassmen filled roles, Fickessen and Pollard to name two specifically, the arrival of the three sophomores proved monumental in the team's development.

Luke Lagera, Fred Robinson and Todd Reesing all broke camp with the varsity team after anchoring a successful freshman team whose season got lost against the backdrop of the varsity's winless season. Kyle Reesing remembers that his class wanted to set the tone for the youngsters. He knew each would play a significant role in any success Lake Travis would have, both immediate and future.

"We wanted to show the younger guys how to do things," Kyle Reesing said. "We self-policed a lot of things. We encouraged and pushed the younger guys – my brother, Fred, Luke – they were the young guys on varsity our senior year and we wanted them to grow. They got an early taste of success and it translated for them. The tone was set and put in motion the right way."

Dicus recalled the work the seniors did to lay the foundation. It became evident early on that his first team would fight until the final whistle, a stark change from what he'd heard of the previous team.

"That first group – Fickessen and that group – established the work ethic that was going to be required," he recalled. "Todd's group was a talented group – Luke Lagera, Fred Robinson – and we had them coming up, playing for us as sophomores. We knew we had good kids coming. That's the thing that parents always commented on: kids were fighting to the end."

Like his brother, the younger Reesing also needed a position change to see the field immediately. He'd quarterbacked the freshman team, but with Bird experienced and intimately familiar with Dicus' offense, he wouldn't play much in that role. Unwilling to merely hold the clipboard and bide his time, the younger Reesing convinced the coaches that he could play receiver as well as back up Bird at quarterback.

"I didn't want to sit on the bench," Todd Reesing said. "I don't enjoy doing that. So I was able to talk them into giving me a shot at receiver and I ended up getting a spot as a starter."

He also held down jobs as the kicker and punter. Robinson and Lagera earned spots in the starting lineup as receiver and running back, respectively, and the season got off to a promising start.

Playing Anderson at home, the Cavaliers took the opening kickoff and scored immediately, setting the stage for an exciting season – something fans had been waiting for. That first game went back and forth, and in the end, Lake Travis had something it hadn't seen in more than a year, a chance to win. No one realized that more than the younger Reesing as he lined up to attempt a field goal with the score tied.

"We had a chance to win the game at the end of regulation and I pushed the kick wide right and it went to overtime," he said.

In overtime, Anderson scored first and kicked an extra point to take a 38-31 lead. The Cavaliers responded quickly and scored to pull within 38-37. Dicus eschewed going for the tie to extend the game and went for two points to win. The try failed, but that doesn't mean the team did. And it wouldn't be the last time Dicus would go for two in a key moment.

"We ended up losing, so [it was] a pretty rough start to my high school football career, blowing a chance to win the game for all the seniors who had just come off an 0-10 season," Todd Reesing said. "I was pretty down in the dirt but they picked me back up after that."

While he took the loss hard, others saw a silver lining in his personal dark cloud. Many close to the program considered the game much different than simply another loss for lowly Lake Travis. The game served as a wake-up call: Lake Travis could compete, battle.

"Coming that close to a win was a new experience," said Pollard. "Even though it started the same way as every other season, by losing, we had a little taste of accomplishment, like we'd won something even though we came up a little short. That was a victory for us, taking them into overtime, considering our past two years. That was a step in the right direction. We didn't win the game, but we saw tremendous improvement."

"I remember the comeback we made against Anderson at home," Little said later. "We ended up losing, but we got a lot of respect that night. The kids played hard, and in that first season, even though we lost, you could tell with the crowd, you could see the excitement. It was a coming out party for the program. We lost the game, but we showed promise. They saw the payoff of the work [Dicus] was doing."

In one game, Dicus all but disproved what Sadler and his staff believed the year before. Lake Travis, with its stereotypical student-athlete, could indeed compete in football.

"It was the same kids, but they were able to bring out the talent," Little said of Dicus and his staff. "We were a well-coached group, and people began taking notice and talking about how the program had turned around. Jeff should get all the credit."

While the Lake Travis fans and even players had been encouraged by the moral victory, Dicus made it clear that losing, past history aside, would never be acceptable. He hadn't been happy following the loss, and the players took note. Pollard remembered.

"But it wasn't a win for Coach Dicus in his mind at all. It was not okay to lose, so by seeing that, that helped push us toward not accepting losing. Before, if we lost we got the normal talk. 'You played hard, gave it everything you had,' pat on the back type stuff, and that's why we started accepting losing. But seeing how mad it made him that we lost, and to know that he didn't expect that and he made it clear that we shouldn't expect that, and that started changing things."

The rest of the 2003 season flew by, and the Cavaliers continued to grow by leaps and bounds. While they kept moving in the right direction, they kept coming up short in close game after close game.

"All of our pre-district games we lost but I don't think we lost any of them by more than a touchdown," Pollard said. "In most cases we outplayed the other team, but the one reason we didn't pull it out was that we didn't know how to win. It wasn't until we got into district when we got our first win that we kind of got the taste of what it was like. It was amazing to finally get over the hump."

The Cavaliers finally got over that hump at Del Valle on Sept. 26, ending a stretch of 18 consecutive losses. Lagera got the Cavaliers off on the right

75

foot with an 81-yard touchdown run midway through the opening quarter. He added another touchdown in the second quarter as the Cavaliers took a 15-0 lead. But outside of Lagera's running the offense struggled, thanks in part to Del Valle's ball-control offense, and Lake Travis' defense took center stage. Despite allowing more than 360 yards rushing and 400 yards in all, the Cavaliers only surrendered two scores, and when Lagera added a third touchdown to cap a 144-yard night, the Cavaliers celebrated a 22-12 win.

"It was a good feeling, walking off the field," Dicus told the *Lake Travis View* following the game. "Our kids finally got the opportunity to see what it feels like to walk off the field as winners. Every ounce of sweat, every minute of time, it is worth it. The kids deserve this win."

The Cavaliers beat Lockhart the following week 28-6 in front of a packed house on Homecoming. Bird connected with Todd Reesing and Pollard for first half touchdowns, and Lockhart managed only a late score to avoid a shutout. Bird enjoyed one of his best Lake Travis days, completing 22 of 27 passes for 270 yards without an interception.

Kyle Reesing knew the Cavaliers were on to something when the annual grudge match with Dripping Springs arrived the following week. His team had gotten into a groove and itched to avenge a 42-14 beat-down on their home field the previous year. The Cavaliers did, beating the Tigers on their field, winning 38-29 for the most significant win of Dicus' early tenure. Lake Travis led 25-7 at the half and withstood a late Tiger rally. Pollard caught three first-half touchdown passes to lead the charge.

"The most satisfying win of all of them that year had to be against Drip after they had beaten us the past few years," Pollard said. "Everybody had beaten us the last couple of years, but having to hear everything about the rival school and going to their place my senior year for their homecoming and embarrassing them was definitely the most memorable game of my career there."

Reesing agreed.

"The turning point for me was the Dripping Springs game," Reesing said. "We stuck it to them and kicked their butt. They had kicked our ass the year before – ran for something like 300 yards on us. We went into their house and gave it to them. To me, that was the turning point. We created a buzz, beating our big rival. After that game, even leading up to it, we travelled well. But we came back home and the crowds were raucous, into the games. Even though the record didn't translate – we were 3-7 or whatever – we could have won four of the games we lost. We played good teams close, and that was a big transition for us, knowing we could compete."

After beating Dripping Springs, the Cavaliers didn't win again, falling to New Braunfels Canyon, Bastrop and New Braunfels in succession to finish the season 3-3 in district play, one spot out of the playoffs. Despite the season's frustrating end, the Cavaliers kept the big picture clearly in focus. Figuring out the team could compete with their rivals turned out to be more important than simply looking at wins and losses. But Lake Travis insiders remained the only ones taking notice.

"The rest of the season we were in games," Todd Reesing said. "It was competitive, we weren't getting blown out, but we just couldn't quite get over the edge. You could feel that we were on the edge, and I think a lot of people started to see that we were being competitive, but there still wasn't quite that level of respect, the excitement around the program. It was kind of, okay, we didn't go 0-10, we won some games this year, we were competitive, but there still wasn't a whole lot of buzz around the team."

Looking back on that season, Dicus knew the program had taken off, and success would come quickly.

"Even though the record doesn't show, our first year at 3-7, things were looking promising because we knew what we had coming back," Dicus said. "We just had to get back to work. We had Todd coming, and he was excited. We had the receivers. We had some defensive kids. Ronnie and Mike DeWitt. Ed Novess had his boys."

Todd Reesing took over at quarterback. He knew Lake Travis would be better in the summer before the season. Dicus wanted the team to participate in the UIL-sanctioned 7-on-7 passing league in the summer, and with Reesing, Robinson and Lagera, Lake Travis thrived. The coach remembers the team doing well even if he couldn't be directly involved with those workouts or competitions.

"Todd's group made it to the state 7-on-7 tournament," Dicus remembered. "Todd's dad Steve was a big supporter, Gale Gilbert, Hardee McCrary. Jack Fickessen as well."

The 7-on-7 proved a precursor. The new quarterback, who hadn't had much formal quarterback coaching and had spent his sophomore year catching passes rather than throwing them, had a good feel for the talent that would take the field around him.

"Coming into the next year, I think there started to be a little bit more excitement because I think people kind of realized that our class that were sophomores were going to be juniors and had played a lot of guys who had played as sophomores," he said. "We could have a chance to have a pretty decent team. But there probably wasn't anyone that really expected we were going to be as successful as we were."

The Cavaliers started quickly developing into impressive football players. Even people who hadn't had a great deal of interaction with the program at that point sensed things had changed. Specifically, they noticed that Lake

Travis didn't feel like a football program starved for success.

"They lost the first game I covered, the first game of the 2004 season to Taylor," said Kleiner. "They only lost by a touchdown, and it was a high scoring game. I thought that for a team that had been 0-10 [two years ago] they looked pretty decent. I didn't know much about them yet. I knew they had Todd Reesing, Fred Robinson and Luke Lagera. Thinking back, I remember covering the Meet the Cavs event, and nobody was acting like it was going to be a down program. I don't remember a lot of negativity. I don't know if that was Dicus or what."

The 2004 team succeeded in large part because its quarterback, an athletic if undersized leader who described himself as a backyard quarterback who could throw, hit it off with a coach who understood that each position needed to be coached. Todd Reesing and Dicus became inseparable, spending as much time together as rules allowed so that the quarterback could develop and improve.

"I had never been properly coached on footwork and fundamentals, on how to keep my shoulders and what my release point should be, how to read a defense, how to read pass coverage," Reesing said. "He came in and pushed me. He pushed me to be better. I spent tons of time with him watching film when the rest of the team wasn't there. We were constantly meeting, going over our packages, or schemes, getting on the same page."

It worked. With Reesing taking snaps and working with offensive standouts such as Lagera and Robinson, Lake Travis' football fortunes changed, dramatically and quickly. That 2004 season started with a loss at Taylor, and as he had at the start of the 2003 season, Reesing shouldered the blame. Despite leading his team to 35 points, he remembered two interceptions that hurt in a 42-35 loss.

"We came out that year, I had a terrible first game as a starting quarterback," he said. "I think I threw a couple of interceptions, so I got real down about that. I think we ended up losing, but after that I think we rattled off, I don't know, a bunch of wins in a row."

Eight of nine, to be exact, but winning eight of nine never came easily. The season's second game at Anderson started slowly, and the Cavaliers found themselves staring at a large early deficit. In bringing the Cavaliers back, Reesing put those old backyard quarterbacking skills on display.

"The second game, they were down huge to Anderson, and I saw the funniest play of my life," Kleiner said. "They were in the red zone with about 20 seconds left in the half looking to score. Todd gets the ball and he's scrambling around. I guess he doesn't realize that the clock is running out, and he gets tackled by one of his own offensive linemen. They went and scored on the next play, and they came back. I remember making a big deal of it in the paper."

The Cavaliers came back and rolled past Anderson 58-30. With Lagera breaking off long run after long run and Reesing and Robinson developing into a lethal combination, the Cavaliers' offense became one of the area's best. The offense put up big numbers in wins over Lockhart, Hendrickson and Elgin to enter district play 4-1. The four wins midway through the season were the school's most since 1999 and marked the third highest total, for an entire season, in the school's varsity history. And the season had only reached its midway point.

In district play, Lake Travis faced its two toughest opponents right off the bat. New Braunfels couldn't contain Reesing and company, and the Cavaliers outscored the Unicorns 38-31. The following week, Reesing never got untracked against a feisty New Braunfels Canyon defense. A scrambling interception late in the first half killed a scoring chance, and the Cougars won a surprisingly low-scoring affair on a last-second field goal, 10-9.

"It was a real close game, besides the Taylor game definitely my worst game," Reesing said. "So the two games where I played real poorly were the two games we lost. Imagine that. Surprise, surprise, the quarterback plays bad, you don't win."

His performance aside, looking back Reesing understood what had happened to his team. Lake Travis wouldn't lose another regular season game, including a shootout against arch-rival Dripping Springs, 42-35 to claim the school's first district title.

"We got on a roll that year," he recalled. "After that first game, I kind of got those first game as a quarterback jitters out of my system and then kind of settled in after that and we got on a roll. The way Luke was running the ball, me and Fred were seeing eye to eye and no one could really cover him back then, and our defense was making plays, too. It was a solid season and I think people were blown away that we went from 0-10 to kind of competitive at 3-7 to all of a sudden winning the district and going to the playoffs as a first place seed."

The team's performance blew everyone away, but the bigger news had become that they started coming to games so they could be blown away. As former Lake Travis basketball player Guy Clayton said, people love winners, and Lake Travis football now had a solid fan base. The players realized what they'd accomplished. Reesing remembered what his brother had gone through, where apathy didn't begin to describe the community's feeling toward Lake Travis football.

"Toward the middle and end of that year, you started seeing more fans in the stands, a little bit more excitement around the school from the students and the staff and the community," he said. "So that was fun, to be a part of that turnaround, to go from seeing how disappointed my brother was and how much him and all his friends wanted to do well and were practicing hard and doing everything right and weren't able to attain that success…to be a part of that and see it take place with my own brother, and to be a part of the turnaround the next year, to get over the hump and finally win the district for the first time.…It was pretty fun, it was a blast."

Those Cavaliers became the school's second playoff qualifier. Their match-up took them to the Alamodome in San Antonio for a Bi-district battle with nearby Alamo Heights. As they did throughout the second half of the season, Lake Travis' offense continued to put up points. But so did Alamo Heights. Reesing recalled two things about his first playoff game. First, he sustained, in his words, a mild concussion in the first half.

"That was the only time I had a mild concussion at the end of the first half," he said. "It was the only concussion I had in my whole career. I went in at halftime kind of dazed, but luckily they cleared me to play in the second half."

And so that, in 2012 coupled with the eight years that passed since the game took place, may be why he can't quite remember the vivid details of how the game ended, but he didn't completely forget. The teams had battled back and forth for three quarters with Alamo Heights gaining a slight upper hand. Lake Travis began driving, down by three, late in the fourth quarter. The Cavaliers faced a fourth down and short inside Alamo Heights' territory. Reesing tried to draw the Mules offsides with a hard count, and it worked. One defender entered the neutral zone. Reesing called for the snap and went to a knee, securing, he thought, the five yards and the first down. Only the officials hadn't thrown a flag. Taking a knee had killed the play, and Alamo Heights went on to score a clinching touchdown.

"I think there were a couple of official calls that I still don't agree with that I think cost us the game, but that was so long ago now it's hard to remember exactly what happened," he said.

Disappointing loss aside, the Cavaliers had won their first district title and reversed the program's fortunes faster than anyone could have imagined. For their play, Reesing and Robinson earned a number of post-season honors, as did many of their teammates. The quarterback took home most of them, including District 25-4A MVP and the Associated Press Conference 4A Offensive Player of the Year. He completed 195 of 296 passes for 3,157 yards and 29 touchdowns against just eight interceptions. He also ran for 344 yards and five more scores.

The community relished in the team's success. While fans celebrated, the players went back to work, hoping that the 2004 season would be the tip of the iceberg, that greater success loomed just out of sight.

6: The Rise of Youth Football

As Lake Travis' nucleus of Luke Lagera, Todd Reesing and Fred Robinson prepared for the 2005 season, their senior campaigns, another class of players matriculated through the middle schools and into the high school. The class that would follow Lake Travis' big three showed promise through the years in Lake Travis' youth football program, and those close to the Lake Travis Pop Warner program felt, despite the varsity's recent struggles, big things could happen.

"We were all spokes in the wheel," said Keith Harvill, a coach and one of the founders of Lake Travis Pop Warner. "It was pretty cool. We thought one day our high school team would win a state championship. That was our ultimate goal [in Pop Warner]."

Harvill had worked with Veryl Johnson 10 years earlier to establish a youth football program that could help teach the basics to aspiring football players. Johnson, the grandfather of Lake Travis youth football, had made it his mission to bring Pop Warner football to the community after moving there upon his retirement in the mid-1990s.

"I think he had coached it in Montana or somewhere like that," Harvill recalled of his friend, who passed away after battling cancer in 2006. "He had been involved when his kids were growing up. This was his gig. He loved it. He was a blessing to Lake Travis and to those young people."

Having retired from corporate America before moving to Lakeway, Johnson made it his mission to know, smile at and help as many of Lake Travis' youth as he could. He worked part time for the school district as a parking lot marshal, but his main responsibility - and passion - became watching Lake Travis' students compete in any and all sports. Johnson seemingly knew every Lake Travis student by name, and he loved every minute of the time he spent watching "his" students compete.

Johnson, Harvill and a core group of other parents, Joe Borowski, Bill Taylor, Brad Beaty and Kyle Spillar to name a few, worked tirelessly to develop the program, taking it from a small organization that fielded just two flag football teams in the beginning to a thriving organization that fielded several teams at every age group/weight class. Harvill recalled the organization's early struggles and Johnson doing whatever he could to overcome them.

"When Veryl made up his mind, look out because he was going to get it done," Harvill said with a smile. "We had this old maroon truck that we loaded up and took everywhere with all our equipment, and we looked like the Beverly Hillbillies in it."

Early on, the parents who coached drew on their expertise devised from their former high school playing days to teach the players. The coaches learned quickly that conditioning drills and other high school football staples from a generation gone by wouldn't work with 70-pound beginners.

"As early coaches, it took us a while to get our act together," Harvill said. "We had played football, so we started putting the kids through drills that we'd done in high school, and man, that wasn't the way to go. Bill Taylor was one of the guys who really helped us get organized and stay grounded. He had three running plays and three passing plays, but his teams worked on those plays until they could run them perfectly."

As players came into the program, Taylor ended up coaching some of the players who'd go on to star at Lake Travis, Lagera chief among them. Harvill recalled a story Taylor told about having called his young quarterback at home one night.

"One night Bill Taylor calls him and they're talking, and Bill finally tells him he can't hear him," Harvill said. "Luke says, 'Hold on coach, I need to take my helmet off.' He loved football so much that he had his helmet on all the time."

Harvill's self-described hillbillies struck oil as the community grew. The program grew along with it, drawing in young, promising players and parents with well-developed football pedigrees who lent their expertise to the founding coaches. While Taylor and Harvill coached the likes of Robinson and Lagera through their Pop Warner careers, Harvill noticed even more talent in the group that followed. That group included Garrett Gilbert, Cade McCrary, Austin Pollard, Ryan Erxleben, Tyler Williams and Mike DeWitt, to name a few.

From former University of Texas players who had settled in Lakeway such as Robert Brewer, Bert Vasut and Alan Williams to former NFL quarterbacks Gale Gilbert and Oliver Luck, the coaching that the youth of Lake Travis received grew beyond what ordinary parents could provide. Gilbert played his college football at California, where he took part in the famous Stanford Band game against John Elway's Cardinal. As a pro he played on five Super Bowl teams as a back-up quarterback to Jim Kelly in Buffalo and Stan Humphries in San Diego. Luck set many passing records at West Virginia before playing several years for Bum Phillips' Houston Oilers. Luck would go on to become the athletic director at West Virginia after stints as the President of NFL Europe and the Houston Dynamo of Major League Soccer.

"There were other organizations in Central Texas with coaches who had been athletes, but we were fortunate," Harvill said.

Gilbert said his family's arrival at Lake Travis had nothing to do with football. He'd heard about Austin from a teammate in Seattle and as his playing career wound down, he and wife Kim began looking for the best place to raise their two young boys, Garrett and Griffin.

"We knew we didn't want to go back to California, and we were seriously open to anything...Austin, we were looking at Denver, Colorado, just good quality places to live and raise kids," he said. "We bought a house in River Place at the corner of [Ranch Road] 2222 and [Ranch Road] 620 and it was out in the middle of nowhere at that time, and that was just to get down here. We knew the school systems were good, it was Leander-Cedar Park and it was rated pretty good at the time. But once we'd been here for a couple of years and Garrett was starting school, [Kim] got more active finding things out, and the Lake Travis school district and Westlake were both rated really high, with Westlake being better. It just came down to us finding this place out here versus there."

When the Gilberts finally settled in their Bee Cave home, they met some neighbors and discovered they all had kids about the same age, and that the kids had similar interests, mostly revolving around sports. They had little to no idea about the community's high school team.

"At that point your only focus is on that age group," Gilbert said. "We heard how bad the football team was up at [the high school] level, but that was so away from our thoughts. It was five, six years down the road. I think Garrett was in second grade in 1997. Kids' sports, the LTYA was in its infancy, and [we were] getting involved and being around that group, that group of friends and parents. We didn't know anybody who had kids in high school, and that [high school] stadium wasn't there yet."

The Gilberts had become close to several other families who happened to have athletic ties to the University of Texas. They bonded and remain good friends today.

"Alan Williams, Hardee McCrary, who had obviously just gotten the job at UT," Gilbert said. "I met Bruce Ruffin and Spike Owen, and it just ended up being this neat little deal, and they all had kids about the same age and coaching Pop Warner."

McCrary had joined Mack Brown's football staff at the University of Texas and served as the football program's recruiting coordinator before stepping down in 2003. Ruffin and Owen both starred on the diamond for

Texas before playing Major League Baseball. Williams and Vasut played football at Texas in the mid-1970s, when Darrell Royal still coached. Brewer quarterbacked the Longhorns in the early 1980s. He's best remembered for a Cotton Bowl-winning touchdown run against Alabama in 1983. All sent sons through the Lake Travis schools, and each son followed in his dad's footsteps, playing football or baseball, sometimes both and sometimes other sports as well.

After his stint as president of NFL Europe, Luck chose central Texas, and Lakeway in particular, as his landing spot. His son Andrew was heading into middle school at the time, and he wanted to learn American football after spending his early school years in Europe. So Oliver, like the other athlete-dads, got involved with Lake Travis Pop Warner to help coach his son's team. He recognized then that the parents working with their kids knew their football.

"We had been in Europe for 10 years," he said. "I remember I was impressed with the people the LTYA had in coaching and on the board. For a youth program of 10-11 year old boys, it seemed like a pretty competent group of guys with football knowledge.

"Of course I'd like to think that the coaching back then led to the dominance [today]," he said with a wry smile.

For his part, Gilbert said he just tried to fit in where it made sense. As a former NFL quarterback, that meant he'd coach offense and work with quarterbacks in particular. His son, it turned out, had begun to develop into a promising quarterback.

"Now, I knew that Garrett at that age could throw it better and more accurate than other kids his age, so that was natural and easy for me to coach offense and quarterbacks," he said. "It was convenient in that sense."

Watching Andrew Luck today – the top pick in the 2012 NFL draft after a college career that saw him named All-America as well as a Heisman Trophy finalist – it's difficult to imagine him playing organized football for the first time in Lake Travis, but there he was, pictured in a June 13, 2011 *Sports Illustrated* story wearing his red Lake Travis Wildcats uniform sporting the number 43.

"[In the first year] I was working with [Thomas Loth's dad] and Andrew and Thomas split time at quarterback," Oliver said. "Back then everyone played everything, and it was Andrew's first year in football having been in Europe. He was learning the game for the first time. I think he also played some tight end and defensive end. The next year, Thomas was too old for our team and Andrew became the quarterback."

The Lucks left Lake Travis for Houston after Andrew's sixth grade year, where Oliver had become the president of Major League Soccer's Houston Dynamo. Andrew would later attend Stratford High School before earning a scholarship to Stanford. His career played out nicely from there. To think that Andrew, learning the game at Lake Travis, may not have been the best quarterback in Lake Travis' Pop Warner program sounds odd, but another talented quarterback emerged one year behind him: Gilbert's son Garrett.

Between 1997 and 2003, various Lake Travis Pop Warner teams earned championship banners. In 1997, the flag football team went undefeated to claim the Central Texas Pop Warner title. In 1998, Lagera quarterbacked the team all the way to the state quarterfinals in the junior pee wee division. The following year, with Loth at quarterback, Robinson and future Westlake High School standout Max Minor at running back, the team won its first 11 games and reached the state semifinals. In 2000, playing in the peewee division, the team – which kept its core players together – again reached the state semifinals. In 2003, teams from two divisions won Central Texas titles and advanced to the state semifinals.

Harvill said the Lake Travis teams stayed together on purpose.

"Pop Warner was a lot different in other areas," he said. "Some leagues stacked teams, we tried to balance ours and keep those groups together. We wanted success to come across the board. We thought that synergy was important to us. Look at Cade [McCrary] and Garrett. They played together all through Pop Warner."

While Harvill thought one of the two groups, Lagera's group and Gilbert's group, would contend for a high school state championship, others including some of the parent-coaches couldn't see it. Gale Gilbert said none of the coaches imagined then that the Pop Warner success would translate to the high school.

"There was no way for us to foresee or predict what would happen," he said. "You could see when they were freshmen they were good, but there's no way to see, with maturity [how it might happen.]"

Hidden on a web page that hangs off of www.laketravis.com is a site documenting that era of Lake Travis Pop Warner football. It includes a team records section, and some of the players listed there went on to become standouts at the high school or college level, either at Lake Travis or other schools both near and far. It shows that Minor, in three years, remains the organization's all-time rushing leader. He'd become a starter for neighboring Westlake and helped lead the Chaps into the 2006 5A State Championship Game. The records show Garrett Gilbert, in his only year on with this group of players, holds the organization's all-time passing mark. Fitting, because he'd go on to set the state's all-time high school passing mark as well. At high school, Robinson would finish his high school career ranked among the state's top five in career receiving yards. The 2003 junior peewee roster also includes Cayleb Jones, who'd star at Austin High and earn All-America honors before enrolling at the University of Texas to play his college football.

Did the coaches and parents who started working with the young players know that types of success the future would hold? Did they realize that back in the late 1990s they were working with the players who would lead Lake Travis to seven consecutive district championships, much less five consecutive state championships?

"That thought never really entered my mind," said Luck. "I kept focusing on coaching Andrew and his buddies, and that was the important thing for me."

Gilbert said that, despite the coaching staff's collective resume, it didn't seem to him that he had been part of a group of super-coaches, nor did it appear the young athletes were destined for unrivaled success.

"At the time, there's no way you could look at it like that," he said. "We were dads who happened to play sports, and our kids ended up being pretty good at their level all the way up. When it was football season, that's what we were working on. When it was basketball, same deal. It wasn't like we thought we had something special going on."

But looking back, it's hard to not see something special appearing for the first time. The success the teams enjoyed at the Pop Warner level had to make Johnson smile. Though he'd never get to see the success translate to the high school, his organization had played a big role in sending fundamentally sound football players to the school district.

"Veryl had two rules: have fun and have fun," Harvill recalled. "Then we'd worry about everything else. The goal was to keep kids involved. It's work for those little fellas and we wanted to make it fun."

Harvill said the entire Pop Warner staff took pride in seeing their players move up to both Lake Travis and Hudson Bend middle schools and find success.

"It became a numbers game," he said. "We had lots of kids and when they got to the middle school they'd had lots of fundamental practice. Believe me, it's a big difference having three years of football under your belt when you get to seventh grade than if you show up there for the first time."

As Lake Travis' population grew, the district eventually opened Hudson Bend Middle School to relieve crowding at Lake Travis Middle. For athletics, football in particular, former high school coach and middle school coordinator Keith Tuck said, the move effectively doubled the playing population and further helped with the development of talent.

"That was the key because then Lake Travis started getting their numbers," he said. "The second middle school was huge because it allowed them every year to pick from 120 freshmen, not 60. It allowed 120 seventh and eighth graders to play the game and not sit and watch or get in only three plays a game or whatever. The youth program exploded."

As the high school football coaches came and went, they all made it a point to help out the youth football program when they could. Harvill said each coach bent over backwards to accommodate almost any request the organization made of it.

"Every high school coach was great, very accommodating," he said. "We were always there bending their ears. We'd come back wanting to do all this fancy stuff, but Bill Taylor reminded us to keep it simple. They let us use their fields. They were very accommodating."

The high school coaches all saw the value, both in teaching fundamentals and in establishing a system that stretched all the way to the high school program. Tuck, in his two years as head coach, made it a point to offer opportunities for the youth football coaches to work with his staff. It didn't hurt that his son Jeff played in the league alongside Garrett Gilbert.

"My staff used to do clinics with the youth program coaches, and so I feel like we helped get that off the ground as well," Tuck said. "I can remember Jeff played on the same little league team as Garrett Gilbert, a bunch of the kids that later became stars. You knew they were good even at a very young age."

In his years, Jim Shewmake spent plenty of time watching the youth games. He could tell that the young Gilberts, Robinsons, Lageras and others could play, that they seemed to be more natural players than some of their young contemporaries.

"We had done camps for the youth football teams and let them play on our campus," Shewmake said. "We wanted to create an atmosphere. We watched all of the fifth graders play. I knew they were good, but the kids coming through were football smart, athletic smart. These kids knew what to do. They were well-coached and they had savvy."

Knowing that these would one day be the players making up the high school program, Shewmake took steps to make sure they felt welcome at the high school. He went to his athletic director, Jim Taylor, and got permission to invite the Pop Warner program to use his game field for their games every Saturday. The development thrilled the Pop Warner officials beyond belief.

"At first they were playing at the middle school, and I went to Jim Taylor and said we should let them play on our field on Saturdays," Shewmake recalled. "When I approached the organization, they were shocked. They asked why we wanted them to do it, and I just said, 'Why wouldn't I?' It created a great atmosphere in the stands."

Along with giving the young players an opportunity to play on the high school field, Shewmake wanted to encourage his high school players to get involved with the younger generation as well.

"Our kids came in to watch film on Saturdays, and when we were done they would stay and watch the games," he said. "It was a win-win situation. It was cool to work hard and to play football. Our kids understood that the Pop Warner kids were our little brothers and that one day, with our support, they will follow in our footsteps and make us proud. We wanted to support them."

And they were definitely worth watching, if not supporting.

"Matt [Jones, Shewmake's offensive coordinator] and I would watch these games and say, 'Wow,'" Shewmake said. "They were doing things as fifth graders that eighth and ninth graders didn't do. I knew it would be a great help to the football program. That group had [Todd] Reesing, Luke Lagera and it was a great class. The influx of people moving out to the area, the Pop Warner program took off. There was a group of parents who wanted their kids to play football, and it just snowballed. It was really fun watching those kids play."

After Shewmake left and the district suffered through the Charlie Sadler experiment, Jeff Dicus arrived and rekindled the school's interest in the youth program. Like Shewmake before him, he met with the Pop Warner coaches and put together coaching clinics for them so they could learn what the varsity was doing and implement its concepts at their level.

"We got involved with them," Dicus said later. "[We] had clinics for them. We taught them our offense and some of the fundamentals that we would like them to teach. I remember when they had their big Saturday camp where they send kids to different stations to learn, and our kids were out there helping with that. We were heavily involved, so our football program was exposed to those younger kids. Every year it got bigger and bigger."

Assistant coach Kevin Halfmann was on the staff during Tuck and Shewmake's coaching tenures before leaving. He rejoined the Lake Travis staff with Dicus in 2005 and noticed a difference in the way the entire football program's structure had changed. Young players had become familiar with the principles of the high school's scheme, and by the time players reached the two middle schools, they began to work in earnest on what the high school players did. Dicus' spread offense was entrenched in both middle schools, and the defensive scheme was being taught there as well.

"At the middle school, the quarterback wasn't in the shotgun so much, but it was still the same plays," Halfmann noticed. "Plus, they were running our defense, so it was more so than any time in the past. Even with Shew, the middle school hadn't been affected as much as what Jeff had done in those two years."

Dicus said he could trace future success to the lessons that began at those Pop Warner camps. As the players graduated Pop Warner and went through the middle schools and into the high schools, they played under the same system, making the same types of calls that the high school team used and made. That, as much as anything, helped contributed to the beginning of Lake Travis' record-setting run.

"As far as Garrett's group, I've told everybody that if you look at what that group of kids did from seventh, eighth, ninth, tenth and eleventh grade when they won the state championship, they ran the same offense and same defense for five years straight and went through the same off-season for five years straight," he said.

The relationship between Pop Warner and high school continues. Following Dicus' departure, his successors, Chad Morris and then Hank Carter, made it a point to continue to bring in the youth coaches and parents, to make them feel a part of the program. All of the Pop Warner dads and coaches go to a clinic at the high school," said Guy Clayton, a Pop Warner dad and also a member of the school board. "The coaches walk all of us through everything they do behind the scenes. It helps us dads by getting us involved and interested in the high school program. Then our coaches can incorporate part of what they do at the high school. We don't run the exact same offense that they do now, but we may get there. The Lake Travis coaches are unbelievable about giving us access to the program. It's really, really cool to see."

Success has kept the community interested in football, and it starts early. A look around the stands at any Lake Travis game, home or away, reveals a diverse group that spans all ages. It's parents and classmates of the high school players for sure, but families with kids knee-high to a high school senior spend their Friday nights at football games as well. The youngsters may not completely understand what they see, but they do understand two things: the high school team wins, and they want to be a part of it when the time comes. They know that the season kicks off in August and ends around Christmas and the community always gets a present in the form of a state championship.

"All the kids are into it," said Guy Clayton, a 1990 Lake Travis graduate who now sits on the school board. "My son is 10, and he's been playing Pop Warner for five years. All he knows about the high school is that you win every single game you play and a state title. They just don't know any different. All these kids, that's all they know."

But in 2005, those titles existed only in dreams.

7: Reesing's development

Following the success of 2004, Jeff Dicus could hardly contain his excitement heading into the 2005 season. Not only had he taken Lake Travis from the point of despair following that winless 2002 season to a district championship two years later, he had the core of that district championship team coming back, led by its quarterback, the reigning 4A Offensive Player of the Year in a division that included some much more heralded quarterbacks.

That Todd Reesing earned one of the state's top honors hadn't gotten lost on the coach. It seemed, however, that his quarterback's ability had gotten lost on college scouts and recruiters from the state's football powers. As a senior with a growing resume, Reesing faced one challenge that no amount of practice could ever overcome: his height. In 2012, Reesing said his official height, the one you get at the doctor's office, not the one you tell Rivals.com or your friendly college sports information director, is five feet, 10 and a quarter inches. Big-time college football programs don't look at sub-six-foot quarterbacks. Right or wrong, they just don't.

They do, however, look at 5-star rated quarterbacks with prototypical measurables. Two of Reesing's contemporaries, Matthew Stafford at Highland Park in Dallas and Jevan Snead at Stephenville, had been high on almost every major college program's radar. They both also played at high schools in Lake Travis' classification, and they had also started for their schools as juniors. As a high school junior, and a very successful one at that, Reesing couldn't grasp that fact that neither he nor his favorite target, also undersized Fred Robinson, hadn't gotten any major Division I offers. He felt slighted, and he used that to create a chip on his shoulder that stayed with him throughout his playing career.

While he'd won player of the year honors, Reesing admitted that he remained very much a work in progress. He'd never had formal quarterback coaching, at least not until his sophomore year of high school when Dicus took over the Lake Travis program. It was then, even with Reesing as a back-up quarterback to Nick Bird, that he began to take the first steps toward developing into, at that point, Lake Travis' most successful quarterback.

"I could throw the ball well, but I had never been properly coached on footwork and fundamentals, on how to keep my shoulders and what my release point should be, how to read a defense, how to read pass coverage," he said. "[Dicus] came in and pushed me. He pushed me to be better. I spent tons of time with him watching film when the rest of the team wasn't there. We were constantly meeting, going over our packages, or schemes, getting on the same page."

During the 2004 season, the coach and quarterback spent a great deal of time together, and Reesing took to the coaching like a duck to water. The results showed. Sure, Reesing suffered backyard quarterback flashbacks from time to time, but in those instances Dicus made sure that Reesing understood he couldn't deviate from the system, that the other 10 players on the field counted on him to stick to the plan.

"He made me more responsible than anyone else on the team," Reesing said. "If I screwed up, he let me know about it by yelling at me more than anyone else. He wanted the team to know, wanted me to know that just because I'm the quarterback and I might do well in some games, 'You're still going to get yelled at and I'm still going to expect you to do things the right way.' That's his way of pushing me to be a leader and to be better."

Reesing has always been as competitive as Dicus, so he didn't mind the extra attention and responsibility. In fact, as a senior, he flourished with it.

Heading into the season, Lake Travis expected to have its three-headed offensive monster back. The Cavaliers had enjoyed a solid spring practice season and had dominated the competition during the summer 7-on-7 play.

"Coming off the season, everyone was pretty excited," Reesing remembered. "We were bummed out because we knew we were better than going out in the first round, so after the few weeks you get to kind of get over that and enjoy winter break and what not, we came back in the spring, and I think the coaches, everyone in the community, the parents and especially the football players, we knew that we could be real good the next year, with having pretty much all of our key players back and the addition of some younger players who were going to be helpful and be playmakers. We had a great off-season. We went out and just dominated most of the 7-on-7 tournaments we played in. We really just were clicking on all cylinders."

Reesing and Robinson could play pitch and catch all day long if necessary, but they didn't need to. When opposing defenses dropped back to try and contain the duo, Luke Lagera would be there to run through all of the vacated space. As a sophomore and a junior, the running back had rushed for better than 2,500 yards, and he was expecting big things of himself as a senior. But a major hurdle emerged before the season really even got started. Lagera's senior season ended before the team's first official snap. In the team's final preseason scrimmage, at home against Lampasas, Lagera went out for a swing pass. Reesing delivered the ball, and as Lagera went to cut upfield, his knee gave out.

Former *Lake Travis View* sports editor Dan Kleiner remembers the 2005 team as the best Lake Travis team he covered.

"That second team I covered [2005] was the best one I saw," he said. "They had [offensive lineman Richard] Kopczinsky, [offensive lineman] Ronnie DeWitt, the big three. What happened to Luke still makes me cry."

"Luke Lagera got hurt in the fall scrimmage," Dicus said. "Oh man. That kid was one of the hardest workers. Bless his heart. It would have been nice to have him and see what we could have done. [The injury] took a very explosive running back away from [us]. [Luke had] 4.4, 4.5 speed, [was] one of our hardest working young men."

Without Lagera, the Cavaliers needed to re-think their running game. They could survive, they knew from experience, on the Reesing-to-Robinson combination, but to be great and go beyond the first round of the playoffs, they'd need more. Help arrived following Hurricane Katrina in running back-receiver Joshua Joseph from New Orleans.

"Then, going into the season we lose Luke in one of the preseason games, and with him, coming back off an all-state type season with Fred and I, that was a pretty huge set-back because if we'd have had him we'd have been even better on offense," Reesing said. "But then we had Josh [Joseph] come in after Katrina and he was able to fill the role of Luke, not quite as good of a runner but was a big threat in the passing game as well."

While Joseph learned the Cavaliers' system and found his role, the offense hit the ground running and never looked back. The Cavaliers scored early and often and games got out of hand quickly. Through the first half of the season, Reesing figures he only took a handful of fourth quarter snaps. In five non-district games in September, Lake Travis outscored its opponents 224-56. Reesing appeared poised to shatter his state MVP statistics.

"We were rolling through," he said. "I think I started the first five games with maybe 20 touchdowns and no interceptions. It was just tearing it up. When you're in the zone like that it's almost too easy out there. It was like we're playing the JV team. All these teams, they really just had no chance against us."

Things didn't get much tougher in district play, at least early on. Facing their toughest opponents from the 2004 season, the two New Braunfels schools, the Cavaliers set the tone early and let the other district schools know that the road to the title would go through them. On back to back weeks, Lake Travis went to New Braunfels and beat the Unicorns 38-16 and then Canyon 35-14.

Reesing remembers the Canyon game. Looking to make amends for what he called a poor outing in 2004, his play approached quarterbacking perfection. He hit on a number of passes in a row and the Cavaliers never looked back. That game seemed to send the Cavaliers on their way toward another district title.

"I think Canyon was the best team we played and I think they finished the year 9-1, and that was my best game of the year," he said. "I think I completed something like 21 passes in a row that game and was just in the zone. So we came off a huge win there and we were flying high. We had a lot of confidence."

While Reesing and Robinson received all of the accolades, Lake Travis was far from a two-man team. Dicus went out of his way to explain to people, Kleiner included, that the offensive line was a big key to the team's success, so Kleiner started paying attention to their play.

"I started paying attention to them and saw Richard Kopczinski, one of the tackles," Kleiner said. "He was the perfect combination of business and fun of any kid I interviewed. I remember a game at New Braunfels, and Ronnie DeWitt scored a touchdown. I'm interviewing DeWitt after the game, and Kop stands behind him during the whole thing just dancing, and it was stupid and it was fun. He was a funny guy who never gave you the standard answer. He was a humble, funny kid. There were so many kids who played roles, and they were all good. That was the thing about that team. They were a group, it was a package deal. They were the group that made it happen."

***

In Reesing's years as quarterback, DeWitt developed into the team's most bruising lineman, the most recent in a trend that stretched back into the mid-1990s. An all-district selection twice and an all-Central Texas pick once, DeWitt would go on to earn a scholarship to Tulsa University. While the Cavaliers hadn't produced the most athletic, most polished football teams through the years, the school always seemed to have one lineman who'd earn a Division I scholarship.

In the 1990s, when running back Ben Reid sparked the offense with his speed, he often found holes opened by the likes of Jake Stoetzner (6-foot-6, 290 pounds) and Dustin Wuest (6-foot-3, 270). Stoetzner's family, ironically enough, helped draw the Reesings out to Lake Travis from the Tarrytown neighborhood in the mid-1990s. Stoetzner's father Tom had been Todd Reesing's godfather, and the Reesings would travel out to Lakeway to watch Stoetzner's Cavaliers play on Fridays. Stoetzner earned all-district honors in 1995 and 1996 before accepting a scholarship to play at Tulsa, where he started off and on for two years. Wuest's Lake Travis career overlapped with Stoetzner's. Wuest graduated following the 1997 season and earned a scholarship to Vanderbilt University, where he earned letters in 1999 and

2000.

By the 2000 season, Lake Travis' most prolific offensive lineman had emerged. After starting in 1999 as a sophomore, Robert Turner became a leader for Lake Travis' first playoff team. Turner stood 6-foot-3 and approached nearly 300 pounds, but he proved more than just a big body. Turner's strength turned out to be his raw power, and as a senior on a struggling team he still averaged nearly nine pancake blocks per game. His play at Lake Travis earned him a scholarship to the University of New Mexico, where he became a consensus all-Mountain West Conference selection. Though undrafted, Turner became Lake Travis' first NFL player when he signed and stuck with the New York Jets prior to the 2007 season. Jim Shewmake, who coached Turner in the 1999 and 2000 seasons at Lake Travis, remembers him as a humble, respectful, easy-to-coach player. Justin Pollard, who played with Turner for one season, called him the best lineman ever to play at the school.

By the time Reesing graduated and Garrett Gilbert took over as the varsity quarterback, the Cavaliers had been producing at least one large, skilled offensive lineman with each class. Paden Kelley emerged as an all-state tackle who made it his life's mission to protect Gilbert's blind side. He'd earn a scholarship to the University of Texas, where he became a mainstay of the offensive line rotation and a part-time starter in 2010-11. In Gilbert and Kelley's senior season, another high-quality lineman emerged: sophomore Taylor Doyle. As big as Kelley if not as quick, Doyle gave that Lake Travis team a veritable book-end package, and the only drama came when the unit bickered, playfully, amongst themselves over who deserved the blame on the rare occasion Gilbert felt pressure. Doyle would earn three letters at Lake Travis and follow Kelley to Texas.

***

Lake Travis' offense, with DeWitt, Kopczinksi and company providing Reesing plenty of time, cruised through the rest of October, scoring 38 points in a big win over Marble Falls and 45 more at Burnet in a 45-28 win. The 28 points Burnet scored marked, to that point, the most Lake Travis' defense had given up all season. Through the first eight games, the Lake Travis defense gave up only 12 points per game. As it would later turn out, Burnet's offensive success might have been the first sign of any crack in Lake Travis' proverbial armor.

At 9-0 with another district title in hand, the Cavaliers set out to complete a perfect regular season against Dripping Springs. While the defense struggled, the offense continued to roll. The Cavaliers had given up on trying to establish a consistent running game without Lagera, but Reesing and Robinson continued to lead the way, and the Cavaliers scored with little trouble. Dripping Springs' offense kept pace, though, and that had become a problem. If the defense's struggles the previous week at Burnet weren't a sign, what Dripping Springs accomplished in the regular season finale got the Cavaliers' attention.

"Dripping Springs, our defense just couldn't stop them that year," Reesing recalled. "We scored at will but they were scoring pretty easily as well. They were able to hang around that game for a long time. I think our defense showed a little weakness by giving up a lot of points to a team that wasn't that great on offense. So that might have been the first tell-tale that once we get into the playoffs we're going to face some issues. But at the time we didn't think too much of it."

At the time, the Cavaliers thought they had a chance to make a run in the playoffs. Those who watched the team felt the same.

"I thought they would win a state title," Kleiner recalled. "I will admit that I don't understand the game of football, but I tried to get to the heart of why they won the game. But then they started winning every game. I probably thought they were better than they really were because the players become like celebrities because you see them in a certain light. I thought they would win the title in 2005, but I really didn't know what was going on anywhere else."

Reesing said the team had been frustrated at going out in the first round the year before and wanted to take at least one more step. At that point, he said the team hadn't thought about making a deep run, but they knew deep down they could.

The 2005 playoffs began with a familiar foe: Alamo Heights, the team that had kicked Lake Travis out of the playoffs in the first round the year before. The rematch excited Reesing.

"I was excited about it because I had a lot of friends that played on the Alamo Heights team, guys that I had met in high school who I actually hung out with and stuff," he recalled. "It was pretty exciting getting to play them again because I was pretty bummed out from the year before."

He nearly got bummed out again. Coming off an undefeated regular season and highly ranked, the Cavaliers proceeded to play their worst game. For three quarters, very little that they did gained them any ground, much less momentum, against the stubborn Mules. Late in the fourth quarter, Alamo Heights led 21-17, and Reesing remembers watching the Mules drive for the touchdown that would have wrapped up the win.

"Our senior year, we're 10-0 thinking we're going to make a run at the state playoffs and then finding ourselves down late in the fourth quarter when they have the ball getting ready to score and seal the game," Reesing said. "I was sitting there on a knee thinking I can't believe we're going to lose to the same team again."

But a funny thing happened as the Mules drove for the clinching score. They never got there. A crucial penalty not only stopped the drive, it pushed them out of field goal range. With less than two minutes to go, Lake Travis had the ball and a chance. That's all Reesing needed.

"They had a huge penalty on offense that really set them back out of field goal range when they had a chance to pretty much put the game away, and I remember I was on a knee on the sideline thinking, 'This is over. We went 10-0 and then got upset by the same team as last year,'" he explained. "And we kind of had a miracle call there and they shot themselves in the foot and gave us a chance with the ball back."

Acting quickly, the Cavaliers' dynamic duo connected on a post pattern for a huge gain on the first play, which sent the sideline and the Lake Travis fans in the stands at the Round Rock ISD Athletic Complex – better known as the Palace on Parmer Lane – into a frenzy. Several plays later, Lake Travis crossed inside the red zone, and finally the Cavaliers faced their last chance. Reesing recalled the timeout that occurred with his team facing a fourth-down-and-three in the closing seconds.

"I remember I just went over to the huddle with Coach Dicus and looked at him and just said, 'Give me the ball.' So we just called a quarterback sweep to the right. At that point there was just no way I wasn't going to get to the end zone."

Looking back at the moment nearly a decade later, Reesing recalled the play with ease. He took the snap and headed for the corner. There were defenders, but they couldn't get to him. He turned the corner, saw the end zone and dove across when he got close.

"I think I added a little bit of drama and jumped/dove into the end zone when it wasn't really necessary, but nonetheless, we somehow were able to pull that one out, pull that one out of our ass, so to speak."

He said he couldn't get to the sidelines quick enough after the winning score. While the overall game hadn't been a thing of beauty, he said the final minutes had been a dream-come-true.

"As a kid growing up as a quarterback, that's all you ever dream of, getting that chance to have the ball with less than two minutes to go and you have to drive your team to victory," Reesing said. "So the opportunity presented itself, and I went from crying on the sidelines so to speak to in the huddle excited as can be to lead my team. To go down to hit the big deep pass play to get the drive started, to scramble around and make a few plays to get us down to the red zone, and then to have it come down to a fourth-and-three, to have them call a play and to go over to coach and say, 'Hey, give me the ball, I'll make sure I score,' and then to get that score and run off the field and celebrate with all your teammates, and have all the four years of hard work you put in pay off and actually win a playoff game. That was pretty exciting and to do it with a lot of guys who were really good friends."

The Cavaliers escaped with a 24-21 win. They took a collective breath and then went back and thought about the game as they prepared for an Area round playoff match-up with Austin McCallum. In prepping for the Knights, Reesing recalled the team thinking that they couldn't play any worse, and if so, they might still enjoy a long playoff run.

"After that game, we're thinking that's probably the worst game we've played all year on both sides of the ball, so to think we came out of a win with that, and we're thinking, 'Okay, we're going to play a McCallum team who Canyon had already beat that year, and we should be able to handle these guys no problem,'" he said.

But they found a problem. McCallum had a talented quarterback in Trey Henderson, who teams had trouble containing, and the Knights had been scoring points in bunches late in the season. Entering the game, McCallum had won six in a row, averaging 40 points per game while giving up only eight. McCallum's defense didn't concern Reesing going into the game, nor did it challenge him during it.

The quarterback tore the Knights' defense apart, passing for five touchdowns and more than 300 yards. Robinson, as usual, caught most of the passes, amassing more than 200 yards and a trio of touchdowns. McCallum, though, matched Reesing score for score, and the only trouble with a shootout soon reared its head.

"On offense all we thought was that we had one of the best offenses in the state if you look at it statistically, and with what we've done we can outscore anybody," he said. "That was probably the case, but that doesn't mean you're always going to have the ball last. But it was one of those games that went back and forth, back and forth, and unfortunately they had the ball last and we couldn't get that stop on defense. I think that was kind of just the story."

McCallum scored the winning touchdown just moments from the end. Telling the story proved difficult, and possibly heartbreaking, for Kleiner.

"I remember the last article that season," he said. "I quoted a 5-year-old boy in the stands who was talking to his older sister. He turned to her and asked why people were sad, because the team only lost one game [all season]. Mike DeWitt overheard it and just laughed. I remember the team all coming together and crying. It was hard to watch. I remember the picture we ran in the paper of a kid, Dan Frey, looking down at his helmet. They just loved it so much."

Assistant coach Kevin Halfmann remembers the game. He also remembers thinking that the Cavaliers could make a run deep in the playoffs if they could survive McCallum, and that run, coupled with the future that he had seen, could be the beginning of something special.

"We had a talent level with that group that was unbelievable, and we could see with our younger kids that we had some potential coming up," he said. "To get beat by McCallum, I mean we should have won it that year. We played tired against McCallum, mentally and physically tired, and it bit us that game. If we beat them, we win it all."

Little did anyone know, or say, at the time, but it wouldn't be long for the potential Halfmann and the other coaches saw to get realized. But on the heels of a surprising, disappointing, season-ending loss, there was only closure for the class of 2005. Reesing looked back on his career with fond memories, none better than the relationship he formed with his head coach and the potential he reached because of Dicus' guidance.

"He was the first quarterback coach I ever had, the first person who actually taught me how to be a quarterback," Reesing said. "Before, you're just playing the game because you're an athlete and you can throw the ball. Now, he was someone who was teaching me about the game, about how to play the position properly. I think because of that, that's what he did and the rest of the coaches did with their players and that's how the team got to the level of success we had."

Reesing's 2005 performance earned him Central Texas Player of the Year honors, but strangely nothing on the state level. He'd improved his numbers dramatically. He led the state in completion percentage at 72.3, passed for 3,341 yards and 41 touchdowns against just five interceptions, and he led the team in rushing with 756 yards and eight scores. Robinson, for the second year in a row, earned second team all-state honors after benefiting as Reesing's favorite target. For his career, Robinson remains fifth all-time in Texas history in career receiving yardage with more than 3,700.

Looking back, Reesing thinks the duo fell victim to two things: the mythical reputation of the 5-star recruit, and their size.

Stafford earned the state's top 4A offensive honor after leading Highland Park to the Conference 4A, Division I title. He was also the top recruit in the state and earned a scholarship to the University of Georgia before becoming the first pick in the 2008 NFL draft.

"It was weird," he said. "My junior year I was player of the year, and then my senior year they gave it to Stafford. I got the player of the year my junior year, and then my senior year I had astonishingly better statistics and a 10-0 record, and I didn't even get honorable mention all-state. Not that it was anything that really pisses me off, it's just kind of funny to think about it. Touchdowns, interceptions, yards, completion percentage and record were all a lot better my senior year, but I think that's when you get to the politics of the guys who are the big-name recruits. You know Stafford was the number one overall guy. There was Jevan Snead, who was a big name guy who ended up at Ole Miss, so I think the fact that they were the big-name recruits just kind of pushed me off to the side."

Not only did the big-name recruits push him off the awards podium, they kept him from getting recruited by the major colleges. Stafford and Snead didn't shut him out personally, rather it had been their attributes compared to his that made Reesing, and Robinson for that matter, afterthoughts. Reesing eventually secured a scholarship to Kansas University in the Big XII, but Robinson didn't, and that bothers the quarterback more than any perceived slight he endured.

"Fred's size, just like it did for me, it set us all back as far as recruiting's concerned," Reesing said. "The thing is there are more short wide receivers that excel than short quarterbacks. The fact that, with the stats that he had, that he ran real crisp routes and never really dropped the ball, and didn't get one school – not even a Houston or Baylor or SMU that wanted to give him a chance – I still just don't understand that."

Reesing understood why the big schools weren't calling on him, and he used that as motivation to improve. Dicus said that the quarterback's heart and drive, fueled in part by his anger at not being heavily recruited, drove him to succeed both at Lake Travis and at Kansas.

"The competitor in Todd was the biggest thing that will stick out," Dicus said. "Winners win at everything they do, and that's Todd Reesing. He was very intelligent, very smart, just his heart and his will to win overcame his size big time. Obviously it took him to the next level at Kansas. Todd was always one that his work ethic and his will to win rubbed off on everyone else. He had that charisma, a personality about him that was very infectious to everybody."

At Kansas, Reesing went from unheralded recruit to program savior in two short years. He'd win the starting quarterback job as a sophomore and lead the team to its best season ever, 12-1 and a win in the Bowl Championship Series' Orange Bowl against perennial power Virginia Tech. When his career ended in 2009, Reesing held 26 school records. The Lake Travis graduate finished his career with 11,194 passing yards and 90 touchdowns.

More than the records, Reesing remembers what he and a bunch of other recruiting afterthoughts accomplished in a magical season.

"We were a team comprised of one, two and three-star rated guys by the recruiting services, and my second year we go 12-1 and win the Orange Bowl," he said. "It just goes to show it's not always how you're rated coming out of high school. It's about finding the right guys with the right mentality."

One of Reesing's biggest fans said watching him progress from little brother to high school and then college football standout makes him smile.

"It was an amazing experience," said older brother Kyle. "His sophomore year [at Lake Travis] was the only year we've gotten to play sports together, and it wasn't just football. It was baseball too. It was great to be on the team together. I was proud, and then to watch what he did – become the 4A offensive player of the year in the state over guys who are now playing in the NFL – was a tremendous accomplishment. And then to see him go from not being recruited by anyone in the state to go to a school like Kansas and completely turn that program around, get the Orange Bowl win and be considered for the Heisman Trophy, that's stuff you wouldn't have thought possible in a million years. I'm proud to say that's my little brother. I like to think that I had a little hand in that, pushing him when he was younger to keep up with us older kids, but I can't. It all goes to the hard work he did, and when he got his opportunity he seized it and ran with it. My hat's off to him. It's been the big highlight of my life seeing him do those things."

While Reesing took Lawrence, Kansas by storm, his alma mater kept prepping for the 2006 season. Despite Reesing's and Robinson's graduation, optimism ran high because many felt the next influx of varsity talent would be even better. Coaches had kept an eye on the next class for years. Dicus required his assistants to get involved with and keep up with the teams at Lake Travis and Hudson Bend middle schools, and those coaches liked what they were seeing. As Lake Travis' varsity team began to take flight upon Dicus' arrival, the middle school teams followed suit.

"We kind of knew how things were stacking up," Halfmann said. "We could start looking at personnel and personnel moves based on what we had coming up. In the past we might have known one or two kids but their freshman year was like the first time we'd seen them. Sometimes it's a pain in the butt having to go to middle school practices and games, but there again, Jeff changed the expectation of the coaches too."

Football at Lake Travis had changed. If Dicus expected great things and supreme commitment from his players and staff, fans had begun to expect big things as well. One former quarterback, home on a break from college, hardly recognized his former team at the 2005 game against Dripping Springs.

"I came back and Lake Travis is playing Drip, and every game since I came back, I'd go stand with [former Lake Travis head coach Keith] Tuck over on Drip's sideline because, save for coach Halfmann, I didn't know anybody on that staff anymore," said Greg Wiggins, who quarterbacked Abilene Christian University in the early 2000s after graduating Lake Travis following the 1999 season. "It was Reesing's senior year, and he made two or three throws that I'd never seen a quarterback make, and at 5-10, 5-11 whatever he was, I knew then that Lake Travis was playing a totally different level of football than we ever played."

He also knew that trend had only just begun. A quarterback whose reputation preceded him stood poised to take over. Wiggins remembers the first time he came across a young Garrett Gilbert.

"They have this passing camp at Hardin Simmons," Wiggins said. "I was at ACU, so to try and make some money I work at the summer camp at Hardin Simmons, and these seventh graders come out from Lake Travis. I knew a couple of kids. One of them turns to me and says, 'This quarterback's going to play in the NFL.' I thought , 'Who is this little [kid] and what does he know about football?' and there's grown men looking at a seventh grader throwing the football, and Garrett Gilbert is making them think holy crap. That was the first time I'd ever heard of Garrett."

No one received more attention or caused more promise than Reesing's heir apparent. As a freshman, Gilbert quarterbacked the junior varsity on Thursday and then stood on the varsity sidelines on Friday nights, where he'd watch Reesing and get first-hand experience on varsity football. At 6-foot-4 with a strong, accurate arm, Gilbert looked the part of a big-time quarterback. He had the pedigree as well. His father Gale enjoyed a long career in the NFL and played on five straight Super Bowl teams. From early on, as soon as Garrett told dad he wanted to play football, Gale tutored and groomed his son to play quarterback at the highest level. People knew about Gilbert, and expectations followed.

"The expectations, especially for Garrett Gilbert, were high," Kleiner recalled.

While Gilbert's arrival at the varsity level signaled a changing of the guard on the field, Dicus continued to work with athletic director Jack Moss behind the scenes to continue upgrading the program. Both coach and athletic director subscribe to the theory that to be a great team, you must play, and beat, great teams. That 2005 team handled its non-district schedule with such ease that Dicus wanted to beef up the early competition to make sure his team would be battle-tested for the games that mattered. While non-district games were important, they hold no bearing on a team's playoff positioning, and Dicus and Moss believed that playing a tough team in September paid off in October and November, when playoff competition begins.

"If we were going to get better at football, we needed to upgrade who we played," Moss said. "He started playing 4A and 5A schools. He knew if we were going to get good, we needed to beat the best."

That began in 2006. Dicus stopped playing Taylor, Anderson and Elgin. In their place, he secured a two-year series with 4A power Texas City, where he had worked as an assistant coach when the Stingarees won the state title in 1997. The first game between the schools would take place in the Alamodome as part of the now defunct HEB Kickoff Classic. He also added a series with 5A Westwood, which like Lake Travis wanted to grow its football program. And most significantly, Dicus and Moss worked with local Chick-fil-A owners to establish the Great Lakes Showdown, a yearly match-up with 5A Westlake, the high school from the neighboring school district that had long been the program by which all other Central Texas teams measured themselves. Two restaurants, one from each community, put up a trophy, and the teams met at the start of the season every year from 2006-2011.

Gilbert's debut in 2006 couldn't have gone better. The sophomore stood tall, passing for 357 yards and four touchdowns against Texas City. Lake Travis trailed 14-7 after the first quarter when Gilbert hit Cohl Walla for a five-yard score to tie the game, and after Texas City took a 20-14 lead, he connected with Hunter Armstrong from 21 yards out to give his team a halftime lead. Second half touchdown passes to Austin Wrinkle and Jason Bird kept Lake Travis on top, but the Stingarees had tied the game early in the fourth quarter and had the ball looking to reclaim the lead when Lake Travis' defense made a crucial play. Riley Percivill stepped in front of Blake Appfel's pass and returned the interception for the winning score, and the Cavaliers prevailed 41-34.

While the defense delivered the win, Gilbert stole the show, setting in motion what would become a storied high school career.

Another Cavalier made his varsity debut against Texas City after moving to the area from Louisiana. Following Hurricane Katrina, Bryant Lagasse and his family began looking at places to live because New Orleans had changed so much. They had their pick of anywhere and eventually settled on the Lake Travis area.

"The more we looked at Lake Travis, the more we liked it," Dave Lagasse, Bryant's father, said. "We were a football family, I had coached a little high school football back in New Orleans, and these guys grew up playing [youngest son Colin was a middle schooler at the time]. I coached them in their youth football programs, so that was an interest to us. They had just come off of Todd Reesing's season. It was good to at least see that. We knew the record was bad prior to that, but it was like okay, maybe it's on the turn. Then we got here and fell in love with it, and to this day we still kind of pinch ourselves. It's a bit ironic, of all places we could have picked if you just pinned something on the map it ended up being here in so far as us being a football family and the outcome of what has happened here."

Bryant, a junior, made quick friends with his new teammates during the late summer and had earned a starting spot in the secondary by the time the season opener came around. Coming from a private, all-boys school in New Orleans, adjusting to Texas high school football and all that it stood for proved challenging.

"Even the old [Lake Travis] facilities were better than what was back home," he said. "When that new weight room was built, that was pretty shocking to see something that big. Trying to explain to friends back home when we first moved here, I don't think they really understood how big of a deal [football] was here."

Football has always been a big deal in Texas, and since Lake Travis had discovered success under Dicus, it had finally become a big deal in Lake Travis. So much so, in fact, that district planners included upgrades to the football stadium and the creation of a new multi-purpose facility that featured a 40-yard covered turf field as part of a bond election. Voters had the choice to allow the school to borrow the money to build the facility, or they could vote it down.

They approved the facility by a large margin, and eventually the district would gain recognition during the 2010-11 professional football season that ended with the Green Bay Packers winning Super Bowl XLV in Cowboys Stadium. Winter weather slammed the Metroplex that weekend, forcing the Packers and Pittsburgh Steelers to scramble for covered practice facilities. One team ended up using Highland Park High School's indoor facility, and football pundits couldn't believe that the Scots had an indoor facility, one of two in the state. The other, part-time Lake Travis resident and Packers coach Mike McCarthy pointed out, stood in Lake Travis.

If Lake Travis' new weight room and under-construction field house seemed state of the art, Lagasse couldn't have been prepared for what awaited when he played in his first game.

"The very first football game I played in was in the Alamodome," he said. "Coming from playing in an ISD stadium – we didn't even have a home stadium in New Orleans – to playing my very first football game in the Alamodome, I couldn't even focus in the first half. I played terrible actually. They almost pulled me out of the game. Then I started getting into a groove, but to be playing in a huge stadium like that, that was a really big introduction to Texas high school football."

From the frying pan that had been Texas City, Gilbert, Lagasse and the Cavaliers jumped into the fire against Westlake, the area's established program with a long history of success, both at the district level and beyond. The Chaps featured former Lake Travis Pop Warner star Max Minor, future Texas Longhorn kicker Justin Tucker and future Arizona quarterback Nick Foles. The Chaps frustrated young Gilbert, and while the sophomore didn't throw an interception, he struggled to move the Cavaliers. In the end, Foles and company left Lake Travis with the Great Lakes trophy following a 37-14 win. Those Chaps would go on to reach the Conference 5A Division II state championship game.

Another tough loss followed as Lake Travis struggled against another 5A foe in Westwood. The Cavaliers never got on track offensively and the Warriors blew them out 35-3.

"The hardest I was ever hit in high school was in that Westwood game," Gilbert recalled. "I remember just curling up on the ground from it. It was a rough game."

From there, however, Gilbert settled in and the Cavaliers rattled off seven straight wins to close out the regular season as district champions for the third straight year. And like Reesing in his first playoff game two years earlier, Gilbert's team came up short against a physical team from Hays, and the season ended quietly in the bi-district round.

Bryant Lagasse remembers being impressed with how the season went, even though the team lost early in the playoffs.

"After every game, seeing how organized the program was, I'd never seen teams throw the ball like that," he recalled. "I was still amazed at how good of an offense that was and how good football was in Texas. That team, that year was actually really good. We just didn't make it quite as far."

Youth, with a core of sophomores, didn't pan out for the Cavaliers in 2006, but it would.

"Garrett's sophomore year, our talent was young," Halfmann recalled. "We faced Hays and they just whipped us, beat us."

The loss didn't deflate the Cavaliers. Knowing that the sophomores would improve with age – Gilbert included – receiver Austin Pollard said expectations were high as the team dispersed for winter following the loss.

"From day one after we stepped off the field after losing to Hays, I remember Coach Dicus in the locker room," Pollard recalled. "He went around to everyone who would be returning next year saying just remember this feeling, remember how painful it is. We knew we were going to have a very good team my junior year because we had Cohl Walla who would have been a junior and was an amazing athlete. Cade [McCrary] was a junior. I was a junior. And we had Garrett with another year of experience. As a sophomore he was tearing it up, but we knew with him as a junior we had a great shot because he was going to be that much better. "

And so the Cavaliers went back to work following winter break, and things would change. Just how dramatically, no one knew at the time.

8: Calm before the storm

Heading into the 2007 season, left disappointed by the previous season's early playoff defeat, those closest to the Lake Travis program could see that big things – possibly unprecedented things – had become possible.

"But then the next year, I don't know," assistant coach Kevin Halfmann said. "It was just a different group. It was Mike DeWitt's senior year, Bryant Lagasse's senior year. Zack Peckover. They weren't the talented group, but they were the leaders who had the mentality that we could get this done. Going into the season, we had high expectations. We had the talent to do it. We had the leaders to do it. And we could see kids stacking up."

Garrett Gilbert returned for his junior year at quarterback, and following a 2,800-yard sophomore year, he had become a focal point of major college recruiters. His surrounding cast, by and large, returned as well, including a talented trio of receivers that featured Jason Bird, the offensive coordinator's son, Cohl Walla and Cade McCrary, the son of former University of Texas assistant coach Hardee McCrary. Gilbert's father Gale could see the potential for a big year.

"After that sophomore year when they lost in the first round, I think at that point they could go deep the following year because they had talent," he said. "The receivers – Cade, Cohl Walla, [Bird]. The offensive line."

The receiving corps also included junior Austin Pollard and senior David Foley. Junior running back Chris Aydam had emerged as a dual threat runner and receiver. With Peckover and junior Paden Kelley, the offensive line looked like a formidable wall to protect Gilbert.

The Cavaliers also had some talent on defense, though by many accounts head coach Jeff Dicus and his staff put the onus on the offense. DeWitt had gained experience at inside linebacker. Punter Ryan Erxleben had moonlighted as a defensive end. Marcus Pate and Sean Robinson returned to the secondary with Garrett Culwell, and a young Ian Lazarus had arrived on the scene as a hard-hitting safety who would start as a sophomore after injuries to open the season.

The players had taken Dicus' 2006 season-ending message to heart. Pollard said the core group of players who had played together since they were eight years old had high expectations of themselves, and they began to work on those expectations as soon as off-season began.

The hard work extended past the players. Dicus credited the attitude of everyone involved, starting with the parents. After four years of watching the staff in action, seeing how they related to the kids, how they pushed, demanded and got results, parents had allowed the coaches to do what worked for them.

"Parents allowed us to coach their kids," Dicus said. "That was the neat thing about parents there. They trusted us. They saw the love and organization and passion that we had for what we were doing. Every little success we had along the road just kept giving the kids confidence in what we were striving to accomplish."

The Cavaliers also began working on a new mantra – to finish games strong.

"Dicus brought in a big philosophy of finish, finish the game, playing hard in the fourth quarter," Pollard recalled. "That was our big deal. The fourth quarter was huge for us. He really pushed that and I remember we worked as hard as we've ever worked before going into that junior year. We really worked our tails off. We had the talent. It was just another year of experience that topped it off from sophomore to junior year."

Dicus would reinforce this emphasis by wearing a small, checkered flag in his back pocket during games.

Lagasse, entering his senior year as a captain, said the Cavaliers made it their goal to win state, though deep down he didn't know if anyone really believed they could do it. Lagasse thought winning state turned out to be something every team said at the beginning of a season to motivate itself.

"I think we had higher expectations the next year, but we also lost kids that year that we didn't think we could replace," Lagasse recalled. "On the defense, kids like Bryce Bird. We thought they were gods. I guess the expectations were higher, but we weren't sure how much higher. It was state, but I think every year you always say that's your goal. Realistically, I'd come home and think that's a great goal, but can we really win state? Think of all those teams out there. During off-season, guys like Zach Peckover would get state chants going. But realistically, in the back of my head, that'd be great if we could win state, but can we really do that? That was our goal, but I didn't think it would really happen."

Not that anyone could blame him for thinking that way. The march to a state title is so often forged over years of close calls and progress deeper into the playoffs. The furthest Lake Travis had made it to that point had been the second round, four games short. State could never have really felt right around the corner. A team had to be close to feel like it had approached the precipice. Losing in your backyard in an Area playoff game didn't come remotely close.

But Dicus always believed. Even after three years of essentially running in place once the playoffs rolled around, he could see ultimate success at the end of the journey his team had undertaken. He couldn't have seen just how bumpy that journey could get.

As they did the year before, the Cavaliers opened with Texas City, this time on the road. Bird couldn't play due to a suspension, and the Cavaliers started slowly. Texas City led 23-7 before Lagasse recorded a safety late in the half. Lake Travis' offense awoke in the third quarter. Gilbert began carving apart the Stingarees, connecting time and time again with McCrary, who had stepped into Bird's spot. When the pair connected for the final time, a 26-yard score midway through the fourth quarter, the Cavaliers had wrapped up a 32-31 comeback win. Gilbert passed for 326 yards and four touchdowns. McCrary caught 12 passes for 207 yards and three of the touchdowns. The season had definitely gotten off on the right foot, even without one of the team's best players.

Week two brought the Cavaliers' second match-up with Westlake. The Chaparrals had graduated much of the 2006 team that made a surprising run to the 5A, Division II championship game – including quarterback Nick Foles and running backs Bron Hager and Max Minor. Facing a Westlake team looking to rebuild, Dicus had high hopes that his talented 4A squad could pull the upset and serve notice. What followed, though, constituted an epic disaster.

Despite rebuilding, the Chaparrals proved feisty. Lake Travis got off to a quick start and led at the half thanks to two Gilbert touchdown passes and Robinson's 80-yard fumble return. But the Cavaliers melted down in the second half. Gilbert endured his worst game as a high school player – throwing four interceptions — and Westlake scored late to take a 28-21 win. Following the game, Dicus fought back tears as he knelt in disbelief in an end zone at Chaparral Stadium. Years later, the game still bothered him.

"That loss to Westlake was a wake-up call to everybody," he said. "We had opportunities there at the end and we just didn't cash in. But, it made us regroup and made us understand that we can be beat if we don't take things seriously, work harder and do the little things that were necessary, and I think everybody kind of tightened the screws and we went on the good run."

The Cavaliers had played that game without Aydam, and with his return, things started to improve, though there would still be roadblocks and hurdles to overcome. Lake Travis gutted out a defensive-minded win over Westwood the following week. Gilbert scored two touchdowns on quarterback sneaks in the 18-10 win, and the Cavaliers quietly put the loss to Westlake behind them. The next week they began District 25-4A play with a solid but ultimately uninspiring 30-14 win over Burnet. Gilbert threw for 283 yards and three touchdowns. Bird had his third consecutive game with at least seven catches and 100 yards. The Cavaliers got out to a huge lead but never really buried the Bulldogs the way a championship team would have.

After four games, Gilbert had thrown for more than 1,100 yards and nine touchdowns. More importantly, he'd been able to shake off a troubling start in which he suffered six interceptions in the first two games. Aydam joined the lineup for the Burnet game after dealing with a shoulder issue, and while he managed just a modest 16 yards on 10 carries, his return added to the Cavaliers' cadre of weapons.

But behind the scenes, a storm had developed. The early results weren't quite what the coaches had expected. Rumors began to fly, telling tales of player displeasure and unrest, coaches who yelled rather than encouraged as the pressure mounted.

"I think we were all a little frustrated," Gilbert said. "It was building. We just weren't playing as well as we all knew we could."

As the team approached its fifth game, it had also reached a crossroads.

9: The Storm

The 2007 season, and quite possibly the Lake Travis football program entirely, turned on events that led up to what would have been an ordinary district game against middle-of-the-road Vista Ridge. According to all parties involved, the week got off to a rough start and spiraled out of control from there. Sometimes teams have to stare down adversity to make it out the other side, and the Cavaliers gave adversity a good, long, uncertain look.

The Cavaliers stood 3-1 heading into the early October match-up with the Rangers, and on the surface things looked relatively normal. It appeared the offense had begun to somewhat find itself following some unpleasant struggles with 5A foes.

But, assistant coach Kevin Halfmann said, behind the scenes problems had begun to surface, and though they may not have come to a head that week, the events would play a much larger part in the program's future following the season. Getting back to work after defeating Burnet, the team struggled through Monday's practice, and head coach Jeff Dicus didn't like it. It set in motion what became the most pivotal week in the program's history.

"Monday was a bad practice and Jeff was going off, fixing to make them run for a dirty locker room," Halfmann recalled. "And he told me he was going to do it again on Tuesday."

Dicus didn't recall the Monday practice but remembered quite well that the team left the locker room dirty following Tuesday's morning workout. The school day began with an athletic period: not quite standard physical education but teams could meet and use the time to lift weights, go over film, and do everything but dress in full pads and hit. As they did each day, the players went through their morning workout, showered and prepared for the rest of the school day. As usual, coaches brought in breakfast tacos for the players, and the players devoured them quickly. But when Dicus came out of his office for a final word with the team before the period ended, he saw a mess. The coach, for whom organization and respect of both person and property were of tantamount importance, took offense. A situation had developed, and he planned to deal with it like a football coach, or any other coach, often dealt with situations involving discipline.

"The situation was that we fed tacos to the kids in the morning [athletic period], and there was garbage left on the floor in the locker room in the brand new facility," Dicus said. "The kids left tacos and wrappers on the floor, and I told them that morning that if we were going to disrespect this place, there would be consequences, so you better bring your running shoes to practice and we were going to get some running done."

The players don't really remember if they left the facility a mess, though Garrett Gilbert assumed that Dicus did indeed have a reason to be aggravated, and this grievance sent things over the edge.

"The place was probably trashed, but I think it was more than that," Gilbert said later. "I just think it was the straw that broke the camel's back. We were all frustrated. I don't think it was any one thing. The season just wasn't going quite how we wanted it to."

Other players agreed with Gilbert's assessment. None pointed to the dirty locker room as the breaking point. Some said they had simply grown weary of the constant yelling. Others had different thoughts.

Bryant Lagasse, one of the captains, had grown frustrated. He shared his frustrations with his parents but didn't tell anyone else. He reached his breaking point following the 30-14 win over Burnet to open district play.

"After Burnet, there was no victory celebration at all," he said later. "It was just not fun. Practice wasn't fun. Watching film wasn't fun. I'd come home saying I wanted to quit. The whole team was gathered around saying this isn't fun. We were winning but it wasn't fun."

Austin Pollard, then a junior, said the coaches had always been tough on the players. He also said he had heard rumors about player unhappiness, even threats that they'd walk away from the team.

"I remember there was a rumor going around that some people were getting kind of fed up with… kind of the coaching and they claimed they were going to walk off," he recalled later. "Would they have ever done it? No, they never would have actually walked off the field. It was just high schoolers getting upset."

Pollard recognized and accepted the style by which the staff coached. They practiced tough love. Some players appreciated and accepted it. Others didn't.

"Coach Dicus and his staff were very strict and very ... it was their way or the highway," he explained. "They were very strict. I don't want to say drill sergeant, but kind of more in-line type of thing. I think it just started to add up. These guys, some of them were seniors and they'd been going through it the last few years. Then we had some shaky games and just the constant getting yelled at and stuff – which, I'm not saying they were out of line, they were just coaching but that was their style of coaching. It works for some people. It just kind of got to some people the wrong way. Do I think it was wrong? No. It was just their style."

Parents who attended practiced had noticed as well. Dave Lagasse, Bryant's father who'd coached high school football in New Orleans before the family relocated to Lake Travis in the aftermath of Hurricane Katrina, said Dicus' ability to organize things and command discipline may have hindered his relationship with the players.

"We were out at practices a lot, and he was doggedly after these kids," he said. "And after something like that Burnet win, he put subs in at the end of the game and got scored on, and he tore into the entire team on their lack of effort for giving up a late score with subs in. And the kids couldn't enjoy the victory. So that's why that all came to a head."

"We didn't know that everyone was experiencing the same thing like when Bryant would come home and say, 'I'm done, I don't want to play anymore,'" said Laurie Lagasse, Bryant's mother. "We didn't want to say anything to anybody because we just thought it was Bryant. We knew he wasn't enjoying it, but we didn't know the full affect until some of the moms asked me about Bryant. Leigh Anne [Pollard] for one. And then we kind of knew there was something going on. It wasn't just one kid getting yelled at. There was something going on."

Dicus maintains the issue revolved around the messy locker room, and he remained determined to make his point.

There isn't a high school, college or even professional team sport athlete who hasn't endured a coach's wrath for missed assignments, unheeded direction, lack of respect or any number of other violations of team rule or policy, either written or unwritten. Running during practice – wind sprints, gassers, 40s, whatever the coach calls his drill of choice – remains commonplace, both as a form of conditioning and discipline. Players who run because they don't follow directions learn that following directions avoids extra running. Even at Lake Travis, Dicus hadn't been the first coach to threaten a team with extra running for poor discipline. In the late 1990s, Jim Shewmake often told inattentive players that they could practice football or practice track, their choice. Invariably, they chose football.

According to Dicus, players became wary of what awaited them at practice as he dismissed them that morning.

"We let them go, and throughout the morning, kids were texting each other and called their parents to tell them they were going to be punished."

Harry Hatch, a junior linebacker at the time who wasn't seeing much of the field, remembered walking in to the chatter in the locker room.

"I remember walking into the locker room, and a few guys were all sitting there bitching, saying if Dicus made us bear crawl, they were walking off. I didn't even care at that point. I wasn't even playing, so I didn't want to hear it."

Gilbert never wanted to take a side. He understood why frustration was mounting from all corners of the program.

"It was a little bit that we weren't playing as well as we should be, a little that we were doing up-downs every couple of days just because – it was just stupid stuff. And everyone was kind of, 'Well, it wasn't me, why am I getting punished?' I think it was a little bit stupid from our perspective, and then someone called their parents."

Nearly five full years after it happened, Dicus could still recall what happened next as if it happened yesterday. The coach said a few of the parents who found out about his plan to discipline the team felt it necessary to go over his head. Several called Lake Travis High School Principal Charlie Little. What those parents told the principal remains a mystery to Dicus, and he could hardly understand or stomach the events that followed.

According to Dicus, Little, without checking with the coach, Athletic Director Jack Moss or anyone on the football staff, called a meeting of the senior football players, without him, in the school's cafeteria. Little acknowledged the meeting, though he said he did nothing to keep it a secret.

"Sometimes as a principal people don't understand that what happens in football affects the school," he said later. "Sometimes you as the principal have to get involved. I know kids and what they need are positive experiences. At the end of the day, if you're not enjoying something you won't be successful at it. I'm not win at all costs, and at the end of the day it's about the kids being treated respectfully. Everything I did was working with Coach [Dicus] and Moss. It wasn't a secret. I wouldn't do it [meet with kids on a team without the coach] without a good reason."

Pollard knew about the meeting. The administration had heard the rumors of a player walk-out and didn't dispel them as the frustrated rantings of high schoolers. Little wanted to make sure the students didn't do anything they'd regret later.

"But once word got out about that, the administration got a little worried and kind of stepped in," Pollard said. "I know that there was a group of us that got invited to a meeting earlier in the week by Charlie Little, and he just sat us down and asked us what we thought of the coaching and what we thought was going wrong, things like that, and if he needed to step in and do something. That's all that really happened."

The principal said he had one purpose for the meeting, to encourage and provide a forum for the players to air their concerns in a positive way and have them heard.

"At any situation, there is a breaking point," he said. "I do recall some things. If a coach has a player's heart, he can do and say almost anything to that player. Can we agree on that? What is the bigger issue is when you have lost the support of the seniors. Obviously, there were strains at that point. That season was so remarkable, but it wasn't about state at that time. It was about mediating and problem-solving for the kids. For an outsider, I can see that it was an atypical situation, and it was not something I did before or had to do again.

"For the most part, I let the players get together and outline their concerns. I left the room, and they were alone for an hour or so. I encouraged them to address their concerns with coach, rather than walking off the team, which had been discussed. I told them it was your year and you need to share [your concerns] with coach in a productive way. I let them have time and they made arrangements to share concerns with coaches. As a principal, it's not unusual to try to prevent [bad] things [from happening]. I needed to provide an avenue for kids to discuss their concerns in a productive way."

Gilbert, as a team captain, attended the meeting. He said the players held their own meeting once Little had spoken, and the players resolved then to come together and do whatever it took to improve, win, and play well regardless of what took place around them, regardless of who called the shots from a coaching or administrative level.

"In that meeting, me and Mike DeWitt and a couple other guys took the lead, but everyone had a hand in it," Gilbert said later. "It was guys that had responsibility on the team. Our attitude just changed after that. We didn't have to get along with the coaches, we just had to win."

According to Dicus, following that meeting with the players, Little summoned Dicus and Moss to a meeting in a conference room along Diane Frost, an assistant Lake Travis ISD superintendent.

"Charlie Little called a senior-only meeting without my knowledge or coach Moss' knowledge, and I don't know," Dicus said. "A couple of parents had called Charlie Little and complained, and the next day, which was a Wednesday, Coach Moss and I got called up to a conference room and met with Charlie Little and Diane Frost. The meeting was about how I was mistreating kids and didn't care about the kids."

Little, however, didn't recall the meeting that infuriated Dicus. Little said he often met with Dicus and Moss and believes they certainly discussed the situation.

"I would meet with Coach Moss and Coach Dicus regularly," he said. "I think we met over this but I can't remember. I'm transparent. If I get involved at a level, then we are going to work together."

Dicus' recollection of the meeting remained very different, and he obviously didn't feel like there had been any collaboration about the issue behind everything.

Jeff and Karen Dicus don't have children, so they pour their souls into his football teams. The players become their children, and while Dicus admits that he demands effort and greatness from his players, he doesn't apologize for his coaching philosophy or practice. He may not ever be called the warm and fuzzy father figure, but being a father figure to his players, especially players who may not have a father figure in their lives, has always been a part of the job he relishes. To hear the things he heard from an administrator he felt didn't know him proved upsetting to say the least.

"The thing is, if you're going to throw those accusations out to me, then I would expect you would be around me to see if that is actually legit information," he said. "There was one guy, one guy, that knows who Jeff Dicus is, and that's Jack Moss. Jack was at practices, he was in the locker room, he was at the game halftime, at the after the game speech. He knew exactly what I did, what I said to kids. So, we sat there and they pretty much let me have it. I was berated. It was a bad day. That was an emotional meeting because voices were raised. I felt disrespected because what they were saying was not true. Only myself, Coach Moss and my staff knew it, what was the actual truth. So I left. I didn't go to practice. I didn't know how I was going to react."

Moss, Dicus' greatest ally, would only say that he doesn't blame Dicus for how he reacted to what he had heard.

"There was no question at that meeting that there were decisions being made that upset Jeff," he said later. "I don't blame him for being upset. Things were said that shouldn't have been said."

Generally speaking, the assumption the Dicus didn't care about the players didn't sit well with the players themselves. Pushing hard and not caring are very different things.

"I never really disliked the guy. I didn't like him, either, but he's not a bad guy. He really did care about the kids, so I was surprised that there were these rumors going around that he might get fired," Hatch said. "He did so much for the program, but he also did things a different way and it pissed people off."

"Yeah, they pushed us hard, but that was their job," Andy Erickson, then a sophomore, said. "I never thought twice about it. To be honest, our practices were more intense when Dicus left."

Moss said following the meeting, he asked Little and Frost to leave the room so he and Dicus could talk. Following that conversation, Dicus went home. Then he and Karen went to Dicus' parents' house in nearby Georgetown, just north of Austin, to do some soul-searching and think about the difficult decision that he now felt he had to make.

The meeting with Dicus, Moss, Little and Frost came as news to the players. As far as they knew, they had their meeting with Little and went back to business as usual. Except their coach wasn't around.

"Nothing really came about that [meeting], but then when either Thursday or Friday came around and Coach Dicus wasn't even around," Pollard recalled. "We weren't sure where he was. We didn't even know if we were going to have a coach or not."

Dicus took the better part of two days to figure out his immediate future.

"So I missed that Wednesday practice, and Coach Moss and I talked Thursday morning and talked about my decision to keep coaching or to resign," he said. "That's what I was contemplating because I didn't care for how it was being handled. Talking to Coach Moss, and he was like a second father to me."

Halfmann recalled that Dicus hadn't been on campus following the meeting, but the team carried on and did the work it needed to do to prepare for Vista Ridge.

"The kids just rallied together as a team and said, 'We can do this, we can do this,'" Halfmann said. "And they really bonded and came together as a team. The kids just said, 'It's up to us, we're the ones playing, we can do this.'"

Little didn't realize or recall that Dicus had taken leave to think things out, but it didn't surprise him.

"I don't really know," Little recalled. "He didn't have any teaching responsibility so if he took off for a couple of days to get his head straight I wouldn't have known. It wasn't uncommon [for me] not to see him every day because he didn't have to come to the main campus."

"We had no idea where he was," Gilbert said. "It didn't seem like anyone knew."

In the end, Little recalled and surmised that Dicus must have met with the team, discussed key issues and came to a consensus on how they'd go forward. He didn't attend those meetings, so he based his opinion on the results that followed.

"Coach Dicus is old school, but he listened to his program," Little said. "If you ignore it, you do that at your own peril. The kids got with Dicus and then look at what happened to the program. He had to be involved with that. They started winning and never looked back, but up to that point they didn't look like they were having much fun. Somehow, they bonded and moved forward, and it wasn't because I had a meeting with some players."

While his team prepared for the game at hand, Dicus reached his decision and rejoined the team in time for Friday's game. The team didn't see Dicus until the afternoon of the game. Gilbert recalled offensive coordinator Jerry Bird led the team's Friday breakfast and, with no real plan in place, resolved that he would move from the booth in the press box to the sideline if Dicus never showed up. The uncertainty of the situation didn't seem to bother the quarterback.

"To me, it was a big deal, but we had a game, we had to focus. This was adversity and we've got to focus on what's in front of us," Gilbert said. "I'll never know what he was doing those few days."

Hatch and Pollard said the coach returned in time for the game and spoke to the team prior to its taking the field for a game they'd ultimately win, though their respective reactions to what he said differed greatly.

"He started tearing up when he was talking to us, left the room for a few minutes, then came back," Hatch said. "And I just thought, 'Are you kidding me?'"

"I remember he came in and gave a very heartfelt speech and he was there for the game and we were able to pull it off," Pollard said. "It was a very close game. It was a game that should not have been that close. They weren't a very good team. I think there were just so many distractions going on that week that we all went in thinking we didn't have to try very hard, we kind of thought we had it. The distractions had us thinking somewhere else and it was a game that turned out to be closer than it should have been."

The Cavaliers and Rangers played a back-and-forth game littered with turnovers and poor execution on Lake Travis' part, and it nearly proved costly. Trailing 33-28, Vista Ridge drove on the Cavaliers and faced a first-and-goal at the Lake Travis six-yard line.

"I hadn't played a lot to that point, but I was in on that drive for some reason," Hatch said later. "I made a tackle for a big loss on first down."

A penalty pushed the Rangers back further. But another big play had them back within the 10-yard line on fourth down with a chance to win on the game's final play.

"I remember I cut out to the flat on the right side and the quarterback threw the ball over my head," Hatch said. "I turned around, saw the open receiver and thought, 'Oh no, we're going to lose this.'"

But Marcus Pate dove to knock the pass down, preserving the narrow win.

"We ended up pulling out that win Friday night," Dicus recalls. "I think it made everyone much stronger. In my 28 years of coaching, that was the most difficult 60 minutes of my life."

Halfmann concurred with the head coach's assessment.

"We could have folded in that Vista Ridge week," he said. "And they just got through that game and it just kept gathering momentum."

Looking back years later, Little said much of the credit for keeping the team on track during that week goes to the assistant coaches, but he also credited Dicus for the part he played once he met with the players and heard their concerns.

"The position coaches are the unsung heroes for that transitional week," he said. "They kept things moving forward. All of those guys related [to the players] at a level that helped overcome. No one wanted [Dicus] to be more successful than I did, and at the end of the day, he is key with the kids. Something happened and he was able to get them focused and moving forward."

Dicus had not forgotten about the incident that set the week in motion – the messy locker room. When he met with the players, it was back to business as usual, at least as best it could be. They did run for leaving the locker room in a mess, but the team remained intact.

"We did get punished, but it wasn't that bad, and Coach Dicus was there," Gilbert said. "Obviously, it was a big turning point in our season. I remember looking around during the punishment to see if anyone was going to get fed up with it and just walk off. But I think it was all talk."

"We got back on a roll and the kids, the seniors, that day of the meeting were going to boycott and quit," Dicus said. "No one quit. We did a little running, not much. We just wanted to make sure they understood that what they did was wrong. They are going to respect our new facility. Once we got into the playoffs, it seemed like that didn't even happen because we were so engulfed in what we were trying to accomplish. We had a great opportunity."

The football program stood at an interesting crossroads. One parent felt that, at least in part, the discipline that Dicus and his coaches had worked to instill helped the team weather the storm of a tough week.

"It took a group of kids who were pretty dang strong-willed, who in the first part of the season defied Dicus, and I don't think it was in a bad way, but there was a separation and they kept it together," Gale Gilbert said. "The kids took it on their back and the coaches stayed with it and everything just melted together perfectly that year."

Others felt the coaches – Dicus in particular – took the week's events to heart and made adjustments that benefited all.

Bryant Lagasse remembers fun returning to his view of Lake Travis football, and that started with the head coach. Lagasse said things had loosened up, and Dicus had begun interacting with the players in a way they hadn't seen before. To this day, he doesn't know who talked to Dicus, if anyone. He just knows things changed for the better.

"I don't know how it was settled," he said. "All we knew was that it did a 180 from having the worst senior year to Coach Dicus having a 180 and…I don't know who talked to him, I guess it was Mr. Little or someone, we don't know. I guess someone did because practices totally changed. He started being more fun, too. He started playing music, I mean he was always playing music, but he started getting into it at practice, trying to make jokes. Once practice became fun, we started playing a lot better. Our team did a 180 because the attitude changed, and if it wasn't for that we probably would have lost in the first round of the playoffs again because of how upset everyone was with the season."

Pollard, though, may have seen the first instance of a new Dicus. Looking back on that week's events five years later, he recalled that he had played his worst game as a Cavalier that Friday night against Vista Ridge, and as he approached campus for the regular film review the morning after, he expected to be admonished. Sternly.

"I played terrible against Vista Ridge," he said. "I fumbled twice that week and it was the only time I ever fumbled in my career and it was both in that game. I remember going back on Saturday for film and expecting just to get chewed out. And Dicus stopped me in the locker room and he looked at me and said, 'Don't worry about it. We still have faith in you. We still trust you. Don't let this get you down.' And that was it. I remember that really stuck out to me because that was not what I was expecting at all. That was not the usual response when you fumble twice in a game."

Dicus' greeting stunned Pollard, in a good way.

"That kind of caught me off guard," he said. "You could tell he was a little more into it. He was a little more into how we were feeling and took that into consideration."

And so the Cavaliers went back to work, prepping to take on an overmatched Lampasas squad. The Badgers came into the game winless, and Dicus' squad found new joy in doing what the coach expected. In the 58-14 beating that ensued, the Cavaliers clicked on all cylinders. The 58 points set a season, and Dicus era, high. In fact, the total would exceed the team's best offensive performance to that point in the season by 25 points.

Lake Travis led 28-0 after one quarter and 45-7 at the half. Gilbert ran the offense precisely, passing for 290 yards and four touchdowns with no interceptions. Jason Bird caught 10 passes for 134 yards and a trio of touchdowns. Chris Aydam, now healthy, rushed for 99 yards and two scores. The defense got into the act as well, forcing five turnovers, one of which resulted in a touchdown from Sean Kelley.

The Cavaliers had picked up their play, but they still saw their share of battles as the regular season wound down. After routing Lampasas, Lake Travis gritted out two close games – at Dripping Springs in the annual rivalry game and then back home against a talented Connally squad.

Like so many other teams in 2007, the Tigers had no answer for Lake Travis' Gilbert-to-Bird passing attack. The pair connected 12 times for 172 yards and three more touchdowns. Gilbert completed 24 of 36 passes for 301 yards. Aydam rushed for 103 yards and a score, and the defense held firm when the Tigers threatened late in a 34-24 win.

Against Connally, the Cavaliers jumped out to a comfortable lead and weathered a furious fourth-quarter rally. Lake Travis led 24-0 in the second quarter behind long touchdown runs from Aydam and Colton Volpe, a touchdown pass from Gilbert to Bird and a field goal from reliable kicker Thomas Rebold. Connally added a score just before halftime when quarterback and future Iowa State receiver Darius Darks scored on a sneak. Lake Travis led 24-7 heading into the fourth quarter when Darks went to work, throwing a pair of touchdown passes, including an 84-yarder to Chase Harper to cut the lead to 24-20. Lake Travis responded with a scoring drive capped by Aydam's second touchdown, capping a career-best 178 yard night for him, to push the lead back to a comfortable 31-20 margin. Darks erased any comfort, though, when he and Harper hooked up again for a

10-yard touchdown to pull within 31-27 late. But the Cavaliers recovered the onside kick and ran out the clock, maintaining their momentum as they headed into the regular season's final two games.

But at that point, Gilbert still didn't feel like the team had figured itself out.

"We definitely didn't turn the corner right away. Even as we won, the teams we were playing weren't that great, so it didn't feel like we were taking off. But against Hendrickson, things started to click a little. Cohl [Walla] had two touchdowns, and I remember the offense really working."

Lake Travis' defense buckled down as the regular season wrapped up, allowing only 20 points to Marble Falls and 13 to Hendrickson in a pair of comfortable wins. Offensively, the Cavaliers amassed more than 500 yards in beating the Mustangs 49-20, overcoming a sluggish start to break open a game that stood just 14-7 at the half. Gilbert threw for 370 yards and four scores, and Aydam and Erickson combined for 88 yards and three touchdowns rushing. Gilbert threw for five touchdowns in the regular season finale against Hendrickson, and the Cavaliers felt good about where they stood heading into the playoffs.

What lay in wait for the Cavaliers, and their fans, no one knew for sure.

10: Beyond the Tradition

Lake Travis won the District 25-4A title, finishing ahead of Connally and Burnet. Connally, with the largest enrollment, assumed the district's spot in the Division I bracket, leaving Lake Travis and Burnet in Division II. Both Connally and Burnet lost their playoff openers, so as the first weekend's Bi-District round drew to a close, Lake Travis found itself the only team in position to carry the district's banner.

Heading into the playoff opener against New Braunfels Canyon, Lake Travis players and coaches knew the team had picked up its game, but none really knew what to expect. Lake Travis had won four consecutive district championships but had just one post-season win to show for it in the previous three years.

Expectations entering the season had been high. Players wanted to win the state championship, though many likely had no idea what that meant. Bryant Lagasse thought back to what he, Zach Peckover and the other leaders tried to instill in the off-season and how they'd grown as a group, battling not only opponents but themselves and their coaches before striking an accord, and they simply went out and played. Not only did they play, they played well. Lake Travis had been a good team in the regular season, winning eight straight games following the frustrating loss at Westlake that seemed ages ago. But something happened when the playoffs arrived. Garrett Gilbert grew from standout to star, and his teammates grew with him.

New Braunfels Canyon had traditionally been the type of team that gave Lake Travis fits. More physical than finesse, the Cougars took the battle right at the Cavaliers. The teams had split a pair of close district games earlier in Jeff Dicus' tenure, but as the 2007 playoffs kicked off, Lake Travis wasted little time in sending the message that those previous meetings had been long forgotten.

Playing at Texas State University's Bobcat Stadium, Gilbert found favorite target Jason Bird for a first quarter score and then connected with Chris Aydam in the second quarter for another touchdown. Late in the half the quarterback scored with his legs, and before anyone knew it, Lake Travis had taken complete control. The junior quarterback found classmate Cohl Walla for a pair of third quarter touchdowns and Thomas Rebold's fourth quarter field goal put the Cavaliers up 37-0. Canyon managed a late score against Lake Travis' back-up defense, but the Cavaliers' convincing win told the team's fans that something had changed from previous playoff trips.

"To go into the playoffs, I don't even remember who we played," assistant coach Kevin Halfmann said later. "It was a tough one, how tough they'd been in the past, to beat them and dominate them showed we could really play with a physical team."

Defensively, the combination of Matt Kuenstler and Nick Whitehair up front, Lagasse off the edge and Mike DeWitt at linebacker made life miserable for the Cougars, who never mounted a serious threat.

Gilbert's opening playoff performance approached perfection. He completed 25 of 29 passes for 318 yards and four touchdowns. He also showed an added element to his game by leading the team with 40 rushing yards. While Gilbert had been very good in the regular season – 2,903 yards, 29 touchdowns, 63 percent completion rate and only 10 interceptions – he'd raise his play considerably throughout the playoffs. The performance against Canyon served only as a start, and his teammates were more than eager to go along for the ride.

"Without a doubt, Garrett put us on his shoulders," said receiver Austin Pollard. "He took that team over and he just got hot. He refused to lose. He was a leader through and through. I know people said he wasn't a leader at Texas, and they just don't get how he leads. He's very close with his players. He doesn't have to say much. We would work off his vibe. He was never down. He was always confident. He just took control and we all responded with him."

"Going into the playoffs, I don't think anyone had any special expectations," Gilbert said. "At that point, no one is really talking about going deep in the playoffs. Then we played Canyon, and we just played great, and our defense smoked them."

After dispatching Canyon, the Cavaliers set their sights on Kerrville Tivy, another traditionally tough team that had given Lake Travis fits as a non-district opponent earlier in the decade. Most surrounding the program saw this as a stern test, and perhaps surprisingly, Lake Travis passed it. Playing in San Antonio's Alamodome, the Cavaliers sputtered early thanks to some dropped passes, but picked it up quickly with Aydam scoring midway through the opening quarter on a short run. After Tivy tied the game, the Cavaliers turned up the heat. Sophomore speedster Andy Erickson returned the ensuing kickoff 96 yards and Gilbert scored on a short run seconds later. When Gilbert hit Walla with a 40-yard scoring strike, Lake Travis led 21-7 at the break.

"I still cringe every time I see myself getting caught on that play," Erickson said later. "But that wasn't just a big turning point for us as a team; it was big for me, too. I finally felt like I'd played a big role in a big game."

He'd do it much more often down the road.

Lake Travis reaffirmed its control in the third quarter. Gilbert connected with Bird on a short scoring pass and Rebold added a field goal to up the lead to 31-7. After Tivy scored early in the fourth quarter, Lake Travis pressed on. Bird scored on an end-around to put his team up 38-14 and Gilbert connected with Walla for another touchdown, stretching the lead to 45-14 with nine minutes left. Tivy added two late touchdowns to narrow the margin, but Lake Travis marched on.

Gilbert threw for 319 yards and three touchdowns, and while Tivy's tenacious defense made it difficult for the Cavaliers to run the ball, the team still gutted out 56 yards and a trio of touchdowns. And though Lake Travis had allowed some points late, the defense stood firm when it mattered. Kuenstler, DeWitt, Harry Hatch and Lagasse made life tough for the Antlers, Lagasse leading the way with a trio of quarterback sacks. The Cavaliers had advanced past the Area round for the first time in its history, and people understandably enjoyed the ride.

"That was a fun year," said Dave Lagasse, Bryant's father. "Going from week to week, we as parents were just amazed. 'Can you believe we got by another team? What is going on here?'"

The amazement continued on a drizzly night in San Antonio the following Friday. Lake Travis made the trip south again to take on perennial power Corpus Christi Calallen, which entered the regional semifinal undefeated at 12-0 and ranked second in the state. Many felt that Lake Travis' run, if two playoff wins can be called a run, would end at the hands of the much more experienced Wildcats, and that the game might not be that close. Many got their pregame predictions half-right. The game proved no contest.

Lake Travis threw caution into the misty wind and decided to move away from the pass. Gilbert entered the game averaging about 300 yards through the air, and Calallen no doubt prepared for the Cavaliers' passing attack. But the Cavaliers shredded the Wildcat defense with their legs. Rebold capped an early drive with a short field goal, and then Aydam went to work. The junior easily navigated through gaping holes opened up by Paden Kelley, Peckover and the rest of the blockers on his way to three first half scores. Gilbert showed off his legs with a 60-yard scamper on a designed draw and added a touchdown toss to Cade McCrary. The defense even got in on the act when defensive end Ryan Erxleben stripped Calallen quarterback Jeramie Marek, picked up the ball and walked in for a score. By the time the drizzle stopped and the teams headed to the locker rooms for halftime, Lake Travis led 38-0 and Calallen hadn't done anything.

Lake Travis cruised to a 45-14 win over the state's second ranked team. Walking out of the stadium that night, the two *Lake Travis View* staffers at the game wondered if they hadn't indeed watched the state's second-best team that night, but they weren't referring to the Wildcats. Kirk Bohls and Cedric Golden, *Austin American-Statesman* columnists in San Antonio a night early to cover the next day's Big XII football championship, took in the game and came away thinking Gilbert might be the second coming of Vince Young, who carried the 2005 Texas Longhorns to the national championship. Golden made the comparison after watching Gilbert stride away from would-be tacklers throughout the first half, appearing to gain distance while running relaxed, free and easy. Bohls dubbed Gilbert "Vanilla Vince" in his next column.

For the night, the quarterback completed a modest 15 of 24 passes for 165 yards and two scores. He also scrambled his way to a season-best 116 yards rushing on just five carries. Aydam had carried the day, rushing for 181 yards on just 16 carries. The defense had dominated again, forcing Marek out of the game early and keeping the Wildcats from getting any kind of offensive traction.

Following the win over Calallen, two things had changed. First, Lake Travis wouldn't sneak up on anyone else. Dominating the team pundits believed to be one of the state's best will do that. Second, the Cavaliers began to believe that those preseason chants of "state, state, state" could actually come true.

Later, Bryant Lagasse would think back to that win and how significant it became. Winning a couple of playoff games had been expected. Beating a team with some tradition sent a different kind of message.

"Beating teams like Calallen, those are the teams that win state," he said. "After that game was when I started thinking. I mean, we just beat the number two team in the state. We must be pretty good."

Others shared his view.

"The Calallen game was where they took off running," said Gale Gilbert, the quarterback's father. "When they beat Calallen, they realized they were good."

Lake Travis' reward for beating Calallen was a third straight trip to San Antonio, this time to take on Jones High School from Beeville, back in the Alamodome. Though the Cavaliers had been playing well, coaches and players alike knew that the game wouldn't be easy. Jones' unique offense would test the Cavaliers' defensive mettle despite the unit's playoff success.

"I remember our defense really hit a phenomenal streak," Pollard said later. "The only time they really struggled was in the Alamodome against Beeville Jones."

Jones ran a version of the single wing offense and the Cavaliers hadn't seen anything like it all year. The offense depended on misdirection and sleight of hand, and quarterback Erik Soza had run it well, leading the Trojans to an 11-2 record and into the Region IV championship game.

When Lake Travis kicked off, Jones went to work quickly. On Jones' second play, Soza faked a handoff and all 11 Lake Travis defenders came charging toward the line. That left Luis Mendoza alone behind everyone and Soza hit him in stride for a 52-yard touchdown. Trailing for the first time in the playoffs, the Cavaliers promptly went three-and-out, punting the ball back to the Trojans. On the next play, Soza gave the ball to Mendoza on a counter. The Cavaliers only saw the back of his jersey on his 62-yard touchdown run, and just like that they trailed 14-0. Jones had run three plays and scored twice.

Garrett Gilbert may not have sensed his team had been championship worthy as it entered the playoffs, but reality set in with the deficit in the Alamodome.

"I remember being down 14-0 to Beeville Jones after about a minute, and thinking, 'Wow. This isn't going to end right now? This can't end right now.'"

Jones had Lake Travis rattled, and one of the biggest opposing crowds the Cavaliers would ever see in a playoff game remained fired up, rabid and roaring. Players think back to how Dicus would have handled the start early in the season, fiery, demanding, and intolerant of mistakes. But he had changed his approach following the events leading up to the Vista Ridge game and Principal Charlie Little's impromptu meeting with the seniors and captains. Pollard recalled how the coach responded to him following mistakes he had made in the Vista Ridge game, and he recalled how Dicus responded following the disastrous start against Jones.

"To this day, I think [that was] the best coaching that Coach Dicus ever did in the playoffs," Pollard said later. "He could have completely went off on us, but after they went up on us, we were in the huddle about to go out for our offensive drive and he just looked at us and he said, 'Alright, everybody ready to go now? You all good? Alright, let's go get it.'"

Gilbert's recollection echoed his longtime friend's.

"I remember Coach Dicus calls the whole team in after we're down two touchdowns, and I'll never forget this, and he says, 'You guys ready to play now?' And he was almost joking, and he started laughing. So we all just took a deep breath, and thought, 'Hey, we're here now, let's go.' You have to give a lot of credit to Coach in that moment because after that we really thought we were fine. We thought we were going to get yelled at, and he cracks a joke, and we went right down and scored, stopped them on defense, and then tied the game up."

If the Cavaliers didn't yet have an answer for Jones' offense, the Trojans found themselves in just as much trouble once Gilbert and company got rolling. Gilbert quickly moved the Cavaliers downfield and connected with Bird, who had gotten behind the defense, for a 30-yard score. Lake Travis had broken through, and things began to look up. Suddenly the defense arrived, stopping Soza, Mendoza and company on the ensuing possession. With the ball and some momentum, Gilbert drove the Cavaliers back down the field and hit McCrary for a short score to tie the game.

When Gilbert found Bird for a second score early in the second quarter, Lake Travis had clawed ahead 21-20. Jones answered again, but locked in a shootout, Gilbert wouldn't blink. Down 26-21, he drove the Cavaliers down the field, capping a drive with a 14-yard strike to Walla. Aydam added a conversion run on a trick play – Lake Travis' version of Boise State's Statue of Liberty that beat Oklahoma in the 2007 Fiesta Bowl – to lead 29-26. When the Trojans kept serve to go up 33-29, the Cavaliers returned fire, capping the half with a 10-yard pass from Gilbert to Bird to take a 36-33 lead into the locker room.

After the marathon first half, Lake Travis' defense made some key adjustments and came out much more in tune with their assignments. Jones, which had managed such a quick start early in the game, struggled after the break. Lake Travis' offense, on the other hand, endured no such struggles. The Cavaliers built a cushion on their opening drive of the half. Still a step behind the receivers, Jones couldn't keep up with the Cavaliers' spread. Gilbert picked the defense apart, giving his team a 43-33 lead with a strike to Walla. After Soza scored to give Jones hope, the Cavaliers went back on the attack. Another drive, another touchdown pass, again to Bird, and Lake Travis led 50-40. Jones could only answer with a field goal early in the fourth quarter, and the Cavaliers clinched the game when Gilbert took off under pressure and scored on a 22-yard scamper. For the first time in the post-season, Lake Travis had been tested. They survived 57-43.

Gilbert had turned in a career night. He'd completed 25 of 32 passes for a modest 287 yards with a gaudy seven touchdowns, then one shy of the state single-game record. He also ran for a team-best 73 yards on six carries. Bird got open all night, catching 11 passes for 146 yards and a team-record four scores. Defensively, the Cavaliers eventually caught on to Jones' scheme and forced a pair of interceptions, one each by Hatch and Marcus Pate. They'd suffered their worst performance – 43 points was the most any of Dicus' teams had surrendered – and survived.

Pollard looked back on his coach's sense of calm during the early storm.

"He was very calm and relaxed and we come back and win that game," he said. "After that game, that's when we all really knew that we had a shot here, and that this was a real thing. I don't think anything could have stopped us after that."

Dayton, Lake Travis' semifinal opponent, had been getting lots of flattering press. The Broncos came into the game as winners of Region III, having scored more than 40 points in three of their four playoff games. Quarterback Cody Green, though out for the playoffs with an injury, would go on to play at Nebraska. Wide receiver AJ Dugat had emerged as a dual-threat player as well.

Looking back, Dicus recalls feeling the Cavaliers had an advantage because of their depth. Lake Travis' players played either offense or defense, not both. Dayton, he recalled, would use its top players both ways.

"When we got to Dayton in College Station, they were the most athletic team we played all year, but their studs were going both ways and we felt we had an advantage and could wear them out, which we ended up doing," he said later.

On film, Erickson, Gilbert, and Hatch all agreed that Dayton provided the most impressive display any opponent had shown when broken down.

"I remember being so nervous before that game because they looked so good on film," Gilbert said. "And then we just dominated them. We were playing really well by then."

Apparently those nerves never showed for the team's leader. As the week progressed, though, Pollard recalled suffering a case of nerves. He didn't know what would happen when the team took the field against Dayton's athletes at Kyle Field, so he found his friend, the quarterback, on the sidelines toward the end of practice one day.

"The most nervous I was for a game was the game before the state championship when we played Dayton," he said. "People were going nuts about how they were going to be the ones to stop us and that was going to be our roadblock. They were such a good team, blah, blah, blah. I was so nervous before because I didn't want to lose the game before the state championship, to get that close and lose.

"And I remember the Wednesday of that week, we were in practice, toward the end. They were doing special teams and I was talking to Garrett on the sidelines. I told him that I was pretty nervous about this one, and he just turned and looked at me dead in the eyes and he said, 'I won't let us lose. I promise you I won't let us lose.' And as soon as he said it, as confident as he said it, I wasn't worried at all anymore. I knew we were under control and we killed them."

Though he'd throw his first playoff interception against the Broncos, Gilbert made sure he kept his promise. When the dust had settled, Gilbert passed for a career-high 474 yards, completing 34 of 40 passes with four more touchdowns. Dayton's defenders couldn't cover Bird or Walla. The duo combined for 25 catches and 301 yards with four touchdowns. The Broncos couldn't stop Aydam either. The running back rushed for 140 yards and caught five passes for 83 more, scoring twice. Lake Travis' defense got back on track as well, forcing four turnovers in a 49-13 whitewashing.

The Cavaliers, now dubbed the state's Cinderella, had reached the state championship game against storied Highland Park, which had also enjoyed one of the strongest seasons any team had put together. The Scots entered the championship game 15-0 with all the experience, plenty of momentum, the knowledge that they had been the favorites from the time teams broke camp in August, and they were sitting on their 700th win. They rank among the state's all-time leaders in wins and state championship appearances and had won the 2005 title behind quarterback Matthew Stafford. The 2007 title game would be the school's sixth appearance. Their toughest playoff game had been a 21-point win over Frisco in the Bi-district round five weeks earlier, and many felt the Scots would be too tough for the Cavaliers to handle.

The Cavaliers knew all about the Scots, their players, their reputation. Pollard heard about the Scots' two-headed quarterback combination, athletic Dutch Crews and strong-armed Winston Gamso. He learned about stud receiver Chase Davis and his talented counterparts. The coaches told the team it would take an epic performance from the Cavalier defense to keep the Scots in check. But they also reminded the players that because no one expected a Lake Travis upset, they had nothing to lose.

"Coach Dicus just kept saying all the pressure was on them. We were just there," Gilbert said. "That Highland Park team was really good. I met a lot of guys in college that played there, and they're still mad. They hate us."

And why not? The team that perhaps embodies the history, passion, and tradition of high school football in Texas faced an upstart with no history. Dicus had worked hard to build tradition at Lake Travis. He used the word often, and while it's impossible to create it overnight, the Cavaliers did their best.

While they surely remember the game, Lake Travis fans also have equally fond memories of the send-off the team received. The team met early on Saturday morning, Dec. 22, at the field house to load up for the ride up to Waco. The game would kick off at 2 p.m. at Baylor's Floyd Casey Stadium. It should have taken the Lake Travis entourage roughly two and a half hours to make the drive from Lakeway.

As soon as the team returned from College Station after beating Dayton, Karen Dicus, the coach's wife, went to work setting up something special.

She worked with Lakeway's Stokes Signs Company to get something made when she encountered a hurdle: the City of Lakeway's sign ordinance, which doesn't allow signs or banners on the side of the road. When she heard that, she went straight to the council and pleaded her case.

"I remember the sign company for the sendoff," she said. "They told us the city of Lakeway wouldn't let us put signs up for the team. So I called them to ask. They said the city was a different entity from the school, but I reminded them that their entity goes to that other entity. And they called us back and said that we could do it. It was phenomenal how the community joined in and the pieces to the puzzle fit."

When the team pulled out of the parking lot and headed out to Ranch Road 620 to begin heading north, they found the highway packed with cars. Supporters had turned out and lined the road, cheering the Cavaliers as they began their journey. Signs had been placed everywhere. Fans stood outside their cars and waved. From inside the buses, the sight took players, coaches and administrators' breath away.

"No other event that will ever take place will compare to the first time we left for Waco," said Jack Moss, the school's athletic director from 2003-08. "From the school to the [Mansfield Dam] bridge, there were cars everywhere lining the road. Four years before that, you couldn't even get 500 people to the stadium on Friday night."

The head coach smiled throughout the ride out.

"I'll never forget leaving for the state championship game and going down the highway with everyone out there," Jeff Dicus said. "That was a good emotional time because you were excited to see parents excited about what was going on."

Leigh Anne Pollard, Austin's mom, saw everything. If Disney had made a movie about that day, it wouldn't have come out as well as the real thing.

"This is the movie moment right here," she said. "We have video of the bus route, the parade that went through to escort."

Dave Lagasse watched the team leave and head north before he and his family got in their car and began the journey. Looking back on those events five years later, he can take in the bigger, more complete picture of not just the day but the season as well.

"That whole season, that first season, that's where I came to realize everything that went into it," he remembers. "The story with the shakeup of the team...it's a little bigger than a small story but it's still relatively small to what happened with that team. It was really about it takes a village to raise a team. To see everybody involved in the community, putting signs in the windows, decorating the buses and then lining the streets. [Bryant] said he had tears in his eyes riding out. To see that many people come out, it made this seem like such a small town Texas. The community came out. It was their team and everybody supported it. We had great crowds throughout the playoff run. Everywhere you went within the community, people were talking about it, buzzing everywhere with the excitement of getting to state. And of course, that has never died down to this day. The community support, up and down the line, people – old couples who don't have kids here or grandkids here but live here, they attend every game. They know the kids' names, they follow them religiously and they're the ones out on the street with a little sign."

As the team crossed the bridge in front of Mansfield Dam, parents who had gone ahead to the other side released black and red balloons, one more show of spirit before the team hunkered down for the ride.

Traffic turned out to be brutal and the drive took longer than expected. In fact, the school's band got caught in traffic and didn't make it to the stadium until midway through the first quarter. But when the Cavaliers took the field to begin their preparations, they noticed that the visitors' stands at Floyd Casey Stadium were beginning to fill up. As Dave Lagasse noted, the community had adopted the team, and they had turned out en masse to see the season's finale. From the field, the view made everyone on it smile, Halfmann said.

"Being the first time of course, in any kind of game like that, being down on the sidelines, and look up and see our crowd, it was phenomenal," he said.

Even though Lake Travis came in the overwhelming underdog, Dicus and his staff decided they would take every opportunity to go on the offensive. The Cavaliers would let Highland Park know that they had every intention of winning, that simply getting to the game for the first time in their history hadn't been their season-long goal. The plan, simple enough, would be to try and grab an early lead, keep the offensive momentum that the Cavaliers had built in their five playoff wins going, and hope the defense could slow down Highland Park's equally potent offense.

In Lake Travis' first five playoff games, the Cavaliers had upped their offensive production from 33.9 points per game to 46.6 points per game. Gilbert averaged only 20 more passing yards per game than his regular season total, but he was much more accurate, connecting on 73 percent of his tries, throwing 20 touchdowns and just one interception. The defense stepped up as well. While its scoring average climbed slightly from the 20.9 points allowed per game in the regular season thanks to the performance against Jones, in the four other games the Cavaliers gave up only 15.8 points. After the championship game, Gilbert looked back and gave credit to the entire team.

"We realized what we were playing for in the playoffs," he said on the field after the championship game. "Our seniors are great leaders, and we are all team players. We just sort of flipped a switch. We all played really well when we needed to."

They needed to play well in the championship game, and it became evident from the outset that they would.

Highland Park took the opening kickoff and marched across midfield before the Lake Travis defense stepped up. On third down near midfield, Gamso dropped back to pass. Bryant Lagasse, rushing around the end, got there before he could get a pass away and dropped him for a sack, forcing a punt. Chris Morris' punt pinned the Cavaliers deep in their own territory, and the first time Gilbert brought the offense out, they scrimmaged from their own eight yard line.

Undaunted by the negative field position, the Cavaliers kicked things into high gear. Gilbert looked to Bird on the first play and found him for 19 yards, erasing the bad field position. Two plays later, the quarterback took off and gained 13 yards to convert a third-and-one. He found McCrary alone for a 39-yard gain to the Highland Park 12. On second down, Aydam slipped out of the backfield, caught a screen pass and followed his escort of blockers into the end zone. The score set the stage for the game's first dramatic moment. In studying film of Highland Park's field goal defense, Dicus noticed a tendency, and he planned to exploit it the first chance he got. So the Cavaliers faked the extra point. Instead of putting the snap down for Rebold to kick, McCrary picked it up and sprinted for the left end of the line, Rebold trailing in option position. McCrary saw a hole and went for it, leaping through a tackle into the end zone for the conversion and an 8-0 lead.

Highland Park coach Randy Allen felt the pressure. The Scots answered with a drive of their own. Gamso completed passes to Michael Thatcher, Morris and Chase Bellinger and scrambled for 12 yards to the Lake Travis seven yard line. Lake Travis corner Sean Robinson knocked away one potential scoring pass, and when Erxleben sacked Gamso on third-and-goal, the Scots faced a choice. They lined up for a short field goal, and as Dicus did on Lake Travis' kick attempt, Allen called a fake. Crews converted with a strike to Jack Murtha for a touchdown. Not wanting to fall behind, Allen elected to go for two. The Cavalier defense stood tall. Hatch sacked Crews, and the Cavaliers stood clinging to an 8-6 lead.

As the opening quarter drew on, the weather became a factor. A stiff north breeze began cutting through the otherwise sunny afternoon. The breeze became a constant wind, quickly driving the temperature down and also taking its toll on the play on the field. Drives into the wind proved much tougher than drives with it, and that would become crucial late in the game. But early on, teams tried to adjust to the cold and maintain their focus.

"It was cold, very cold," Austin Pollard recalled. "We weren't expecting that. We all thought it was going to be hot so none of us were prepared for that."

If the falling temperatures bothered the Cavaliers, they didn't let on. They simply kept their heads down and tried to make plays when opportunities presented themselves. And those opportunities came often.

Highland Park kicked off into the wind, and Erickson returned it to midfield where Gilbert went quickly to work. He found Bird for 26 yards into Highland Park territory, and after a short run from Aydam looked for his favorite target again. Bird motioned from the outside into the slot, started up the field and made a turn toward the flag on a corner route. He entered the game with a state-record 146 catches on the season, so he figured to have at least one and likely two Highland Park defenders tracking him everywhere he went. But when he made his break to the corner, he found himself all alone, the only player on that side of the field. Gilbert's spiral fell softly into Bird's sure hands, and Lake Travis led 15-6 late in the opening quarter.

The scoring continued as Highland Park enjoyed the wind at its back in the second quarter. Lagasse sacked Crews on the second quarter's first play, but on the second play, Crews got even, hitting Bellinger in stride on a slant pattern. The receiver cut between two defenders and didn't stop until he'd covered 84 yards for a touchdown.

Back came the Cavaliers, though. From his own 21, Gilbert found McCrary on a 12-yard curl, but when the defender fell down, McCrary took off. Running into the wind, he ran out of steam before he could score, and the Scots tracked him down at their own nine yard line. Gilbert found Bird open for eight yards, and Aydam took care of the rest, bulling in for his second touchdown, giving the Cavaliers a 22-13 lead.

To that point, the offenses had been striking quickly, so quickly that the defenses had little time to catch their breath. Lake Travis' longest drive of the opening half took just 2:54. Two of the scoring drives lasted less than 1:21. It had been that way throughout the post-season for Lake Travis, and Lagasse remembers it both as a blessing and a curse.

"Most of the time I was too tired to watch the offense," he recalled. "We knew what was going on because they scored so much we were always on the field. It was almost too fast. Offense scored again, back on the field."

Highland Park took its time following Aydam's short touchdown run. Crews got the Scots started, mixing runs and short passes with success. When he came out following an 11-yard completion to Morris, the Scots had reached the Lake Travis 23 yard line. Gamso entered and Erxleben greeted him with a sack. Lake Travis' pass rush, led by Lagasse and Erxleben, kept getting home, something that had been happening with regularity throughout the playoffs. By the time the team reached Waco, Lagasse said the coaches had grown so confident that he and other players had some freedom to blitz whenever they saw openings.

"As the season went on they gave me more freedom, and by the time the playoffs hit, mainly it was just blitz, blitz, blitz," he recalled later. "I got a knack for it, and in that state game, I was almost so comfortable with it that I could do more stunts. Me and someone would be like, 'This time you go outside and I'll go inside.' Teams weren't expecting it in that spot kind of thing. I guess that's just how it went."

Despite Lake Travis' constant pressure, neither Gamso nor Crews wilted. After picking himself up, Gamso connected with Seth Gardner for 20 yards and capped the drive with a short scoring pass to Morris, who also added the extra point. The Scots' long drive took 12 plays and 4:33, an eternity based on the game's early flow. Highland Park's defense obviously enjoyed the rest, forcing the game's first three-and-out as Lake Travis lost a yard on its next wind-hampered possession. Erxleben managed to boom a 36-yard punt into the wind, but Highland Park looked to take some momentum.

Momentum, though, can be a fickle, fleeting thing. Inspired by their stop, the Scots looked to connect on a big play. Gamso found Davis on a quick slant, and the receiver looked to break free with a clear path to the end zone. But Robinson didn't quit on the play. Lake Travis' senior corner not only tracked Davis down shy of the goal line but managed to get the ball loose. When the fumble bounced into and through the end zone for a touchback, Lake Travis had dodged a monumental bullet. Coaches immediately knew that play would be crucial.

"You look at plays that defined Lake Travis, and the play that Sean Robinson made will define us because of that effort," Dicus said later. "He could have very easily just gave up and let him score."

"Sean Robinson played the game of his life," Austin Pollard recalled. "He was in charge of that receiver and he forced that fumble on the one yard line and the ball went out of bounds. He played the game of his life."

Though they had dodged a bullet, the Cavaliers couldn't escape Highland Park's pressure. The offense still struggled against the strengthening gale and Erxleben's next punt netted just 14 yards. Highland Park regained possession near midfield, determined to make up for the previous turnover. Gamso started with a pair of quick completions, the second to Gardner for 28 yards to the Lake Travis 12. Two Thatcher runs moved the Scots closer, but Gamso's third down pass fell incomplete, leaving the Scots with a decision on fourth-and-short from the Cavalier five yard line. With the clock showing less than a minute before halftime, Allen elected to take the lead with a short field goal, but the Cavaliers had other ideas. DeWitt broke through the line and blocked Morris' kick. Pate picked up the bouncing ball and returned it to the Lake Travis 32 yard line. With 34 seconds left, the Cavaliers had the lead. They had no plans to sit on it.

"We wanted to attack," Bird said after the game. "That's how we've played all year. We attack, we have fun, we keep moving the ball."

He promptly caught two passes from Gilbert to get the Cavaliers out to their own 48, and Gilbert spiked the ball to kill the clock with 15 seconds left. Then he uncorked a throw that Lake Travis fans remember vividly. With the wind howling, he sent Walla deep down the Highland Park sideline. Amidst heavy pressure, he stepped up and threw a rainbow through the wind while being hit. He never saw Walla get behind the defense, haul in the pass and dive across the goal line. He heard it, though.

"Never in a million years should that play have happened," Gilbert said later. "It was so windy, I didn't think we'd pull anything like that off."

Describing the play on the field after the game, Gilbert calmly gave the credit to his receiver.

"That was a huge play," he said. "Cohl ran a great route to beat the defender."

That's Gilbert's style, never too high, never too low. His teammates and coaches, though, knew the magnitude of the moment.

"We thought we'd struggle a little bit because it was so windy and we threw the ball so much, but Garrett was able to get the ball through that wind," Pollard recalled. "I remember right before halftime he threw a 50-yard bomb to Cohl Walla into that wind and it was one of the best throws I've ever seen."

"That was a huge momentum swing for us at the end of the half," Dicus said on the field following the game. "It allowed us to go into the half on a positive note."

The 52-yard touchdown gave Lake Travis a 29-20 lead heading into the locker room, where coaches furiously worked to make some adjustments that could slow down Highland Park's attack. The Scots had amassed more than 300 yards, punting only on their opening drive. The two big plays from Lake Travis' defense loomed large over the half, and many believed Lake Travis' tenuous lead wouldn't last.

If halftime stemmed Lake Travis' momentum, the Cavaliers still had one key card they could play. With the option for the second half, the Cavaliers elected to put the wind at their backs in the fourth quarter, putting faith in the defense to keep the Scots in check while they had the wind. If the Cavaliers could keep their lead through the third quarter, a Highland Park rally would be that much tougher in the final quarter.

So the second half began with the Scots kicking off with the wind, and the coverage team pinned Erickson down at the Lake Travis 13 yard line. Aydam lost four yards on first down, and two plays later Erxleben punted into the wind, a 32-yard effort that gave the Scots the ball on Lake Travis' side of midfield.

Gamso used his legs to get the Scots marching, and when Lagasse sacked him on a flea-flicker, Lake Travis' defense looked like it had gained some momentum back. But Gamso responded quickly. Two completions to Morris moved the Scots to third-and-short, where Gamso found Davis behind Robinson for a score, closing the Lake Travis lead to 29-27.

The battle intensified, and everyone on the Lake Travis sidelines knew it.

"We came out for the second half and it was non-stop intensity," Pollard said. "I remember having butterflies the whole game because it was back-and-forth and the game was so close right to the end."

Lake Travis still couldn't move the ball into the wind, but the defense began to hold its own despite spending most of the third quarter on the field defending its own territory. Highland Park's next drive started in Lake Travis territory but ended with a punt after Gamso fumbled a snap to move the team out of field goal range. Morris' punt pinned Lake Travis back at its own 11 yard line, and with 2:46 left in the third quarter, Lake Travis knew it needed to come up with a drive to help out its defense. They also wanted to keep the ball long enough to end the quarter and put the wind at their backs again.

Things started slowly. Gilbert misfired on first down. A delay of game penalty moved them back into the shadow of their own goal posts. Facing second-and-long, Gilbert took the shotgun snap in his own end zone, avoided some pressure and scrambled for just a single yard. On third-and-14, he found Bird over the middle for 17 yards to get a precious first down. The Cavaliers gained another when the Scots jumped offsides on third-and-five. When Gilbert and Bird connected twice more, the Cavaliers had killed the third quarter clock and advanced near midfield.

Two plays into the fourth quarter, Lake Travis decided to take a shot with the wind. Gilbert sent Walla down the seam on a skinny post but under-threw the pass ever-so-slightly. Highland Park's Johnny McKnight made the Cavaliers pay, making a leaping interception in front of Walla. It would be the Cavaliers' only turnover, and only Gilbert's second interception of the postseason. The defenses had clearly made their adjustments. The two teams traded punts, and the net effect left Highland Park with the ball at its own 20 yard line, still trailing 29-27 with 7:53 left.

On the first play, Gamso made his only mistake of the game. Pate intercepted a poorly thrown pass and returned it deep into Highland Park territory. While much of the yardage got erased on a penalty, the Cavaliers saw their best chance of the half, taking over at the Scots' 33 yard line. After Gilbert scrambled for 11 yards and the Scots were flagged for holding, the Cavaliers lined up at the Highland Park 12. Dicus reached back into his bag of tricks and called on Boise's Statue of Liberty. Gilbert looked right and faked a pass, putting the ball behind his back. Aydam grabbed it and cruised around the left side of the line, running untouched into the end zone. Just like that, Lake Travis had a 36-27 lead with 6:53 left. Highland Park would need two scores, and time and the elements both worked in Lake Travis' favor.

For a minute.

Gardner fielded the ensuing kickoff and nearly broke the return. Lake Travis' coverage team finally forced him out of bounds at midfield. Two completions and a pass interference penalty later, the Scots were knocking on the door. Gamso crashed through it on a touchdown sneak, and only 43 seconds after Lake Travis had gained some breathing room, the Scots erased it, closing within 36-34 with 6:10 left, plenty of time for a rally if they could stop Lake Travis.

And stop Lake Travis they did. The Cavaliers managed to run two minutes off the clock before punting, and Erxleben's 43-yard punt gave the ball back to the Scots at their own 29 yard line at the 4:10 mark.

While the Lake Travis offense preferred to keep the ball to run out the clock, maybe even score and restore the cushion, they remained confident that the defense would do what it needed to do to preserve the lead.

"Our defense has come up big during the season, against Connally and Vista Ridge, when we needed them to," Gilbert said following the game. "Granted, that wasn't against this level of competition, but we had confidence they would make a play."

The defenders relished the opportunity to stand up and secure a win after the offense had taken Lake Travis so far.

"We weren't worried," said Kuenstler, the senior defensive tackle. "We knew we would get the job done."

Well, that became easier to say afterward.

The job proved difficult. Gamso and Highland Park stood intent on making this drive their best of the season. Quickly, efficiently, Gamso went to work as Lake Travis dropped back into zone coverage. He found Morris for five yards and Bellinger for 21 to move into Lake Travis territory. Another completion to Bellinger moved the Scots to the Lake Travis 36 yard line, and Dicus called time out to settle his troops.

On the next play, Tanner Kyle sacked Gamso for a loss on second down, but the Scots marched on when Gamso found Gardner to convert on third down, moving the ball to the Lake Travis 31. On first down, Gamso rolled right and tried to hit Davis in the end zone. Davis snuck behind Pate, but Pate jumped up at the last minute and the pass hit him in the back, falling harmlessly to the turf. After a penalty backed the Scots up, Gamso hit Bellinger for 10 yards to the Lake Travis 26. On third down, Gamso scrambled, but DeWitt knocked him down after a short gain, leaving the Scots facing a fourth down at the Lake Travis 25. Allen called time out as the Scots faced fourth-and-four, their season on the line with 1:45 left. The wind ended up a deciding factor. A 42-yard field goal into the gale would never make it. The Scots had to go for the first down.

On the Lake Travis sideline and in the defensive huddle, chaos reigned. Lagasse, who had registered three sacks to that point in the game, stood hell-bent on getting a fourth. He knew the coaches were giving orders, but he couldn't hear anything.

"With all the adrenaline pumping, I couldn't tell you what was said," he recalled later. "I was just trying my best to sack the quarterback."

Hatch, a junior inserted into the starting lineup during the playoffs, remembered the coaches surprisingly sticking with the zone scheme.

"They were eating us up on that drive, and we were on our heels. The zone just didn't seem to be working anymore," he said later. "And [defensive coordinator Dave] Nelson was sitting there saying, 'We're fine, we've got this.' I'm thinking, 'Uh, no, we don't.'"

Hatch remembered breaking the huddle, seeing the Scots line up and snap the ball. He dropped back into his zone and started looking for receivers. He found one in his zone, open. Austin Mai, the fourth receiver in the Scots' four-receiver set, hadn't been thrown to all day. Hatch wasn't the only player to see Mai open. Gamso saw him too, and before Hatch could close in, Gamso let fly with a pass that hit Mai in the stomach. And fell to the turf. Incomplete.

"He was wide-ass-open, and the quarterback put it right on him," Hatch said. "When he dropped it – 'We just won the state championship! I cannot believe we just won the state championship!' It was pretty crazy."

"The game was on the line for us and I really didn't know what to think or feel watching it," said Bird after the game. "But our defense came up big and won the game for us."

Five years later, Lagasse still couldn't put what he saw into a complete thought. "When I saw the ball drop...."

The Lake Travis sideline erupted.

"And then when that guy dropped the ball on fourth down, it was like your heart just leapt," Pollard recalled. "It was a feeling that you can't describe, the instant joy that you had just won."

Lake Travis hadn't won yet. One more first down would kill the clock for sure, and Gilbert delivered with a 12-yard run on third-and-six. He handed the ball to the referee and sprinted toward his sideline as the clock ticked down. He never made it. The onrushing mob of Lake Travis players and fans met him on the field to begin the celebration. Fans of all ages, all sizes, took part. It lasted for what seemed like hours.

"It was amazing to see the field – everyone stormed the field and the little kids trying to pick things off your body, trying to get wristbands and gloves," Pollard said. "It was amazing."

The coach, standing with his wife taking it all in, summed it up following the game.

"So much work went into this from so many people," Dicus said. "Five years ago people said you couldn't win at Lake Travis. Well, look at us now. It took a lot of hard work, belief in our system and support from everyone in our great community. This is just unbelievable. I'm so proud of our seniors, proud for our community."

Former Cavalier linebacker Mark Kuenstler went to the game with his mother to watch his younger brother Matt anchor the Lake Travis defensive line. He said he'll never forget the way he felt.

"Oh boy. Next to marrying my wife, that was the greatest day ever," he said later. "It was just phenomenal. That was incredible. It was quite a team. They had disciplined coaching and Garrett Gilbert, and that was all they needed. He was throwing that ball through that wind, the prettiest spirals you had seen. In my opinion, he was the best high school quarterback who's ever played the game, hands down. He was phenomenal."

Dicus agreed with the sentiment.

"Garrett really stepped up the way he played big time, and I think it elevated everyone else's game as well," Dicus said during the celebration. "He is definitely the catalyst for what we do."

Years later, Dicus added to his description.

"Garrett was unbelievable. He was special. One of those special kids, like Todd Reesing, Luke Lagera, that you just think the world of because of who they are and their work ethic and their passion to succeed."

Looking back later, people could put what happened into perspective. The championship season proved to be a wild ride full of highs and lows, comebacks and stands.

"That playoff stretch where they just caught fire, week to week it was like we were all on this joyride," Dave Lagasse said. "We just didn't want it to end and they kept pulling off wins."

The school principal enjoyed the ride as well.

"Each game went down to the wire," Charlie Little said. "And then at state, that was the most thrilling, exciting game you've seen. That's when I realized how unusual and rare it is to win because you can get beat at any place at any time. I felt like Dicus went into that game with a different attitude. He changed things up and made some gutsy plays to get ahead. It was exciting. That's when I realized how it was pretty amazing."

Joy and community pride surrounded everyone.

"Everyone was just hugging and high-fiving and it was a great feeling, and I had a family member on the field and it was a big deal," said Mike Maroney, stepfather to junior defender Jon-Michael Paul. "It was a lot of fun in Waco that day."

The players beamed with pride as well. They had come a long way, not just in their careers but in that 2007 season.

"This is wonderful," Matt Kuenstler said after the game. "I've never felt anything like this before. This is well worth everything we've been through, all the hard work."

The parents enjoyed watching the celebration with the players. For some, it wasn't just the culmination of a couple of years of hard work at high school. For the Gilberts, Pollards, McCrarys and others, the journey began much earlier, so the smiles were bigger.

"That whole experience was really cool because of the group being together for so long," Gale Gilbert said later. "With Hardee [McCrary] and Alan Williams, Walla's dad had done coaching with us…the whole group had been together and seen success. They got brimming with confidence that they couldn't be stopped and that became evident playing Highland Park that someone was going to make some plays. I think we could play that Highland Park team 10 times and maybe only win two or three. That was a good team. There was a lot in that game that the defense hadn't done before."

Even years later, others recall everything that took place, the stories that lived behind the scenes at the time, some good, some bad, some heartbreaking. Leigh Ann Pollard said knowing all of those stories made the win much sweeter for the parents.

"One of the things I respect about the parents of this particular team is that you have to know the stories behind so many," she said. "The Lagasses came from Louisiana after Katrina. Matt Kuenstler was facing the last days of his mother's life. She was dying of cancer and she was holding on until they won. She died in February [of 2008]. Austin's struggle was with his injury and what had happened to him, and he was trying to come back strong. And I could list others. There were so many things happening in these boys' lives that they pulled together through them and with the help of – one of the pillars of strength was Coach [George] Oakes, a man of God, one that gave them direction."

Mark Kuenstler, who would marry Christin Pollard, Austin's brother and Leigh Ann's daughter, remembers how his mother, Loretta, felt during the playoff run.

"My mom saw that game, and it was the last game she saw," he said. "That's one of the reasons that game was so special for so many people. She was there even when I wasn't going to games. She was still there, with her bells, when she was battling cancer. She was a huge supporter through the years. For her to be able to see them win that title game, it was really something special."

The 2007 Cavaliers became the first school's first state football champions and only the second team to claim a title, following the 1997 boys golf team, which won the 3A state title.

The season didn't just produce titles. It produced records. Gilbert set state records for completions (360) and attempts (546) in a single season, and his 52 touchdown passes ranked sixth (at the time) on the state's single-season list, according to records kept at *Dave Campbell's Texas Football*. Bird, despite missing the season opener, set the state single season record for receptions with 153, shattering the old record of 124. His 1,815 yards ranked fifth on the all-time single season list, and his 25 touchdowns ranked seventh. Like his quarterback, Bird didn't accept much credit for setting the marks.

"It's just a credit to the entire team," he said. "We work hard. We have a great system with great coaches. That's all there is to it."

In their title run, the Cavaliers all, as Gilbert pointed out when asked how he elevated his game for the playoffs, stepped up. The offense as a whole averaged 45 points per game, up from 34 during the regular season, and with good reason. Aydam, after missing the first part of the season, scored eight rushing touchdowns in the playoffs, matching his regular season total. He added two more receiving touchdowns in the post-season, and his playoff average of 116 yards from scrimmage surpassed his regular season average. McCrary, after catching 26 passes for 426 yards in 10 regular season games (including 12 for 207 in the opener), stepped it up, catching 22 passes for 392 yards in the six playoff games. Walla also upped his production.

After averaging 56 receiving yards per game during the season, he upped it to 85 per game in the playoffs. He scored eight playoff touchdowns after managing just five in the regular season. The offensive line, anchored by Peckover and Kelley, kept Gilbert upright and created holes for Aydam.

Then, as much as they prefer to deflect any credit, came Bird and Gilbert. In nine regular season games, Bird caught 93 passes for 1,171 yards and 14 touchdowns. In the six playoff games, he caught 60 more passes for 644 yards and 11 scores. His worst playoff game saw him make seven catches. In the final three games, he averaged 13 catches, 147 yards and almost three touchdowns against defenses designed to take him away. For the season, he scored touchdowns in all but the Westwood game and scored in 13 straight games. And did it as a 5-foot-10 receiver who continuously played bigger than his height.

After completing 63 percent of his passes for 2,903 yards and 29 touchdowns in the regular season, Gilbert picked his play up as well. In six playoff games, he completed 71 percent of his passes for 1,922 yards – 320 per game – with 23 touchdowns – nearly four per game – against just two interceptions. As Austin Pollard said, Gilbert put everyone on his shoulders and wouldn't let them lose. He also wouldn't take credit, which the parents quickly recognized.

"Garrett is a true leader, no matter what has happened to him since," Leigh Ann Pollard said, making a fleeting reference to his rough time at the University of Texas. "My heart got crushed for him. He is a true leader, and when I say that, he takes it upon himself for fault, he'll take it upon himself for anything that happens in the game. But when it came to a victory, he never took it upon himself."

The Cavaliers came back to Austin and enjoyed another first. Local businesses teamed up with the booster club to host a celebration for the team at the recently opened Hill Country Galleria. The team paraded down the Galleria's main parkway in convertibles before arriving at Bee Cave's City Hall, where speakers including Gov. Rick Perry congratulated the team and wished them more success in the future. The city suburb celebrated like a small town, a community united stronger than ever by football. Lake Travis' became the ultimate Texas success story.

More success would come, of that many were certain. Most of Lake Travis' key players had been juniors in 2007, and expectations soared even before the team began meeting for off-season workouts. But January 2008 would not be an easy month for the team. Old wounds reopened, setting in motion events that proved surprising to some but not to all.

11: Dicus' departure

Lake Travis' run to the title drew attention, not just for the players. Several schools had contacted head coach Jeff Dicus about rebuilding their programs, and some of those contacts took place at the end of the regular season. Committed to seeing the 2007 season through, Dicus said he didn't take any meetings until after the season ended, and even then it seemed unfathomable that a coach who had just guided a team to the state title with a strong core of junior players, including a record-setting quarterback, set to return would consider making a move knowing the team would be an early favorite to repeat.

But without a next opponent to prepare for, Dicus couldn't help but think back to the first week in October, when his world seemed to fall apart around him. Among the schools that had contacted Dicus, one interested him above the others: Duncanville, a Conference 5A power in the Dallas-Fort Worth Metroplex that had fallen on hard times. The Panthers had last been to the playoffs in 2004, losing to powerhouse Euless Trinity 39-32 in the second round. The 2006 and 2007 seasons proved disastrous, with the Panthers winning just five of 20 games. Watching what Dicus had done at Lake Travis intrigued the Duncanville administration and they reached out to the coach, who, to their surprise, proved willing to listen.

Upon his introduction at Lake Travis in 2003, Dicus described himself as a program builder. His first head coaching job came at Boerne High School in 1998. Boerne had been 3-7 the previous season and in his three years Dicus got the Greyhounds back into the playoffs in 1999. After a 6-4 2000 campaign, Dicus moved south to Mission, where he inherited a Rio Grande Valley team that had missed the playoffs in 2000. In his second year, Dicus not only had the Eagles in the playoffs but into third round before they lost a heart breaker to New Braunfels. His challenge at Lake Travis may have been greater, but he had the Cavaliers in the playoffs in his second year and had done the previously unthinkable, winning it all, in his fifth year.

"Coach Moss calls me a missionary coach," Dicus said later. "A missionary goes around and helps different cities or countries."

And that's how Dicus felt when he learned about Duncanville's situation. He met with administrators in Duncanville and then back at Lake Travis as well. He said then, and he still maintains that he wasn't sure he wanted to take Duncanville's offer until he heard a sermon delivered at Promiseland West Church by Randy Phillips in January of 2008.

"The speech and the message that he gave that day, it was as if he was talking to me," Dicus said. "We met him afterwards. The message was that I needed to go help another program. It was an emotional meeting."

The message, coupled with the still burning memory of what Dicus went through in October, all but made up his mind. He still wanted, needed, to meet with his friend, his mentor, his rock: athletic director Jack Moss. They met, and both agreed that a new challenge would suit the coach best.

"Things that were said in that [October] meeting were obviously pretty harmful," Dicus said. "I didn't agree with what was being told to both Coach Moss and myself and I felt it was the right time. I needed to move."

Moss agreed that the decision worked for everyone. For all his success, Dicus' drive and complete devotion to all things football didn't sit well with others, namely high school principal Charlie Little, and Moss said their relationship had become oil and water. In every situation, both sides can compromise for the relationship's long-term health. Pick the battles to go to the mat over, give in on others. But that's something Moss said Dicus couldn't bring himself to do. He focused on football, knew the course he wanted for his program and would not waver from that course.

Over time and sparked no doubt by the events of early October, Dicus' relationship with Little all but vanished.

"He and Charlie Little didn't get along," Moss said. "It was a two-sided street and I was in the middle. Charlie asked little things of Jeff – things like coming over to the main high school building and walking the halls – and Jeff worked 24 hours a day on football. He wouldn't bend and the [divide between principal and coach] just grew."

Moss later said he tried to set up a meeting with Dicus and Little, hopeful that a sit-down would result in a peace where the two men could work together. But it never happened, and Moss encouraged his friend to move on.

"It was just time for Jeff," Moss said. "He's a great friend, but sometimes strength can also be a weakness. You want coaches who have tunnel vision, but sometimes you need to broaden that tunnel. Jeff had his road, and because he had that road he wasn't going to change."

And so Dicus made his decision, and make no mistake: he decided to resign. No one forced him out.

"Jeff left on his own, he wasn't fired," Moss asserts. "He came in to meet with me, and I knew he had been talking to Duncanville. He told me he thought he was going to take the job, and I told him he needed to do it. Jeff and I were the same guy. Sometimes you have to decide if the issue is something you want to die over, and not every battle is worth that. Jeff didn't always get that."

The internal conflict that played a role in his departure never made it to the public. Dicus confided in some of the parents he had come to consider friends, but even those close to him agree that he made the best decision he could.

"I think there was some irreparable damage between him and [superintendent] Rocky Kirk, between him and Charlie Little, who was the principal at the time," said Gale Gilbert, Garrett's father. "The kids are the kids, you have to deal with them no matter what, that's what you do as a coach. With the hierarchy of power, I think it was set. Looking back on it, it was great deal [for Lake Travis] in hindsight, but at the time, you're wondering, 'What the heck?'"

Not everyone wondered, even on the football staff.

"We weren't surprised at all when Jeff left," assistant coach Kevin Halfmann said much later.

Some of the players, though, didn't see it coming. They had all lived through the rough patches of 2007 and seen the coach change his style, for the better, they thought. They knew he'd be in high demand following the title, but they never thought he'd leave.

"Yeah, we were very shocked," said receiver Austin Pollard. "I remember there were rumors going around, but there was always a rumor about everything. I didn't think it was actually going to happen. Then he had us all come in to the turf room and he told us. He told us he was leaving and he seemed very upset about it. It was just something that he felt like he needed to do."

"When it happened, I think I felt betrayed and confused. I didn't understand why someone would leave after a state championship," running back Andy Erickson said. "He built this whole football world, and he had it made, and I never understood why he would leave."

To others, Dicus' departure seemed like the inevitable becoming reality. Even if Dicus left on his own terms, it felt like a separation had been in the works for some time.

"I feel like it was going to happen sooner or later," Garrett Gilbert said. "A lot of the kids just didn't get along with him. He did a lot of great, great things for the program, but even when things are going well, sometimes there needs to be a change to be a catalyst."

While message boards offered rumors of his ouster and of a bidding war that Duncanville won when Lake Travis wouldn't match his reported salary, district officials spoke glowingly in the news release announcing Dicus' resignation.

"Coach Dicus has been able to effectively channel the tremendous work ethic and dedication of the coaches on his staff, the wealth of talent that the student-athletes possess and the support of our administration, parents and community. It has been great for our school," said Little.

Years later, Little said the choice to leave had been Dicus' alone, that the coach could have stayed and the administration would have welcomed him back. But hindsight offers a clear picture, Little noted, and given what had taken place that October, maybe it had been best for Dicus to move on and begin building a program at another school.

"I know that there is more drama in that deal [of Dicus leaving]," Little said. "To be honest I didn't always know what Jeff thought, but I do respect Jeff for what he did. He is a program builder and that's his main strength. He didn't have to leave. He'd been very successful. He clearly had kids who responded well to him, but when he left, he probably had to leave for his own growth."

In the district's 2008 news release, Kirk thanked the coach for what he had accomplished and wished him well, saying he understood a coach's need to find the next great challenge in his career.

"Successful coaches, by virtue of their competitive spirit, live for the opportunity to create conditions for success. Often, this means doing so at new places with different challenges," he said in the release. Kirk even hinted that the administration wanted Dicus to remain on board. "We thanked Jeff for his work and contribution to our program, and we re-affirmed our commitment to his continued success at Lake Travis."

Though Kirk hadn't been part of that October meeting, the comments must have rung at least a little hollow in Dicus' eyes, and his decision had already been made. In some ways it had been since he returned to the team for the Vista Ridge game. As he looked back on his exit years later, he remained unapologetic for anything that happened and said he doesn't think he'd change anything if he could go back and do it again.

"I just think we did it the right way," he said. "Obviously you can't do it by yourself. You have to have a great staff. The kids have to buy in. The parents have to buy in. The administration has to buy in. The administration was great, up until that Vista Ridge game. Why things turned? I will go to my grave wondering why. We had a great thing going."

In fact, Dicus said he believes that he'd still be coaching at Lake Travis if the events that took place that week never happened.

"Yes, without a doubt."

Dicus' assertion might emphasize a disconnect that had developed between the coach and the parents. While every parent understood what Dicus found when he took the job in 2003 and what he needed to do to get the program headed in the right direction, many maintain that the coach never changed his ways once he accomplished his early goal. Even those parents who grew most frustrated with Dicus' later style understood what needed to be done in the beginning, and they recognize that Dicus had been the perfect coach for that job. Dicus took over the program in its darkest days and gave it life. He returned excitement to Lake Travis football.

"The heart was Jeff," said Leigh Ann Pollard, whose sons Justin and Austin played under Dicus in 2003 and 2006-07. "Jeff is structure. He's organized. He had a plan and you just followed the plan and everything was good. He knew how to encourage. There was a point that got reached with the kids."

What happened early in the 2007 season had been building for a while, parents felt, and they blamed Dicus and several of his assistants for taking the joy out of football for their children. Many parents decided that when their children had stopped enjoying football, something had to be done. Some called the administration. The principal met with the players. Someone met with the head coach. From the players' point of view, the problem had resolved itself. Football became fun again and it showed on the field. But as it often turns out, situations seldom remain that cut and dry.

But the parents circle back to the notion that Dicus can be the coach who builds a program up with rules, with discipline, with his tireless energy and rigidity. But those same traits that make him ideal to build a program also work against him over time and as successes come. They said his style doesn't lend itself to the long haul. He's not the coach you want to maintain your program's success.

"There were a lot of good times," said Glenn Pollard, Justin and Austin's father. "Jeff was great that first year. If I was a school and in charge of a high school, I'd hire someone like Jeff if I had a bad program to build it up, but he'd only have a two year window."

If everything happens for a reason, Dicus believes a higher power called him to Duncanville from Lake Travis. He has no regrets about coming to

Duncanville, falling back on the message of Phillips' sermon. And after four years building his program, he understands why very clearly.

"Being here for four years now, I understand why the Good Lord has put us here," he said. "Not a day goes by where I don't think about Lake Travis, the kids, the community. The parents were awesome. The kids were awesome. Coach Moss was awesome. But, being here and seeing what these kids need... Eighty-five percent of our kids don't have a daddy, and I could tell you days' worth of stories of kids and families that are just heartbreaking. It's every day. It's about life and it's about helping these kids become men."

He's fully invested in Duncanville's future. Through 2011, he'd taken the Panthers to the playoffs all four years he's coached there, though they only advanced out of the first round once, in 2010 with a win over Irving Nimitz. His road to a 5A title will never be easy: Region I contains some of the most decorated teams in Texas and has many title contenders each year, ranging from Trinity to Skyline to Southlake Carroll to Allen and more. In his short tenure at the school, the 5A champion has come from his region twice.

It's a challenge, but Dicus wants to take his Duncanville team where he's gone before. He wants the players to become winners and remain winners, both on the field and off of it.

"It's a mindset," he said. "Winners win at everything they do. That's what we are trying to preach to our kids here."

The circumstances surrounding his departure from Lake Travis will in no way take away from what Dicus accomplished there. He coached the team for five seasons, making him the longest-tenured coach in the school's history. His teams went 45-15 in those years, won the first district championships and, of course, the first state title.

His vision in creating the infrastructure that exists today remains a key component of the Lake Travis football backbone.

"Whether you like or dislike Jeff Dicus, you need to be thankful he was at Lake Travis," Moss said.

12: The Search to replace Dicus

While Jeff Dicus settled in at Duncanville and began establishing his program, Jack Moss and the Lake Travis administration went about replacing him.

The search, Moss recalled, proved painless and stress-free. He knew what he wanted in a coach, both in character and in coaching philosophy. He recognized what the Cavaliers brought back, and he knew not to upset the proverbial apple cart.

"Knowing our community, we needed a change in personality but not someone so different that he would blow up [what we had in place]," Moss said. "It was the first time that I'd ever been concerned about how they ran their offense, because we were committed to the spread all the way down the line to Pop Warner."

Senior-to-be Garrett Gilbert had just completed a record-setting season and earned the earliest scholarship offer that the University of Texas coaches had ever given out. As his junior year wound down, Gilbert received his offer on the seniors' national signing day. He came home from school to find Mack Brown's business card waiting for him, along with a phone number to call that night. Once the Texas coach had finished announcing his 2008 recruiting class, he made Gilbert the offer he'd waited for all his life, and the quarterback accepted.

From Moss' standpoint, Gilbert's reputation would serve as an attractive carat to interest potential coaches. Who wouldn't want to work with a can't-miss talent returning with the solid core of a state championship team? And he proved correct. Moss said the district never sought out applications, but they soon flooded his office.

"When we looked for Jeff's replacement, we had lots of interest," Moss said. "We narrowed it down to five and I drove all over the state visiting. None of them actually applied for the position, but the five I visited had won 11 state titles at the 4A level or higher."

The group of interested candidates included Chad Morris, who had won a title as a head coach at Bay City in 2000 before moving on to Stephenville, where he had sent highly-touted quarterback Jevan Snead to Texas and his successor, Kody Spano, to Nebraska. Morris' resume fit the bill, as did his offense: a version of the hurry-up, no-huddle offense he learned at the feet of HUNH creator Gus Malzahn, who used the offense to win a national title at Auburn with Cam Newton as his quarterback in 2010. Moss couldn't wait to visit with Morris, though at first he didn't know why the coach wanted to leave Stephenville.

"There was nothing magical about Chad as a choice. I visited with Chad two or three times, and at the time I remember I was surprised he was interested in us," Moss said. "We met at a county café in Lampasas and just talked about life and coaching and why you coach, everything not particular to football. I just thought this was the guy."

It was in that small town square that couldn't be more Texas if it was pulled out of a John Wayne film that Lake Travis' future success began to take shape.

If Moss had a blueprint of the ideal candidate to follow Dicus, Morris embodied it. Where Dicus had been demanding with a hard edge, Morris appeared equally demanding, but with a style more welcoming and relating to the players.

"With Chad, we needed a personality change from Jeff's style," Moss said. "He was still as demanding of the kids, and we were fortunate to get that guy. He told me from the start, though, that he wanted to get to college."

Morris didn't know anything about the Lake Travis' history, but he did know about the 2007 title team. The school's most exciting moment could also be suspicious. For all Morris knew, it could have been a flash in the pan moment for the Cavaliers.

"One of the things you look at as a coach, is that there are so many teams with two divisions. There are so many teams that will have a good run of kids, and they'll have a good season or two, and then they'll fall off. They build around one group, and that's it," Morris said. "And so you had to wonder if they just had a good group and that bunch and the timing was right."

Hank Carter, Morris' long-time defensive coordinator and right-hand man, recalled the first time Morris brought up the opening.

"Obviously we knew they won the state championship, but I hadn't had a chance to see them. I didn't get a chance to watch it on TV," Carter said. "Didn't know much about the area other than it was on the outskirts of Austin and that it was a growing community."

The one thing that struck both Morris and Carter had been Dicus' departure.

They had no inkling of any drama that might have taken place. They just felt it odd that a school fresh off a state championship and with its entire nucleus coming back would be replacing its head coach.

"Whenever the job came open, I want to say Coach Morris might have even called Coach Dicus to ask him about it," Carter said. "He started calling around, and you know, it was kind of strange to us that you'd win a state championship and the coach moves on, so we kind of wanted to figure out what was going on with that."

Morris did call Dicus, while driving at dusk across the open roads between Stephenville and Abilene.

"I talked to Dicus on a Friday night on my way to Abilene for a coaches meeting. I called him in the car and talked to him about it. He was very honest about it – there'd been a lot of clashing with the parents."

The honesty didn't throw Morris off. The situation seemed tolerable. After all, he coached in a town where after some early struggles, "For Sale" signs showed up in his front yard, courtesy of disgruntled fans. He thought it would be worth kicking the tires to get some more official information before officially tossing his hat in the ring as a candidate. Before he did, he wanted feedback from his top assistants, Carter included. The defensive coordinator said everyone Morris confided in trusted him enough to make a good decision and they encouraged him to let Lake Travis officials know he wanted to interview.

"I guess he set up and applied for the job, and I think it was at the same time [Lake Travis Superintendent] Dr. [Rocky] Kirk was having some surgery done, so Coach Morris maybe interviewed at the time with Mr. Little [principal Charlie Little] and [deputy superintendent] Diane Frost and Dr. Kirk, and he didn't hear anything for about three days," Carter recalled.

The lack of response troubled Morris. Carter said the tricky thing about changing high schools is controlling the news cycle, or at least getting ahead of it. Officials at high-profile schools don't often appreciate their successful coach exploring other options.

"At that point, Coach Morris was really fearful that word was going to get out in Stephenville that he was looking for a job, because you don't want to do that," Carter recalled. "Any time you're at a high profile place, you can't really apply for a job because you don't want your name to come out in the paper when they do the [open] records act and all. Whether you got the job or not, you may have to leave the one you're at because of the ridicule you'd get."

Morris felt the interview went well, and when an offer didn't follow quickly, he decided to withdraw his name and go on coaching Stephenville. Stephenville, after all, remains one of the most acclaimed 4A programs in

Texas, and its annual rivalry with Brownwood ranks among the most heated in all of Texas. But that heat turned on Morris when word got around that he had spoken with Lake Travis.

"I interviewed on a Monday, and Coach Moss told me they'd get with me on Thursday or Friday. At this point, it was going to be the first week of February," Morris said. "Friday came around, and the word had gotten out at Stephenville. I had to justify some things, talk to the superintendent and it was getting pretty heated. Saturday, nothing from Lake Travis. Sunday, nothing. I was pretty much reserved to the fact that I wasn't going to do it. On Monday morning, I called Moss and said, 'I completely understand.' I was hearing [Denton Ryan head coach] Joey Florence was their guy. 'I know how this business works, but just remove my name.'"

Moss told Morris he couldn't do that, to hold on, and he'd call right back. Morris insisted that Lake Travis look elsewhere. A barrage of calls followed, starting with Moss and ending with Kirk's efforts to convince Morris to change his mind.

Carter and Morris had been in a meeting when the official offer came in from Kirk, and following that call the two talked about the offer for several hours.

"I can remember him hanging up, and boy we were in a tiny office there in Stephenville," Carter said. "It was the athletic director's office, we shut the door and I think we were in there for three hours, just kind of hashing it back and forth. We loved it in Stephenville and had obviously developed some great friendships there. And I loved the kids there. My wife and I had just bought a house, a brand new home there a year and a half before. Coach Morris had just put in a brand new pool. We didn't think we were going anywhere for a while. We finally had things going at Stephenville. We had some good seasons and the program was on the rise."

Morris talked about the decision more at his home with his family and Carter as the night went on, but went to bed without having truly made his mind up.

"I remember I'm getting ready in the bathroom the next morning, and my son Chandler walks in while I'm sitting there with my head in my hands wondering what I'm going to do," Morris said. "And Chandler goes, 'If we move, can we have a house with stairs?' All he wanted was a house with a second level. It was a silly little moment, but it put things in perspective for me."

Knowing they could always stay at Stephenville, Carter said he and Morris put together a list of requests – demands would be too strong a word – they'd like to see fulfilled before accepting the position.

"We finally put a list of things together that we felt like needed to happen [if we were going to make the move], and Lake Travis was able to do all of those," Carter recalled. "So we agreed to take the job."

The district confirmed Morris' hire late that Tuesday afternoon, and on Wednesday the new coaches drove down to meet their team.

Like his predecessor, Morris proved a very driven football coach, but his approach couldn't have been more different. Both coaches demanded excellence of the kids, both on the field and in the classroom. But Morris understood what it took to work with everyone, from the superintendent to the principal to the parent of the least talented player on the freshman B team.

"Chad was more of a politician-type," Moss recalled, noting that his new coach took whatever time he needed to make sure those who sought things from him – be it reporters, fans, parents, kids – got exactly what they needed.

Parents could see the difference as well. They all respected the work that Dicus had done and understood what it took for Dicus and his staff to build the program, but they questioned whether Dicus had the temperament to succeed with a team that didn't need building anymore.

"As a coach I think of [Dicus] more as a builder than a maintainer...I don't think...we may not have won the next year," said Dave Lagasse. "The timing could not have been more perfect and we couldn't have been more lucky to get Chad Morris coming in here and the dynamics of what he brought to the table. I think Jeff is organized and is very good at turning programs around."

In many ways, Morris put a different spin on the things that Dicus had implemented when he arrived in 2003. Where Dicus encouraged parental involvement, Morris embraced it. And most of all, parents said, he embraced the players.

"He immediately connected with the kids, connected with the parents, just a whole different style that made it more inviting for parents to be involved with the football program," Lagasse said.

Gale Gilbert agreed.

"I don't know what the word I want to use for Chad is," he said. "He's such a good people person, and of course you're very interested because it's your kid. They were all really good. Our first impression off the bat was that we were really looking forward to working with these guys."

It came naturally in many respects, but the instant connection also came by design. Morris said that he'd developed a plan to implement when he became a head coach, a process that reflects the commitment to all the people that make a program go, from the players to the groundskeepers. Goal one: win the kids over. Goal two: win the parents over. Goal three: win the teachers, students and administration over.

As the new coaches began making their way to Austin to get started, offensive coordinator Matt Green joined Morris and Carter for the first visit, they still weren't quite sure exactly what they had gotten themselves in to. The sporting adage says we don't want to be the one to follow greatness. Only in rare cases have successors found things as easy as their predecessors. More often than not, those who followed legends get lost in historical footnotes. Which coach followed John Wooden at UCLA? Dean Smith at North Carolina? Bo Schembechler at Michigan? Vince Lombardi in Green Bay?

Morris remained positive.

"We had been successful well before Lake Travis, and I knew the ingredients that made us successful, still make us successful," he said. "It's about building relationships. That's the biggest thing. That was the missing ingredient to people at Lake Travis, and that was easy for me."

Carter, looking back on the situation four years after he arrived, recognized that he and his friend had accepted that challenge. What would success for them mean?

"It's not really attractive [for new coaches] to come in following a state championship, but at the same time we felt like, especially after meeting with Coach Moss and looking at what the growth of the community was and looking how the schools and support, we felt like it was a place that was hungry and that we talked about turning it into a dynasty like Southlake [Carroll]," Carter said. "That's what we talked about, obviously not knowing what would follow. "

Circumstances certainly fell in their favor. The 2007 title had been unexpected. Gilbert, running back Chris Aydam, offensive tackle Paden Kelley, defensive end Ryan Erxleben, linebacker Harry Hatch, receiver Cade McCrary and a host of other key contributors were just juniors on that team. Andy Erickson and Ian Lazarus had been only sophomores. The core still had a senior year to look forward to. Barring any other drastic changes, the Cavaliers would enter the 2008 season as prohibitive favorites to repeat. Carter saw those things but still didn't take success for granted.

"Coming in and following a state champion, so many things have to line up to win a state championship," he said. "That year, in 2007, things fell into place, so we were like should we look at it like, 'Boy we have nowhere to go but down,' or should we look at it like, 'We're only scratching the surface, and let's go there and let's make this something really special.'"

So they went about making the program their own, steering Lake Travis on a different path, one they hoped would end with the same result.

13: Different season, same reason

It took almost no time for Lake Travis' new football coaches to get acquainted with and accepted by their new team. Head coach Chad Morris, defensive coordinator Hank Carter and offensive coordinator Matt Green quickly got themselves to Lake Travis after accepting the job, and their first order of business became meeting the team.

They met most of the players and their families as a group the day they arrived, and the players could tell things would be different.

"They connected really well with us and they brought a family philosophy from day one and it didn't take long for us to catch on and buy into it," said Austin Pollard, a receiver on the 2007 team.

The players gathered on a Wednesday afternoon on the artificial turf in the indoor practice facility. Athletic Director Jack Moss opened the meeting by saying that he and the administration had found the best coaches for the team, and that they were now in good hands.

Then Morris introduced himself, and asked the players how they were doing. The response he got threw him and his fellow coaches for a loop.

"Good, coach, how are you?" the team chimed in unison, a seemingly pre-programmed response instilled by the previous regime.

"I looked over and thought, 'That's the first thing that's going to change,'" Morris said. "And that's nothing against Jeff, it's what got the program where it was. He laid the foundation for that program. That was the structure of the discipline, and that's who he was. That's not who I was. I tried to be Art Briles, and that didn't work. So I was going to be myself. I didn't care who I pissed off."

"Coach Carter gives us grief to this day about that response," Garrett Gilbert said. "We were just wired one way at that point."

Gilbert had been the one player with other things on his mind when the new coaches arrived. The quarterback would have his throwing shoulder operated on the next day to repair a torn labrum. Gilbert suffered the injury early in his junior season but played through it. The injury didn't impact his play during the season, Gilbert had set two state records in leading Lake Travis to the championship, but by January, 2008, he told his father, Gale, that the pain had grown.

"We went to California in January and Garrett told me he couldn't throw," Gale said. "He said he couldn't get his arm over his shoulder."

When the pain didn't subside after rest, the family decided Garrett needed to get the shoulder examined, and doctors discovered the tear. Gale Gilbert said the discovery coincided with Dicus' departure and the search that led Moss to Morris.

When the younger Gilbert woke from the anesthesia, he saw Carter waiting by his bed.

"I met them with the rest of the team on Wednesday, but I had surgery the next day," Gilbert said. "And I wake up from surgery, and Coach Carter is sitting right there. I'm thinking, 'I don't even know this guy yet. This is pretty cool. There's something special about these guys, something different.' I'll never forget that."

Morris had been finishing up player interviews that afternoon before he swung over and joined Carter in Gilbert's hospital room.

"I wanted to meet with each player, one by one, to get a feel for what they needed and to let them know that we were here to help, and I was swamped. We interviewed every kid in the program," Morris said. "But I met with Henry that morning and told him, 'When that boy wakes up, you're gonna be right there by his side.'"

Later that night, Morris, Carter and Green arrived at the Gilbert household to get to know everyone a little better. The coaches, the Gilberts and several other parents talked for a while that evening. The resulting relationship proved deeper than relationships that the previous coaches had built in five years.

"They were all really good," Gale Gilbert said. "Our first impression off the bat was that we were really looking forward to working with these guys."

Players noticed the change in coaching style, and personality, from day one. In stark contrast to Dicus' rigidity, where players and coaches – the head coach in particular – kept their distance outside of football functions, Morris, Carter and many other new coaches wanted to spend time with their players away from the game.

Garrett Gilbert and Hatch learned this on the way to the golf course one day. When Carter discovered what they had planned, he asked if he could tag along. The request left the players flabbergasted, in a good way.

"We get to the summer, and me and Harry [Hatch] like to go golfing together, and we're talking about it, and Carter just jumps in and goes, 'Hey, when can I go play golf with you guys?'" Gilbert said. "And we just looked at each other and thought, 'This is our freaking defensive coordinator. This is awesome.'"

A few of the defensive players even took defensive assistant Randall Edwards out water skiing.

"They really wanted to be involved in our lives, and it was awesome," Gilbert said. "It was great."

There were even meetings with the players to see which coaches they wanted back the most. Morris would bring much of his staff from Stephenville, but he also wanted to maintain continuity and familiarity for the players. They named Jason Jaynes, George Oakes and Michael Wall among others.

"It meant a lot to us that he would ask us," Gilbert said. "But then he started looking at film with us, and asked us what we liked to run. We were so involved. He liked certain plays we ran. In one meeting, I drew a screen pass up from scratch, and he loved it and said we needed it in the offense. Coaches always think their way is the best, but he was so open-minded. It did nothing but help."

That player-coach relationships developed quickly caught Carter off-guard, no matter how much the coach wanted to develop them. Morris and Carter kept in mind how hard it had been to earn full acceptance at Stephenville, where for some reason the players and community didn't embrace them as they settled in to replace Briles after he left to coach the University of Houston.

"I can tell you it was so different than when we went to Stephenville," Carter said. "When we came to Stephenville from Bay City, at Bay City we had won a state championship, got beat in the state championship the next year and the third year we got beat by LaMarque, a really good team at the time. We felt like we were a very accomplished bunch of coaches, and a few of us came from Bay City and joined a bunch of the [coaches] from Stephenville. The kids really didn't accept us at first, just because they had been part of the same system, even under Briles going back a long time. We were fearful of that here."

Carter said that while the coaches paid close attention on how to quickly relate to the players, the Cavaliers made it much easier than any had anticipated.

"We really had our ears up looking for that, but boy the kids welcomed us with open arms," he recalled. "It was unbelievable. And so it was different. The coaches, too. There was a lot of friction between the coaching staffs when we went from Bay City to Stephenville, but not here. Coming here was totally different. The kids were different here. I don't know what I expected but they were different from what I imagined: very, very friendly; very polite, they were very willing to work their tails off."

The players understood the new coaches would still demand hard work, respect and focus. But they quickly took to the manner in which the new coaches brought it out of them. Dicus' brand of discipline and motivation centered on a fear of punishment for a job done wrong, as Justin Pollard described looking back at the 2003 season. In Dicus' last year at the school, the players felt he had become unapproachable. Morris, whether he compensated for Dicus' style or simply practiced his own style, let the players know his door would always be open for whatever they needed to talk about.

"Coach Morris from day one had an open door policy," said Austin Pollard. "If we ever needed to talk to him about anything, we could go see him. They brought a very light-hearted approach."

Light-hearted but still demanding.

"When it came to work, we worked, but they were very good at having fun," Pollard said. "We had a lot of fun when we practiced and just being around the facilities, joking around with them."

Carter recognized how and why Dicus and his staff ran the program the way they did, almost with an iron fist. Knowing how far the program had fallen when Dicus arrived, Carter surely understood what needed to be done.

"Coach Dicus was charged with coming in here and taking a program that had not done anything, and so he kind of started at rock bottom," Carter said. "And to do that, you have to come in and be pretty rigid. Discipline is something that you can start with. And I think that's exactly what the program needed and obviously he got it turned around."

In 2008, the program already had a foundation of discipline, so maybe Morris, Carter and company didn't need to come in with a zero-tolerance policy on discipline. The change in philosophy pleased the players.

"We operated a little bit differently than that, and so maybe the kids welcomed that a little bit," Carter said.

As a parent, Gale Gilbert recognized a difference as well.

"With Garrett and with Griffin, they couldn't wait to get up there every day to be around those coaches because the atmosphere they provided was fun," he said. "Yet, when they got on the field they expected and demanded that they work."

Other parents saw the change just as quickly.

"Immediately," said Glenn Pollard. "The kids knew too. The kids took them in and never even missed a lick. When you talk to Coach Morris today and that whole group of coaches, they tell you they couldn't believe how [quickly they were embraced]."

"They thought they were going to have to come in and prove themselves and change the boys' ways or perspectives of things," said Leigh Ann Pollard. "The way we saw it was that the boys just engulfed them, and they are still good friends today."

In addition to Morris' open door policy, players had noticed a different approach when coaches had to put their feet down.

"They knew when to push and when to lay off," said Austin Pollard. "I'd never seen that before. They knew to push somebody, but then they knew the best time to lay off and just explain to somebody. They were great coaches in that way."

And so with everyone getting along from the beginning, the coaches and players embarked on their first spring practices together. If the coaches appeared easy going off the field, players quickly saw how equally demanding and energetic they could become on it. With Morris taking over an offense featuring a record-setting quarterback and his heir apparent in sophomore Michael Brewer, everyone, players included, knew the offense would score and score often. Carter, though, wouldn't allow his defensive players to take a back seat, to let even potentially the best offense in the state push his group around day in and day out at practice. So he coached them with a chip on his shoulder.

"I think we started [to coach defense with a chip on our shoulder] when we came here," he said. "At Stephenville we were known for great offense but also for great football and a lot of that had to do with the guys who were there before who obviously took a lot of pride in coaching both sides of the ball."

He did it, in part, because he wanted people to be excited about Lake Travis' defense.

"Coming here, there weren't a lot of kids excited about playing defense, and I think that's just the nature of it," Carter recalled. "Your more high profile players had been on offense and so that's what little kids were excited to play and that's just the way it was. So one thing we wanted to come in and do was we don't want to win in spite of our defense and we don't want to not win a state championship because of our defense. That's where all fingers would have been pointing if we didn't win in 2008."

Assistant coach Kevin Halfmann noticed that the new coordinator wouldn't accept anything less than excellence from his unit, and he said the only question leading into the preseason centered on how quickly the returning defenders could adapt to Carter's new scheme.

"Really the biggest change was defensively," Halfmann said. "Because with Coach [David] Nelson we were such a non-blitzing, formation recognition defense. To transition into this moving, attacking, multiple coverage kind of college defense, that was the biggest change."

So, to concentrate on defense the coaches made a few personnel changes and then went out and taught the defense to play angry. Part of defense revolves around technique and scheme, the other depends on getting all 11 players to rush to the ball and to be in a foul mood when they arrive. The Cavaliers needed to learn that.

"We came in and we made some changes," Carter said. "We moved some kids from offense to defense. We tweaked some positions there even as we went through the season learning the kids. But the biggest thing we said was that we weren't going to put up with any jawing in practice from our offense or anybody else, whoever we played. We've got pride and we're going to go out and stop people."

Carter's order to his defensive players to stand up for themselves had the defensive coordinator and head coach doubling as referees for the first few weeks. Sure enough, the offensive players, McCrary chief among them, started jawing at the defensive players, including linebackers Hatch and Lazarus, and spirited, full-pad scuffles broke out every day. Everyone interviewed for this book remembers the biggest one between McCrary and Lazarus, a returning starter, short but fiery and relentless who'd become an all-state defender. Years earlier, Dicus and his staff had built a hill into the side of a practice field to help with conditioning. Players despised that hill, but now it played a different role.

"The first day of spring ball in pads, there was fight after fight after fight after fight in practice," Carter recalled. "I think it was the defensive kids wanting to show us coaches that, 'Okay coach, you want us to come out here and not take any crap, and we're gonna show you.' I can remember Cade McCrary and Ian Lazarus rolling down the hill – normally coaches jump in and separate them – but they rolled all the way into these cedar branches in the woods, and I couldn't even get in there to get them out, so I just let them go for a minute. But those are the things you remember about that first spring."

The fighting became an unavoidable result of the environment that had been created.

"We knew it was going to be intense. We would talk daily about how we wanted it to be an intense practice," Morris said. "We kept telling the kids, 'Everybody's on a clean slate.' Doesn't matter who you were, you had to prove something to us. The one I remember most is Cade McCrary and Ian Lazarus. They fought a good 10-15 foot deep in to the cedar bushes. We couldn't get them apart. We wanted to be the toughest dudes in the state of Texas. And the kids took it to another level because they wanted to prove something to us."

Edwards actually became the coach who drove the message home the most to the defense.

"He's one of those country boys from Stephenville, and he can be a mean guy if he has to be, but he's one of my favorite guys," Hatch said. "He'd tell us about how much tougher the guys were in Stephenville, and it pissed us off. None of us had ever been the fighting kind of guys, but I don't know, when we put on the pads, it got nasty."

And so the fights kept breaking out.

"Five minutes into the first day, Jack Hourin and Cade [McCrary] go down, and Cade comes up swinging," Hatch said. "Cade probably fought everyone on the team that spring. I remember probably the third or fourth practice, Cade was getting pissed, and he ran a corner route and I knocked him down the hill. He got up and came after me, and I just walked away, I wasn't even going to start with him. And then the next play, he ran a fade and Lazarus hit him early and they get tangled and roll down the hill into the trees and were just going at it."

It even drove a few wedges between good friends.

"There was a point where Garrett and I just started going at it," Hatch said. "He texted me after practice one day and told me to get the defense to knock it off with the cheap shots, and I told him, 'No, we're going to keep doing it.'"

The order came from defensive backs coach Jess Loepp to hit the receivers as often as possible, rules be damned.

"To this day, Garrett and I still get in arguments about hitting receivers during their routes and what's fair or illegal – it's really not, so Garrett's in the wrong," Hatch said with a wry grin. "We had to prove we were different, that things had changed. I'd fight with Paden [Kelley], just to prove I wouldn't take crap from the biggest guy on the team."

Perhaps more remarkably, despite the ferocity of the battles, when the final whistle blew for the day, everyone went back to joking around and hanging out off the field.

"Sometimes it carries over," Morris said. "But for the most part, you stress the family aspect. It's about relationships. We're still a family. We're still a brotherhood. And when we were done, they were gassed."

"It's cliché and corny to say this, but it's true: we really were all brothers. We really love each other," Hatch said. "Brothers fight, but they get over it. Nothing was more important than our friendship."

With the defense sticking up for itself in practice, the school's offense-only reputation began to change from the inside out. Lake Travis players had to take pride in their defense before they'd show everyone else how far they'd come.

"We wanted the kids on defense to be able to take pride in the fact that, 'Hey, I play defense for Lake Travis,'" Carter said. "We know the offense is great and they're going to get their due, and that's fine. But we want kids to come up through the system who are excited about playing defense too."

While Carter and his defensive coaches instilled a fighting will in the defensive players, Morris took over the offense. Halfmann said once the players and other coaches saw the offense Morris utilized, the transition from 2007 to 2008 became seamless.

"The main thing was that the offenses were similar," Halfmann recalled. "It wasn't going to get Garrett out of his comfort zone. We knew we were going to utilize all those receivers, because we had a bunch of those."

"They brought this exciting offense and exciting defense, new generation spread," said Austin Pollard. "We had a great time running their plays."

Morris learned his offense at the hands of Arkansas high school coach Gus Malzahn. Malzahn developed a hurry-up, no huddle attack that piled up yards and points. When Morris coached at Bay City, his offense struggled. Looking for solutions, he discovered Malzahn and asked the inventor to teach him the principles. Morris proved the ideal student and took what he learned to back to Bay City and then to Stephenville, where quarterback Jevan Snead developed into one of the state's best. He brought the same offense to Lake Travis, where it seemed Gilbert would be licking his chops to get a chance to run it.

But Gilbert had to wait while his shoulder healed. Brewer, the strong-armed apprentice, ran the show, and as the players began to understand the plays and how exciting the offense could be, they also realized the kind of talent their new coach possessed.

"I've never seen or heard, been around anybody, who was better at game-planning a game than Coach Morris," Pollard said. "It was phenomenal how he knew exactly which plays were going to work each week and he did a great job of dispersing the ball out to everybody. He would sit there and tell us, 'This play is going to be there, this play is going to be there this game,' and sure enough, week-by-week, without a doubt, exactly what he told us was going to happen would happen. It was crazy. I still can't wrap my head around how he just knew it so well."

By the time the team had broken for summer, went through 7-on-7 and watched their quarterback regain strength in his throwing shoulder, fall practice began. Both offense and defense had a healthy respect for each other. At full strength, Lake Travis began to prepare for the season opener against 5A Westwood in their new home away from home, the Alamodome. The team made just one major change from off-season to the opener. Brewer, like Todd Reesing years ago, would move into the receiver rotation while backing up Gilbert.

Morris called his future quarterback to feel out his interest and found him sitting on his back porch. Morris explained that Brewer had a bright future under center (or more appropriately, in the shotgun) for the Cavaliers. He would need to learn from Gilbert during the season as his backup, but he had to choose whether to do that as a receiver on varsity or while moonlighting as the junior varsity quarterback.

"I'd never played receiver before, but I told him, 'I can run and catch and I'll learn.' And that was that," Brewer said. "But it wasn't until two-a-days that I realized I was going to play a bigger role than I thought. I was all over the field, I was even at safety for a while. But it was a lot to process. Too much. Over time, I got to focus more on special teams, receiver and quarterback."

The decision, along with playing as the starter in the previous spring, altered Brewer's path forever.

"It helped me so much. I think the main thing is that a lot of QBs don't realize that seeing a game from that side of the ball benefits you," Brewer said. "It's a totally different game. I knew going in how the receivers were thinking. You're supposed to know where they're going to be, but knowing what they're thinking changes everything. I saw the game from a whole different perspective."

With the future safely developing and game day approaching, expectations remained high. Many expected the state champions to repeat, something hard enough to do without changing coaches.

"I know once we got Garrett back and started running practices, I remember looking around thinking we were pretty good," Pollard said.

"We had everything. We had a running back, we had a receiving corps, we had great offensive linemen. Our defense was stellar, they could fly around. They had great speed. And then we had Garrett on top of that. So, yes, we had that feeling that there was no one who could beat us."

To go with that feeling, and the new attitude, Morris changed the Lake Travis helmet logo. Gone was the blocky 'LT' adorned with flames. A new, sleeker 'LT' would replace it, and a star would signify the team's state championship. Many around the program balked at steering away from the logo established by Dicus, but Morris kept them in mind, too.

"I wanted a fresh look, to establish an identity," he said. "But the stars were about connecting the past guys to the present guys. We didn't forget about them, or the work they did to make the program what it was."

A year later, the flames would be gone altogether, and the star count would keep rising.

After all of the changes, parents eagerly anticipated what Morris would bring to the team in game situations. It didn't take long for Morris to make his mark.

Gale Gilbert recalls the team coming out for pregame warm-ups against Westwood. Standing in the cavernous surroundings of the Alamodome, where everything echoes and amplifies the quiet far more than the noisy, players were quiet, focused, stretching. He watched Morris come out of the tunnel and take in his players' body language.

"I don't remember if it was Garrett telling us or if Chad told us first, but Chad walked on the field and everyone is warming up," Gale recalled. "Chad had to tell the kids to smile and have some fun here. Everyone was straight-laced and serious. I think that was one of the first things that broke the ice and let everybody just free-flow from there."

Westwood gave Lake Travis a stern test. Lake Travis' new offense took some time to get going, but eventually Gilbert found his groove, connecting with McCrary for three touchdowns in a 27-20 win. The following week, the Cavaliers avenged their only loss of 2007, beating Westlake for an emotional 38-17 victory. While Gilbert didn't put up spectacular numbers, he picked his spots. He connected with Aydam on a long pass and run for a touchdown that took control late in the first half, and he added two touchdowns on the ground late to ice the win on the Chaparrals' turf.

Afterward, Westlake coaches found the visitor's locker room covered with copies of a newspaper column in the *Lake Travis View* by *Westlake Picayune* Sports Editor Thomas Jones, playfully railing on the idea that Lake Travis would never be as good or as storied as Westlake. It was a motivational ploy that offensive coordinator Matt Green relished throughout his tenure at Lake Travis.

Annoyed, Westlake head coach Derek Long asked Jones why he wrote that column, adding fuel to the Cavaliers' fire.

"But coach," Jones said. "Their sports editor wrote a similar piece railing Westlake in our paper."

Long paused to process the information.

"Shoot," he said. "I guess I need to start reading the paper."

The following week Gilbert did something else memorable in leading Lake Travis to a 35-21 win over Cedar Park. An early interception frustrated the quarterback, and he took out his frustration while making the tackle. His shoulder-slamming collision sent the ball-carrier flying out of bounds and sent the Lake Travis bench and fans leaping to their feet. Lake Travis football had gotten off to the program's most impressive start ever.

At 3-0, the Cavaliers enjoyed a special treat late in September, hosting storied Evangel Christian from Shreveport, La. The Eagles had long been one of Louisiana's best teams and traditionally took on teams from other states in marquee match-ups. Pollard said facing Evangel brought out a different challenge for the Cavaliers, and a different side of their head coach.

"It was something different," Pollard recalled. "It was a team from another state coming into our territory trying to beat us. I remember [what] Coach Morris before the game had told us. It gave me goose bumps. He said, 'You're not defending your school. You're not defending your district. You're defending the state of Texas and what Texas high school football stands for.' It's something that we take a lot of pride in and Evangel Christian had dominated Louisiana for several years, and that was something that was really cool when he was telling us we were defending the state of Texas and what our morals stood for in high school football. That was one of the coolest moments for me."

The Cavaliers took the battle directly to the Eagles. After a back-and-forth opening quarter that saw Evangel take a 12-8 lead, Gilbert went to work. Avoiding athletic rushers with apparent ease, he picked apart the Eagles' defense. A 62-yard strike to Conner Floyd gave Lake Travis a 15-12 lead at the end of the first quarter. Early in the second quarter, backed up at his own 10 yard line, Gilbert dropped back into his end zone and launched a rainbow toward a well-covered McCrary at midfield. McCrary out-jumped the defender, pushed him down and strutted into the end zone for a 90-yard touchdown. His strut earned him a personal foul, and Morris lit him up when he returned to the sideline. But if anyone had been concerned about the team having an edge, that certainly put the fear to rest. Another Gilbert-to-McCrary touchdown pass preceded Aydam's two-yard run, and Lake

Travis took a 39-12 lead at the half. Evangel closed the gap in the second half, but Gilbert's touchdown pass to Pollard provided the final 46-31 margin.

On the night, the quarterback completed 25 of 41 passes for 414 yards and five scores. McCrary and Pollard combined for 10 catches covering 224 yards and four scores. Defensively, the Cavaliers forced three turnovers and blocked a field goal. Jon-Michael Paul led the way with a trio of quarterback sacks.

From there, the Cavaliers headed into district play. The offense kept churning out points and the wins became more lopsided as the season's momentum continued to build. The Cavaliers scorched Killeen for a season-high 50 points and then picked up speed. At Hutto, the Hippos presented an interesting challenge. The Hippos entered the game 4-1 and had been picked by many to challenge for one of the district's playoff spots. Hutto made an early statement by taking the opening kickoff and driving for a touchdown. When the Cavaliers got the ball and Gilbert brought the offense out, he surveyed the defense and saw something he didn't expect. Where most teams had played zone coverage with plenty of cushion against Lake Travis, the Hippos lined up in man-to-man, press coverage with no safety deep. On one of the team's first plays, Gilbert signaled to McCrary and then hit the receiver in stride for a quick 41-yard touchdown, and the rout was on. Pollard returned a punt for a score, and Gilbert added five more touchdown passes before leaving with a 55-6 lead. The next two weeks saw more of the same. Lake Travis blanked Lampasas and Hendrickson by identical 57-0 scores. Gilbert threw five touchdown passes in each game and never took a fourth quarter snap.

By the time Dripping Springs brought a 9-0 record over to play Lake Travis, the Cavaliers looked every bit the part of the best team in the state. Gilbert threw a rare interception early, only his second of the regular season, and the Tigers took an early 3-0 lead. But Michael Streuling intercepted a pair of passes, and the Tigers had no answers once the Cavaliers got rolling. Gilbert threw for two scores, ran for 69 yards and another score and had a 70-yard scamper called back. His ability to get yards with his legs when the Tigers were determined to slow his passing game down proved a precursor to the upcoming playoff run, which began after he torched Marble Falls for 358 yards and six touchdowns in the regular season finale, a 54-14 win.

The Cavaliers, already confident following the 2007 title, became all but certain they'd repeat following the regular season. As a team they averaged 46.1 points per game in the regular season and 52.5 against 4A competition. Defensively, the Cavaliers went three full games without allowing a touchdown and held district opponents to a paltry 7.6 points per game. Gilbert's regular season ranked him among the best quarterbacks in the country. He completed 68 percent of his passes for 3,057 yards with 38 touchdowns and only two interceptions.

While McCrary had been the primary recipient, other receivers had their days to shine as well. That's all part of the beauty of Morris' offense.

"Any receiver had the potential to have a great game and it was just whether or not you performed," Pollard recalled. "Cade was getting a lot of the deep balls and drawing a lot of attention deep, which left a lot of open holes for me down low when I was running my screens and quicks and things like that. It kind of opened up. It goes everywhere around, though, because with what me and Cade were doing, Conner Floyd was open on the other side doing his thing. Because of what we were doing, Chris Aydam was open to run up the middle. One thing fed off the other, and that's just the way Morris' playbook worked, and it came down to what teams wanted to stop which player. When they wanted to stop Cade, I would have a big game. When they wanted to stop the running back, Cade would have a big game, something like that. We all kind of shared it and we all loved it."

With Gilbert able to distribute the ball accurately to so many different receivers, the Cavaliers became even more dedicated to Morris' approach that demanded players worry only about their responsibilities, not to try and do more than they could. Further, the coaches demanded perfection from each player performing his responsibilities, and the players became hell-bent on achieving that standard.

"A lot of coaches say that and preach that, but Morris and them actually meant it," Pollard recalled. "You had your assignment and they didn't ask you to do more than you had to. If you tried to do more than you had to and you messed up your assignment, then the whole play breaks down. It was do 100 percent your job and I know as a receiving crew, Morris told us from day one, 'If you're giving me your all and you're doing your job, I'll get you the ball. I'll take care of you.' And that was the same for everybody. If Chris was doing his thing, he'd get his carries. Morris was very good at getting everyone motivated and everyone bought in to doing their thing. When we built this family feeling, we knew that we could take care of each other. Chris knew his linemen were going to pick up the blocks. I knew that Cade was going to be breaking in a certain point and there would be a nice little hole for me to slip into. We didn't make mistakes much. We were perfectionists on the field and I think that was the big thing."

The Cavaliers took their perfect record into the playoffs and didn't miss a beat, even when defenses decided they wouldn't stand idly by and let Gilbert pick them apart. Because he didn't run very much in the regular season, only 39 times but just 11 in the last six games, teams didn't fear Gilbert's running ability. Or if they did, they viewed it the lesser of two evils when compared with his passing prowess. So teams decided to either drop back and blanket the field with coverage or pin their ears back and rush as many players as they could hoping to get to him before he could find an open receiver. But Morris had his troops prepared, and the Cavaliers kept up their scoring pace, just in different ways.

The team's mentality had changed as well. The uncertainty of 2007, when entering the playoffs and setting the goal as a state title had been little more than lip service, had long since vanished. The Lake Travis train had been rolling since early in the season, and it would take a catastrophic performance against a formidable foe to derail the express.

"There was no doubt about it in 2008," Gilbert said. "We felt like we were going to win a state championship. It was a lot different than 2007."

In the playoff opener, despite howling winds, LBJ decided to drop defenders back and left running lanes open. Gilbert exploited them by keeping the ball 11 times and gaining 98 yards with four rushing touchdowns, all in the first half. He added a 54-yard touchdown pass to Pollard as Lake Travis jumped out to a 34-14 halftime lead. He added two more touchdown passes after halftime and the Cavaliers cruised 55-14.

Lake Travis' second round match-up proved to be the team's toughest, most physical game of the season. Cibolo Steele, a rugged, athletic team quickly building a name for itself on the outskirts of San Antonio, had heard all it could stand about Lake Travis' offense and its flashy quarterback. Despite playing without their own star – sophomore running back Malcolm Brown injured a knee late in the season – the Knights took the battle to Lake Travis. After a scoreless first quarter, the Knights defense broke through, intercepting Gilbert in the midst of a 14-0 run to take a 21-7 lead. Faced with their first significant deficit of the season, the Cavaliers regrouped quickly. After a rough first half, Gilbert led a late drive and found McCrary for a touchdown to close the gap to 21-14 heading to halftime.

Still, the dream season sat on the brink. Another half like the first, and the Cavaliers would have little more than a dominant season cut short by the unforeseen rising giant to the south. For the first moments of the break, players and coaches snapped and tensions ran high.

"They out-physicaled us all first half," Brewer said. "They weren't scared, they didn't care that we won state, they didn't care what our record was. They just stuck their foot on our throats. That was the first defense other than Evangel that had really good coaching and athletes, they were big."

And with one half left to save all they'd worked for, the leaders stood up.

"Things got real at halftime. I remember walking into that locker room and everyone pulled together," Erickson said. "Garrett made a little speech. Erxleben said something. Coach Loepp got heated. We needed to get out there and turn it around."

The Cavaliers knew they'd get the ball first, so coaches worked quickly to make some adjustments on both sides. Defensively, the Knights had run over the Cavaliers, and Carter tweaked a few plays to attack the ball carriers at the line of scrimmage. Morris, meanwhile, reminded his offense to be patient; that their chances would come. But one adjustment that took place had nothing to do with coaches. Steele players, defenders especially, became emboldened following their early interception and began taunting Gilbert and the rest of the Lake Travis offense. That turned out to be a poor decision, Pollard recalled.

"They started to get cocky and started to talk a lot of trash to Garrett, and it was just over from then," Pollard said. "They said enough just to piss him off, and I've never seen someone put a game so much on his shoulders. He had everything to do with every play, whether he was passing it, he would keep it and run it or he would hand it off and try to go throw a block or something."

With their quarterback asserting himself, the Cavaliers drove for a Kramer Fyfe field goal to open the third quarter. Then, Hatch made a key third down tackle to stop Steele's opening drive, giving Lake Travis the ball back with momentum. Gilbert responded, taking the team back down the field and finally connecting with McCrary for a 19-yard score to take the lead. Steele wouldn't threaten again, and when Gilbert scored the second and third of his rushing touchdowns, Lake Travis earned a 38-21 win.

"He crossed the end zone after we'd won and got the nail-in-the-coffin score at the end, I went up to him to celebrate with him and he was just pure exhausted," Pollard said of the quarterback. "He'd given everything he had and it was phenomenal. I'll never forget that game because it was so much fun to watch him just take control."

The game proved so physical, and Gilbert exerted himself so much, that to this day, it's still hazy.

"There were more than a few late hits in that game," he said. "Honestly, I can't remember when it was in the game, but at some point, I was just a little out of it. I got hit somewhere along the way, and all I remember is telling Coach Morris to keep giving me the ball, to let me keep running it."

He ran Steele right in to the ground, and the last of the scores sparked cries of foul from the opposing sideline. With 10 seconds left in the game, instead of taking a knee, the Cavaliers executed another QB keeper from three yards out to extend an already untouchable 31-21 lead.

Players chalked the decision up to their coach believing they'd received more cheap shots than deserved (though, to be fair, Lake Travis dished out a few of its own), and that the touchdown had been a not-so-subtle message. The many stories about Morris' likability and ease with players and parents don't do the riverboat gambler and his competitive nature justice. The belief that "no one can beat Lake Travis except Lake Travis" is not just smart philosophy. It's stubborn assuredness.

"He wanted to break records. He wanted to score," Erickson flatly declared. "He didn't give a shit."

Turns out the coach was trying to send a message, just not the same one the opposition got.

"It was such a heated game. It was battling back and forth the whole way. It was just something, calling a game of that magnitude," Morris said. "But [the touchdown] was more so to tell our guys that when we step on the field, we step on the field and we're going to give everything we've got. It was more so about confidence. We didn't come here to back down. I was trying to set a tone. An attitude. I'm not going to lie to you. I have so much respect for Coach Jinks and what they've done. They're incredible at Steele. But we talk about being the best. That was us making sure we knew who the best team was."

Gilbert took control again the following week in the Alamodome against Alice High School. The Coyotes came in undefeated, but like so many other 2008 teams they couldn't keep matching Lake Travis' offense score for score. Alice did manage to hold a 10-7 lead in the second quarter, thanks to an offense very similar to the one Beeville Jones ran to give the Cavaliers trouble the year before, but the lead proved short-lived. Erickson fielded the ensuing kickoff two yards deep in his end zone, found a seam and sprinted past everyone for a touchdown. Sparked by the score, Lake Travis' defense clamped down while Gilbert and company went to work. The quarterback capped successive drives with rushing touchdowns – his second and third of the half – and then found Floyd for a 53-yard scoring bomb to take a 35-10 lead.

Alice would rally and make things interesting, scoring on three consecutive drives to close within 35-32, and in the middle of the second half, there were definitely more shaky moments by the Cavaliers than they had grown accustomed to in 2008.

But Gilbert remained determined. Up by three, the Cavaliers marched to the Alice 32-yard-line before stalling and facing a pivotal third down. With pressure mounting, and the momentum still on Alice's side, the quarterback stepped into formation, then had an idea.

"Garrett looks over at the sidelines on third down and he gives me the call that he wants to run. Pink Ram, it's a quarterback run for us. He can throw if he wants to, but he makes the call. And it's a huge play for us. I thought, 'By God, if he calls it, he better get it.' He calls it, he goes and scores," Morris laughed. "I told him, 'Great call,' but I had that much confidence in him. He saw it. He wanted it. I trusted him. If he sees something, he's playing, not me. It's the same way I do things with my guys now at Clemson."

Gilbert added another scoring run and Erickson scored the capper in the 55-32 win. When the dust settled, Gilbert had thrown for 241 yards and a score and rushed for a career-best 126 yards and five scores.

The win moved Lake Travis into the Region IV final, which turned out to be a rematch with district rival Killeen. Playing for the first time in Darrell K. Royal-Texas Memorial Stadium, the future Texas Longhorn survived his most rugged performance – he threw two interceptions and lost two fumbles, one of which the Kanagroos returned for their only touchdown – to lead his team to an astounding 71-9 thrashing. While he threw four more touchdown passes, the completion everyone remembers came in the third quarter, when a gangly freshman receiver not listed on the roster snuck onto the field and caught a nine-yard comeback.

"Really my first memory was as a freshman, when the new coaches came in with my brother playing as a senior after winning state for the first time," Griffin Gilbert, Garrett's younger brother and once-gangly freshman receiver, said later. "I got to come up and play varsity for one game with my brother. It's a memory I'll never forget, and to get to go out and catch a pass from him was such an honor. To have Coach Morris actually let me do that was such a privilege and I thank him so much for that."

Decisions like that, allowing a freshman the chance to catch a pass from his brother, helped cement Morris' idea of the program as a family. Though, his previous attempt for the two brothers to connect failed in the first round win over LBJ. The younger Gilbert admitted later that he put too much pressure on himself the first time, and it turned out to be a blessing in disguise, as catching a pass from your future Longhorn brother in DKR is infinitely cooler.

Having dispatched Killeen, the Cavaliers had two more steps to take. Most close to the program, and watching from around the state, figured the second title had become Lake Travis' to lose. Morris didn't count himself among that group, and he kept pressing his team forward, preparing against his standard of greatness. But as Gilbert kept throwing touchdown passes and racking up yards, the coach did some math and set about on a mission of his own. Through 14 games, Gilbert had amassed 4,231 yards, on pace to break both the state's single season record, which he had set the year before, and the career mark held by former Ennis quarterback Graham Harrell, who went on to star at Texas Tech. He didn't tell his quarterback, but the coach had decided he'd do everything he could to help Gilbert earn both records.

Lake Travis headed from one iconic stadium to another to take on Friendswood in the state semifinal. Playing at Kyle Field, the Cavaliers wasted little time putting the game away. Gilbert started off hot, and the

Mustangs had no answer for his passing despite an early injury to top receiver McCrary. As Pollard explained, Lake Travis had no shortage of weapons. McCrary departed after catching one of two Gilbert first-quarter touchdown passes, and when the quarterback sandwiched a scoring strike to Pollard around two touchdown runs, Lake Travis led 35-7 at the half. Gilbert and Aydam added third quarter touchdown runs to stretch the lead further, and the Cavaliers cruised into the title game with a 56-22 win. Pollard enjoyed his best day with 10 catches for 149 yards, and Gilbert finished with 262 yards passing, 132 yards rushing and six combined touchdowns, edging ever closer to the historic marks.

As they had in 2007 against storied Highland Park, the Cavaliers' path to a second title went through another of the state's football elite. Longview had played in two state championship games, most recently as a 5A team in 1997. The program also ranks among the state's top 20 in all-time wins. The Lobos would not back down against the Cavaliers.

Leading up to the game, Lake Travis' coaches had noticed something crucial about the Lobos defense. Against teams that used a faster tempo, Longview's defenders would get lined up before any signals came in from the sidelines and then check with coaches for the call. Once the coaches saw the offensive formation, they'd signal in their call. That strategy had worked well. The strategy, however, didn't account for other teams figuring the signals out, which is what the Lake Travis coaches had done prior to the championship game. Pollard said the discovery helped Morris, already the ultra-successful play-caller, dial up the perfect counter to nearly every defense Longview would try.

"The coaches had seen on film that before the play the Longview defense would get its signals," Pollard recalled. "So what we'd do, we'd go up and pretend we were about to run a play. They'd signal in, and we'd all check to the sidelines. The coaches knew exactly what defense they were about to run because they'd just signaled it. They had picked up through film what each signal meant. So we would just walk up to the line of scrimmage, defense would call their signal and we'd check the sideline and they'd give us an offensive play that would work perfectly for that defense. It was actually pretty funny that they were giving us what they were about to do and we knew exactly how to pick them apart."

Lake Travis didn't need to change anything it did regularly to disguise the fact that they knew what the defense would do. In Morris' hurry-up, no-huddle, the Cavaliers had become so conditioned to get lined up immediately following a play, they only had to delay their customary sideline checks slightly to get their call.

"That's just where good coaching comes in," Pollard said. "We were so conditioned to line up as quick as possible, defenses never had a chance. And if they did at the beginning of the games, we were just so conditioned that they couldn't keep up for four quarters. No matter what team it was, what defense it was, they couldn't keep up with us for four quarters. It was great coaching to pick up the signs on the film and see what each one meant."

Figuring out Longview's defensive calls turned out to be just one advantage Lake Travis entered the game with. Pollard recalled two more things that set Lake Travis apart, not just from Longview but from any high school team that year. One distinct advantage lay in Gilbert, the quarterback who refused to let his team lose.

Gilbert rarely addressed the team, preferring to lead by example. But when the team gathered to take the field for the championship game, Gilbert stood up. When he finished, his teammates knew two things: they would not let him down, and they would send him out on top. Pollard doesn't recall exactly what Gilbert said, but then it wasn't how he delivered his message that moved his teammates.

"I remember he wasn't one to yell," Pollard said. "You could tell looking in his eyes that you could see the emotion and the passion that he has. He started to talk to us and I remember everybody getting really quiet to listen to him. It just gave you butterflies. He talked about how much he enjoyed playing with us and how this was our last game to be together, and things like that. Just the way that he was able to say it and the way he looked at us all, you felt safe because you knew he would take care of us. When he got up and started talking like that, when you know your leader is in check, then it makes everything go away. I remember him talking about how proud he was of all of us."

Morris added his own touch before sending his team out. All of the coaches wrote a letter to each of their designated players about the journey they traveled together that season, which the players read on the way to the game. After all the speeches before him, Morris' final literary touch, and his final message to his players, was a poem. It's called "Who Am I?"

"It's 3-4 minutes long. It talks about working tirelessly, I sweat, I cry, I work hard when no one's around. And every part ends with 'Who am I? I am a Lake Travis Cavalier,'" Morris said. "Well, at the end, it goes, 'I'm about to make history. Who am I?' And that's when I looked at all of them and said, 'I'm a two-time defending state champion.' And we ran out."

With a strategic edge and all the motivation to make history, the other advantage manifest itself as the game went on. Before the team went over to Floyd Casey Stadium, Morris pulled his quarterbacks and receivers into a room and did something Pollard had never seen a coach do. He added a play prior to the game, drew it up in the sand, if you will.

"The other cool thing, which goes to show how good we were and how on another level we were from most high school teams, Coach Morris put a play in the morning of the state championship game, and we never even practiced it," Pollard recalled. "It was a route combination between me and Cade. I would shift in from the outside right on Cade's hip. Cade would break to the corner and I would run a dig."

The insight came when Morris had spoken with Jevan Snead, then the quarterback at Ole Miss and having the season of his career, and Snead suggested a play that countered Longview's defense, something the Rebels had used in a game earlier that year against a similar alignment.

As the game kicked off and the Cavaliers went about their business, Morris found a way to work the new play into the plan. Though they'd never practiced it, Morris still trusted his quarterback and receivers enough that, when the time came, they'd run the play and run it correctly. Of course they justified his confidence.

"It was something we'd never practiced before, and we ran it three times. It went three for three for over 100 yards, and Cade scored a touchdown off of it," Pollard said. "I think the first two went to me, and the third time we ran it I think they expected it to go to me, and so Cade was able to get a step on his man and that was one of his touchdowns. It was crazy to think that was the kind of level we were on. We could put a play in the morning of, never practice it and run it to perfection like we did in the state championship. I thought that was pretty neat."

Lake Travis' performance turned out to be pretty neat, as well. On a crystal clear day fit for a celebration, the Cavaliers scored first on a 26-yard strike from Gilbert to McCrary, but Longview answered. It didn't matter. The Cavaliers then scored three unanswered touchdowns to take complete control. Aydam took a screen pass and used escorts from Kelley and Will Hawk to score untouched, and Erickson and Gilbert added touchdown runs to boost the lead. Leading 28-7 at the half, the Cavaliers added to the lead on another Gilbert run to further extend the margin, and the only remaining drama lay in Morris' quest to help Gilbert earn his records. After the game the coach made no apologies for continuing to have his quarterback throw the ball even as the game had been decided.

"We were going to do it, and I didn't care what people thought," Morris said after the game. "That kid deserves every bit of that, and it's so special for him."

As the clock wound down in the final quarter, Gilbert needed 32 yards to break Harrell's career mark. When the Cavaliers got the ball the final time, they had it on the Longview 34. Leading 41-23, Morris sent Gilbert back onto the field and called pass after pass. Three successive incompletions brought fourth down, but the coach pressed on. Gilbert found Brewer, who made a tricky catch, to earn a first down.

"I still hold that over his head to this day," Brewer joked. "I tell him to go get me a soda because I saved his chance to break the record. He never does it, of course."

Then Gilbert earned his records. A 13-yard pass to Aydam allowed him to break his own single-season mark, and a final strike to Floyd – for a final touchdown – set the all-time record at 12,534, two little yards clear of Harrell.

His teammates understood what it meant to play with a quarterback who had just completed one of the state's best high school careers.

"To this day I feel so honored that I got the chance to play with him," Pollard said. "It was something to watch him play. It's something you can't describe."

"I never thought we were going to lose. I can't emphasize enough how much trust I had in Garrett. No one could stop him. I always thought as long as Garrett was good, we were going to be good," Erickson said. "I looked up to him so much."

Following the season, one that saw the quarterback pass for 4,854 yards with 55 touchdowns and only six interceptions and rush for another 767 yards and 23 touchdowns, Gilbert received the Gatorade-USA Today National Player of the Year award.

The offensive numbers had been prolific. McCrary finished the year with 84 receptions for 1,711 yards and 24 touchdowns. Pollard had 60 catches, 1,022 yards and eight touchdowns. Aydam had a combined 1,410 yards rushing and receiving for 18 touchdowns. Floyd caught 33 passes for 592 yards and seven touchdowns, and Erickson caught 34 for 439 yards and three touchdowns while rushing for 546 yards and six scores. Each individual player's numbers would rival the top players on almost every team in the state, while the leaders obliterated the norm.

The defense had been just as omnipresent, with four players – Crow, Hatch, Streuling, and Todd Perry – all recording 100 tackles or more. Hatch also led the team with eight sacks while becoming one of the most unlikely 4A all-state linebackers in state history.

The precedent had been set by a core class that had achieved the unthinkable. The question now had become whether Lake Travis could reload after losing the most talented class in school history. The new quarterback would be tested. A new offensive star would emerge. And the head coach would lead them on his historic curtain call.

14: Let it be Three

When Garrett Gilbert put on the pads for the last time at Lake Travis, it signaled the end of an era. The piles of yards, the seemingly endless strings of points and touchdowns, and unparalleled leadership all graduated with the national high school player of the year.

If quarterback play dictates much of what the Lake Travis offense does, then the pressure now rested on the shoulders of Michael Brewer. Brewer represented another wave of Lake Travis talent, coming from a wildly successful athletic lineage, and possessing the confidence required of a quarterback at the helm of a team that now had a proverbial target on its back.

It seemed the natural order of things that the 2009 squad would carry the momentum and maintain the school's established place atop the Texas football mountain, but despite the confidence that comes with back-to-back championships, the team still had to convince itself that another championship season could follow. But head coach Chad Morris knew what he had with this newest bunch, especially his quarterback. The trick would be getting the most out of him.

"I knew that with being a first-year starter there were going to be a lot of things I could help with because I'd coached Kody Spano who had followed Jevan Snead," Morris said of his Stephenville quarterbacks that earned Big XII scholarships.

"It started with Michael trusting me, and he did. I had to coach him different than I coached Garrett. He's a different person. He would probably need to run the ball more often with his skill set, and I thought if he got hit a little more early on in his career, he'd settle down and get after it," Morris said.

Morris wouldn't coddle Brewer. He'd coax him into stardom.

"I knew he was a winner. Bottom line. That's where he comes from, his parents and his family. The Brewers have been winners for generations," Morris said. "It was my job to get it out of him. I had confidence in him, even on days when I had to wring his neck, the confidence was still there."

Brewer didn't have Gilbert's size. Their physical presence couldn't have been more different, their styles varied in so many small ways. If Gilbert had been the ultra-friendly pal to everyone around him, Brewer became the collected king of cool. Perpetually tan with light green eyes and a permanent aw-shucks grin, all set under a mop of hair, the casting department at *Friday Night Lights* couldn't have picked the guy better. Gilbert had been the tall, lanky machine on the field with long strides and a bazooka for an arm. Brewer's legs churned and cut quickly, and his quick release shot the ball through gaps that didn't exist. Everyone could see the differences between them. So, Morris' first order of business became making it abundantly clear to the new team leader that no matter what he did, he needed to always remember to be himself.

Every day, Morris parroted the mantra over and over, "Just worry about being Michael Brewer. Don't try to be someone else."

The coach spoke not from a cliché, but from experience, drawing on his aforementioned attempts to be Art Briles.

Besides, while losing one of the best quarterbacks in state history would be a blow, the new guy didn't appear a pushover. Mercurial? He had his moments, but Morris' blunt assessment of Brewer's ability to win games said everything. It wasn't always pretty, it wasn't always a blowout, but only once in 28 starts did Brewer fail to produce a Lake Travis win.

Brewer's first spring as starter got off to a seamless start, much more so than the average debut for most quarterbacks. That had a lot to do with running practice a year earlier as a freshman while Gilbert recovered from surgery. That extra development time getting first-team snaps made all the difference.

"I think if you talk to Michael, he would say that spring of his freshman year catapulted him a full season ahead of where he would have been," Morris said. "We don't win the state championship the year he's the quarterback if he doesn't go through that first spring."

With a foundation of confidence in place, coach and quarterback began the real work of preparing for a season. Morris and his most important pupil to that moment in his career became inseparable. They spent most of their time watching film. Endless amounts of film.

"I think he did a really good job of making sure I watched a ton of film. I watched Garrett and watched defenses. It was good, but in a way it was also a reminder – I wasn't replacing just anyone, I was replacing Garrett.

There was added pressure. But Coach Morris always told me to be me. Don't try to be Garrett or Todd [Reesing], just be Michael," Brewer said.

Being Michael would be easier than anyone probably expected because of the emergence of a player who'd become one of the state's greatest offensive threats.

Andy Erickson had played his part in two championship runs. He spurred the first of many unlikely victories with a blazing kickoff return against Kerrville Tivy in the area championship in 2007, and he was ultimate extra weapon in a season where the Cavaliers didn't need one in 2008. Short but fast, lean but strong. What seemed like an exceptional player in open space became a weapon of far more devastating ability. But his talent hadn't been obvious at the outset of spring practice. Not to him, his coaches or his quarterback.

"I knew he had great talent. I knew he had an air about himself. Not to say he was cocky, he was confident and he was tough," Morris said of Erickson. "He had a tough man approach. Nothing scared him. Nothing would back him down. When you get that kind of mentality coupled with that kind of talent, the sky's the limit. I knew he could be good, but offensive player of the year? No. I didn't see that coming."

With Chris Aydam graduating, a primary running threat left the Lake Travis backfield. From day one, Erickson figured to be the replacement, despite playing a different position. Aydam had been the fullback in the Lake Travis offense, but Erickson would be in a more versatile role, starting at the tailback spot. Erickson's role would be an important one, but as the spring progressed, no one treated him like a franchise back. For Erickson, practice became about being a part of the onslaught, solidifying his role. If anyone saw what Erickson could become in the spring, they're bizarrely holding it in to this day.

"I don't ever remember Coach Morris or anyone else telling me that I was going to be this big guy," Erickson said. "I knew I was going to start and I knew I had a chance to contribute."

***

Erickson arrived in Lake Travis by way of Montana before his freshman year. His father had helped a friend move to Cedar Park, and instantly became hooked on the area. In short order, a whirlwind family tour followed as the Ericksons attempted to find a suitable landing spot in the Austin area. As they looked, Andy visited the prospective high schools, ultimately coming to the realization that he'd attend Dripping Springs, Cedar Park or Lake Travis, based on his parents' housing search.

The family met with football coach Jeff Dicus and athletic director Jack

Moss and remembers being instantly impressed.

"I liked [Dicus] a lot. They were so nice to me. It seemed like they cared so much about everything else that was going on there. My parents could feel that. I wasn't used to sensing it, I was just 15. My coach in Montana was great, but he wasn't like this. Dicus said if I came there to play it could be a life changer," Erickson said.

The reception elsewhere? Not quite as hospitable. Throw in the perfect house, and the Ericksons were sold. Lake Travis became home.

Erickson had played quarterback in Montana, but mostly just because he was the best player on the team. Lake Travis had its quarterback, so he bounced around for a few years trying to find the right position. He played some defensive back, some running back. No spot seemed to fit him perfectly. But that changed in 2009. He may not have been the tallest guy on the team – he's listed as 5-foot-10, 175 pounds as a college junior in 2012 – but he still cut a physical presence. Erickson could be lifted straight out of an Abercrombie catalogue, fit as a fiddle with nary an ounce of fat on his body. Morris had been right. Erickson exuded confidence, and his teammates liked that. He provided much-needed leadership, leadership the team sorely missed when he left.

***

Planting the aspirations for your season on the shoulders of just two players is no way to build a title contender, though, and plenty of other changes made the 2009 team a completely new take on Lake Travis football. The team had different, inexperienced replacement parts for the fine-tuned Ferrari that mowed down the competition the year before. But it still felt right.

"I knew that the potential was there. In the spring of that year, there was a lot of uncertainty. [Receiver] Conner Floyd was really going to have to come on. They had to play well in 7on7," Morris said.

Defensively, the team lost experience and grit, but it returned a fast group familiar with the defensive schemes installed by Hank Carter and Randall Edwards. Linebackers Austin Williams, Quinton Crow and Ian Lazarus would anchor the unit. Jonathan Roberts would plug the middle of the line with Trevor Gillette and Shaquille Marable rushing off the ends. The unproven unit had plenty left to show, but the reinforcements had arrived on both sides of the ball, not just offense.

When spring practice arrived, the intensity remained high. Fights didn't occur as often as they did the previous spring, but they still happened, if for no other reason than the new guys needed to prove they wouldn't back down from any challenge, just as their predecessors didn't. The Cavaliers maintained their intense practice pace, the plays seemed to click the same, and by the end, the offense made big play after big play. The spring game showcased the deep threat that Floyd presented, and the speed Erickson brought to the backfield. Brewer hit his spots. Everything seemed to be on course as planned.

Then, out of nowhere, Erickson had an announcement to make. His girlfriend, Callie, was pregnant.

"I had a meeting with [Coach Morris]. My dad had already told him, but my dad still wanted me to tell coach face to face," Erickson said.

It's a meeting no coach can prepare for, but one that Morris handled as best he could. The school year had come to a close and the football team was setting up to host its summer 7-on-7 tournament.

"It was very devastating to [the Ericksons] at the time. They needed my support more than anything. It's not the first time this sort of thing has ever happened to a player I've coached, and it won't be the last time," Morris said. "I just kept reinforcing that things aren't going to change for us. They'll change for him, but we'll be here, and we're still going to need him."

The reaction surprised Erickson.

"He told me that everything would be all right and nothing's going to change. He told me I had to do one thing, and that was tell the team. I went in after [workouts] and told everybody. I had to formally address that, and it was kind of weird, but it was crazy – everyone was in the locker room, just the guys, and they all got excited. It was crazy, I expected them to flip out. But they were all excited."

But a lot would change, and it would affect more than just the 2009 football season. While the imminent part of Erickson's life and his potential were in jeopardy, Morris tried to remind his new tailback that there was much more life ahead. And it would only get tougher.

"'Your priorities are going to change.' That's what I kept saying. I kept using football as the out to get the education to provide for the family he was going to have. If he took care of business in school and on the field, he'd have a future that could help him build a family," Morris said.

Meanwhile, the football family that had been built at Lake Travis made what could have been a major strain to the team a seemingly uneventful blip. From Erickson's announcement, the team shifted focus to 7-on-7. Brewer settled in quickly, making the most of his second summer with a ton of snaps with the first team at 7-on-7, and it showed.

"I really felt like we were in good shape because everything clicked during that summer," Erickson said. "We were winning like we always did, and even though we got knocked out in the playoffs at the state tournament, it was just a big boost."

Brewer sensed it as well.

"Spring went good, off-season went good. Nothing was different than the previous years. We still felt really good about that," he said. "Every workout ended with, 'Repeat.' But 7-on-7 was when I think we realized we were going to be good. The defense was playing really well; the offense was playing extremely well. That's when I knew the title was ours to lose."

That realization came on the blazing intramural fields at Texas A&M in July. December remained months away. And while the quarterback felt that way, it took a little more convincing for the rest of the group. For Erickson, things started to make sense in two-a-days. That's when his confidence in his new quarterback really started to solidify.

"I realized Brewer was great in two-a-days. He has a great arm, and from the time we started throwing routes, I really believed in him," he said. "But that all really clicked once we put pads on, and the results were pretty good."

A few story lines dominated the football discussion in Central Texas that summer, none more prominent than the Cavaliers' quest for a three-peat. To do that, they'd have to go through an even stronger Cibolo Steele team at some point in the playoffs. Despite new personnel and plenty of formidable obstacles ahead of them, the Cavaliers made little secret that the majority of their preparation from the beginning of the summer centered on an inevitable clash with the Knights.

They had plenty of reason. The black and silver squad returned plenty of people from the team that nearly upended Lake Travis' 2008 dream season, except this time everyone expected that star running back Malcolm Brown would be healthy and stronger than ever after a breakout sophomore season that projected him as one of the country's best running backs. The Knights had their eyes on a rematch, too.

"It's been 365 days — Nov. 21st to Nov. 21st," Knights head coach Mike Jinks said the week before the game finally happened. "We'll be ready to play."

All anticipation aside, the Cavaliers still had plenty of work to do before they'd see Steele. Lake Travis would open the season as coaches' pick at No.1, but only as No. 5 in *Dave Campbell's Texas Football*. Even in central Texas, the *Austin American-Statesman* didn't have the Cavaliers ranked as the area's top team, opting instead for 5A Stony Point.

Lake Travis would again open the season with Westwood, a perennial early season darling of Central Texas media. The Warriors featured Princeton Collins, arguably Central Texas' best running back. Committed to the University of Utah, Collins had gained just shy of 2,000 rushing and receiving yards combined in 2008, and the ability of teams with strong ground games to keep the Lake Travis offense off the field gave this match-up the appearance of a true test, especially one year removed from a dicey 27-20 Lake Travis win with the Cavaliers' strongest team to date.

Leading up to the game, Brewer couldn't calm his nerves. He didn't need the opponent to be formidable. If anyone felt the pressure and weight of championship expectations, he did, and he couldn't, wouldn't, downplay it. He spent every waking hour preparing and thinking about his new role, but the toughest times came when his thoughts would remind him of the daunting challenge ahead of – and behind – him.

"That game was big for me because it was my first start. I was so nervous going into it because I knew all the expectations. I was juggling all these thoughts," he said, coming back to the biggest among them. "It was going to be hard to replace No. 7."

If his teammates knew Brewer carried the weight of the world on his shoulders as kickoff approached, they lent a hand, no one more so than Erickson, who announced his presence with authority. He caught a screen pass from Brewer and took it 34 yards for a score. He broke loose on a 74-yard touchdown run. Another screen pass turned into an 80-yard score. The omnipresent Erickson finished with 164 yards rushing and 163 yards receiving. He ran all over the Warriors, and his teammates followed suit en route to a 55-31 win.

"From the get-go, we were just dominating. We just kept driving on them. Andy had some big runs, and then Coach Morris let me start slinging it around, and that was fun. It got rid of a lot of stress and pressure," Brewer said. "It made everything easier from there."

Brewer's debut couldn't have gone better, the mark of things to come. He finished with 17 completions on 23 attempts for 379 yards and four touchdowns, a Gilbert-worthy line in its efficiency and effectiveness.

Brewer and Erickson hadn't been the only bright spots, signs that the changes coaches had made during the off-season would pan out. Taylor Wrinkle had moved to the defensive backfield and led the team in tackles with eight. Marable had seven, Trevor Gillette had five. Sophomore Colin Lagasse made his varsity debut in the defensive backfield. Pillars of the future of Lake Travis' offense were initiated as a group. Juniors Tanner Gillette and Floyd and sophomore Griffin Gilbert combined for nine catches and more than 200 yards. It had been a perfect start and a perfect night.

Well, aside from those 31 points surrendered, which would wind up being the most Lake Travis surrendered all season.

"One of the coolest things I remember about the game was the student section. We had one of the greatest student sections. Everyone knew we were going to be good, but maybe not quite as good. But I just remember the student section just going completely nuts with how good we were playing," Brewer said. "I'll never forget that."

The start surprised even the most optimistic of Lake Travis fans. Those wondering whether the Cavaliers would contend for that third title felt they had an answer. The hardest part now became managing the reaction.

"At that point, I wanted to give the mentality of, 'This is just what we do,'" Morris said. "I don't want there to be a huge surprise. OK, you won the game, but big deal. It was a great start, you want to build on it, but we're not going to build rings for beating Westwood."

They had no time to celebrate, anyway. Traditional 5A power Westlake loomed on the horizon, and Westlake was pissed off. The Cavaliers had stomped the Chaparrals the previous year, and the Chaps, led by new coach Darren Allman, returned with a squad that would eventually reach the 5A, Division II state championship game.

The showdown didn't really live up to the billing, though. Westlake squandered early opportunities, dug itself a hole and Lake Travis wound up with a comfortable 42-21 win. Brewer improved on his opening performance, completing 23 passes on 32 attempts for 422 yards and a touchdown. Erickson had 200 combined yards. Floyd had 163 receiving yards. The first week hadn't been a fluke, and it seemed clear that the Lake Travis train could set its course for the title.

A seemingly salty test still remained, though, in Cedar Park. The then-5A Timberwolves had been nasty a year before and kept the Cavalier offense in check. The school had a growing reputation and plenty of talent, talent that would turn Cedar Park into one of the state's strongest teams in the coming years. The game felt like the perfect kind to hype. Even the Cedar Park public address announcer declared it the "game of the year in Central Texas" during pregame introductions.

And then it spiraled into an ugly, one-sided shellacking in short order. Lake Travis opened with a 17-0 lead thanks to touchdown runs by Brewer and Erickson and a field goal from Kramer Fyfe. Cedar Park paused the carnage briefly, capitalizing on Lake Travis' only mistake: a Brewer interception that was fumbled and then recovered by Jeff Peden and returned for a touchdown. Lake Travis then scored 27 points before Cedar Park notched a field goal. The onslaught continued until the dust settled with a 54-17 win. At the time, it appeared to be another domination of an inferior team, but in retrospect, it may have been the greatest aberration during the run of five titles. It marked the only game out of six in four years where the outcome became evident early, and didn't do justice as an indicator to the rivalry that would develop between the two teams.

The score, however, had been an exact indicator of the rest of Lake Travis' regular season. Evangel Christian backed out of the second year of its commitment to play Lake Travis, leaving Boerne in its place. The Greyhounds weren't yet officially a registered 4A team, and the Cavaliers cruised 52-0. Then came a clean domination of District 25-4A. Killeen went down 56-31, Hutto 57-16, Lampasas 38-7, Hendrickson 58-15, Dripping Springs 52-0 and Marble Falls 52-7. The Cavaliers secured a sixth consecutive district title, and moved on to play Crockett in the bi-district championship. Crockett entered at 4-6, and the result had been such a foregone conclusion that the Cougars decided to play on a Thursday rather than delay the inevitable, and lost a coin flip that gave Lake Travis one more home game. Lake Travis didn't mind a bit. The Cavaliers had already turned their attention to Steele in the second round.

"The week that we played Crockett, we planned for Steele 70 percent of the time and Crockett 30 percent of the time, if that," Brewer said.

Lake Travis won 58-7, setting up the Steele rematch in San Antonio's Alamodome.

The ballyhooed rematch didn't start well at all for Lake Travis. A snap out of the back of the end zone resulted in a safety, and Steele added to that with a field goal. Then, the interception. After driving into Steele territory, Brewer dropped back on a screen pass, looked to his right, turned to his left and threw. He didn't see the waiting Steele defender lurking behind the wall.

"Usually there's a window you throw into, but there's a guy there and I see him as I'm throwing, and he tips and intercepts it," Brewer said.

Andre Jenkins took it 80 yards for a touchdown, and Lake Travis found itself in a 12-0 hole against a team that could control the clock and keep the offense off the field. All season, the Lake Travis starters had yearned for a competitive game, one they'd be able to play from start to finish. Careful what you wish for, you just might get it.

After Lake Travis spun its wheels and punted on its next drive, Brown found a seam at his own nine-yard line and took off. He seemed destined for pay dirt when, out of nowhere, Lagasse caught up with him and knocked the ball loose. Lake Travis recovered. Reminiscent of Sean Robinson's touchdown-saving-fumble in the 2007 championship game against Highland Park, Morris said after the game that Lagasse's play marked the turning point in the game, and that he would talk about that play for years to come.

"We don't make it without that play by Colin," he said. "It changed everything in that game."

Lake Travis charged down the field from its own 32-yard-line and scored on Erickson's 21-yard run, cutting the lead in half. A quick stop later, Brewer darted up the sideline for a 32-yard touchdown run that gave the Cavaliers an all-too-tenuous halftime lead at 13-12. In the locker room, Morris' halftime message didn't surprise anyone. After months of build-up, the coaches thought perhaps the team had forgotten that it would have to show up to win the big games.

"The talk at halftime was kind of, 'We told you so, you knew what we were getting into, these guys are a physical bunch,'" Brewer said. "We made a lot of mistakes that made it a lot worse. Most games, we make those mistakes and still win by 35, but those teams don't have six DI guys. These guys were good. We basically talked about minimizing mistakes, and as long as we did, we would win."

The Cavaliers opened the second half with another scoring drive to make it 20-12, but when it seemed Lake Travis had captured the momentum, Brown put the Knights on his back. On a seven-play drive, Brown carried the ball for 78 of the 80 yards and scored on a 25-yard run on fourth-and-three. He then ran in untouched for the game-tying two-point conversion.

Then, the game really got interesting.

Steele stuffed the Lake Travis offense on three plays, and Steele defensive back Jake Hatcher nearly took off with what would have been a sure interception for a touchdown, but Erickson broke up the pass at the last second. Hatcher's day got worse on the ensuing play. He fumbled a punt return that Wrinkle then recovered, giving Lake Travis the ball at the Steele 33-yard line.

Three plays later, the Cavaliers made it count. Erickson took Brewer's screen pass 28 yards for the touchdown, giving Lake Travis a 27-20 lead.

Steele put together a methodical, 12-play drive into Lake Travis territory, but the Cavaliers stuffed Brown on fourth-and-two at the Lake Travis 35-yard line. It foreshadowed the biggest moment of the game.

Lake Travis drove to the Steele 25-yard line on its next drive, but had to punt facing fourth-and-11 back at the 33. Brewer executed a perfect pooch punt, pinning the Knights at their own seven-yard line.

With 6:16 left in the game, Steele started its march, chewing up the clock as it rolled along on Brown's churning legs, eventually reaching the Lake

Travis four-yard-line. Quarterback Nick Sergent spiked the ball on first down to stop the clock and set up the final three plays.

On the first play, Steele, which had thrown just seven passes to that point, went with play action and Sergent's pass failed. On the second, the Knights stuck with the play action, and again Sergent's pass fell to the turf with a stadium wondering why Brown hadn't gotten the ball on either play, just yards away from the biggest touchdown in school history. Morris could only watch.

"It was nerve wracking. I'm on one end of the field, and I have all the trust in the world in Henry [Carter. Morris never called his defensive coordinator anything else]. I wasn't intermingling. I had faith in him and our relationship," he said.

So with 17 seconds left in the game on fourth-and-goal at the Lake Travis four-yard line, Brown finally got the nod. A wall of Lake Travis defenders expected it and met him in the hole, dragging him to the turf. The Cavaliers erupted in celebration, and the Knights could only ask what might have been.

"We still had to make a play, and Ian Lazarus did and everyone joined in. It was a euphoria of emotion," Morris said.

"That play was just awesome," Brewer said. "Malcolm's helmet went up in the air, he went down, and then everyone comes flying toward us to celebrate. Just remember thinking, 'Did that just happen?'"

Brown ran for 299 yards on 34 carries and a touchdown, carrying his team offensively, which made the play calls at the end more than a little perplexing. This should have been Steele's crowning moment, to upend the pretty boys from Austin, to establish itself as the new power in Central Texas. To get revenge on the team it should have beaten in 2008. And with the game on the line, Brown's number wasn't called until the ship had taken on too much water. The Knights got cute, and it cost them.

"I was definitely surprised by the play-calling at the end," Carter said afterwards. "They felt like they'd had some success with the play-action pass and I guess they felt like it would work again, and really, it did – they just fell incomplete. We were expecting run. I can't say enough about the way our kids hung in there and battled. They stepped up on the biggest play of the game, and made plays for us all night."

Along its long, arduous path to state immortality, the death of the dream came dangerously close a handful of times for Lake Travis. This had been one of them, and Lake Travis' defense had made the difference. For the first time in three years, the Lake Travis defense came up with more big plays than its offense, and it did so when the team needed it most.

"I just remember going into those last three plays determined not to lose the game. It wasn't going to happen," Lazarus said after the game. "I always visualize that scenario and we came up with a big play."

More than anything, the win proved a relief. And it meant big things were still possible.

"Going into the playoffs, I was really confident. After Steele, that was the moment for me," Erickson said later. "That's when I knew we were going to win again."

Jinks would say after the game that had Steele scored, it would have gone for two and the win. Two years in a row, Steele put a scare into the state's fastest rising power like no one else could, but ultimately came up short. One year later, it would win its first state championship – in 5A. The Knights would also reach the championship game in 2011, losing to Spring DeKaney.

A third round date with Corpus Christi Flour Bluff back at the Alamodome turned into a 52-13 afterthought, setting up the regional championship with Alamo Heights.

Heights had no standouts. The Mules definitely didn't have six DI starters. But they had taken Steele to the brink in district play, losing 34-33. So much emphasis had been placed on preparing for Steele all year that Lake Travis didn't consider an emergent Alamo Heights squad the same kind of threat. The Mules posted a 10-3 record and had also lost 29-0 to 5A Stony Point and 14-13 to San Antonio Clark. It seemed like a case of a good team that simply wouldn't match up with Lake Travis' firepower. Carter mentioned after a review of game film that Heights running back Justin Rosenthal, the heart of the Mules' attack, didn't appear any better than Lake Travis fullback Turney Maurer.

He and his teammates had plenty of fight, though.

The night broke differently than most regional championship nights in Texas, with temperatures in the 20s by game's end. At Texas State's Bobcat Stadium, Lake Travis' players thought back to their last cold-weather experience.

"Man, I just remember how cold that game was," Erickson said. "I don't think we ever played in a game that was close to that cold, other than that first state championship."

After trading short possessions to open the game, Lake Travis jumped on the board first thanks to Brewer's seven-yard touchdown run. Down 7-0, Alamo Heights responded with a monster 17-play drive, paced by Rosenthal and short, crisp passes by quarterback Cullen Mills. Mills capped it with a nine-yard touchdown pass to Bryon Marshall to draw even.

Lake Travis responded quickly, scoring in eight plays, the last a 16-yard screen from Brewer to Erickson, giving the Cavaliers a 14-7 edge with 3:21 left in the first half. It seemed at the time that Lake Travis might start its signature scoring roll, building separation. But Alamo Heights kept eating up the clock, playing to the formula that has always given Lake Travis trouble.

The Mules ate up the rest of the time in the half en route to a 20-yard field goal by Kristian Stern to close within14-10 at the break. A Lake Travis defensive stand forced the field goal after Alamo Heights had a chance to tie the game from nine, four and two yards out, but couldn't get it done. The final stand had been a positive, but the Cavaliers entered the break feeling like they came up short overall.

"We basically came in at halftime and I told the kids up front, 'Look, we didn't play very well in the first half from a defensive standpoint. We only got the ball three times on offense. From an offensive standpoint, we almost had to be perfect. And if this is the way we're going to go out, you guys will really surprise me,'" Morris said. "The kids agreed with me and boy did they respond. We played a great second half, the defense did great and we eventually found some wrinkles and broke through on offense."

The teams battled to a stalemate in the third quarter, and the pressure peaked as the fourth quarter began. But just as Alamo Heights seemed ready to close in, a 35-yard field goal attempt missed wide. The miss proved an eerie reminder of that battle with Steele a year before on the same field, when a missed field goal seemed to give Lake Travis the momentum it needed to close out the game.

But the Mules fought on. Erickson could only tip a pass from Brewer and the Clifton Molak happily gathered in the interception at the Lake Travis 31-yard line. That's when the Lake Travis defense really stepped up.

After a short pass for no gain, Mills suffered sacks on successive plays, first by Zach Watts and then by Tyler Paulsen on fourth down. Both players, who didn't have much of a chance to contribute during the regular season, had stepped up big in the playoffs. Watts spent the entire fourth quarter bullying his way through the heart of a strong Alamo Heights' offensive line. And as sacks by Crow and Paulsen attested, his friends joined the sack party as well.

The big defensive stand gave Lake Travis a boost, and the Cavaliers scored in five plays when Brewer hit Griffin Gilbert in the back of the end zone for a 28-yard touchdown. Fyfe's extra point hit the post, and Lake Travis led 20-10 with 5:19 left.

Heights managed one more desperation drive and capped it with a 29-yard field goal, but the ensuing onside kick slid out of bounds and Lake Travis took over on the Alamo Heights 45-yard line. All the Cavaliers had to do was run out the clock, but on the second play Erickson broke loose for a 42-yard touchdown run to seal the win.

"That's one of the hardest playing teams we've played so far," Erickson said afterward. "It was frustrating early on. They run a 3-3 stack and it was definitely different, but we just had to keep fighting to get that breakthrough. So it was a great feeling to run out that final touchdown and know we were headed to the state semifinals."

For a team known predominantly for its offense, the game turned when the defense found a way to shut down a balanced attack that created problems early on.

"We try to take away the running game or limit their running plays, and they were running the ball on us," Carter said afterward. "I felt like we'd give them short passes as long as we stopped the run and kept them in a lot of third-and-long situations."

Rosenthal proved far stronger than he'd gotten credit for in the Lake Travis film room, running for 103 yards on 22 carries. But the Lake Travis defense stood tall again, showing its continued evolution. The Cavaliers could win because of their defense, no longer in spite of it. The team continued to grow more dangerous and balanced with time.

Pearland Dawson met Lake Travis in the state semifinal at Texas A&M's Kyle Field. The newest school in the Pearland ISD had quickly made a name for itself during a 12-2 season. And the Eagles wanted to let everyone know that Lake Travis didn't intimidate them. Not in the least.

"They have won a lot of games and beat a lot of good teams," Dawson quarterback Darian Lazard told the *Houston Chronicle*. "But they haven't played Dawson yet. So why should we be intimidated? We are going to be ready to play anyone."

Dawson had the personnel. Lazard had committed to the University of Utah, and the team had a built a reputation as a balanced machine. The Eagles relished the showdown, and wasted no time showing it. During damp, foggy, pregame warm-ups, a few Dawson players started talking trash near midfield, then a few more. Soon, a nearly fully engaged brawl looked ready to explode at the 50-yard line.

"I couldn't believe it, it was so intense," Brewer said. "They completely disrespected us and tried to get in our heads and we were beyond heated."

The coaches did their best to restore order, and the teams returned to their respective locker rooms before the game began. Normally, the coaches would go in with a speech in mind for that particular day. But Morris, still wound up from the fracas, kept it simple.

"Well, if that wasn't enough motivation for you, I don't know what is," he said.

"We all just kind of looked up surprised," Brewer said. "Then you started seeing it on everyone's faces. It was like, 'Hell yeah!'"

What followed proved a brutal and relentless assault in the most lopsided state semifinal the Cavaliers have played.

Erickson scored on a 27-yard pass from Brewer, then on a 34-yard pass, and then Brewer ran in from six yards out. The Cavaliers went for two, and Brewer converted with a pass to Floyd. Lake Travis led 22-0 after the first quarter, 43-6 at the half. Lazard, Dawson's brash quarterback, couldn't back up his pregame talk. He threw four interceptions and suffered six sacks. All the bluster, all the anticipation on one side of the field died in a matter of minutes. On Dawson's side, the game became a funeral for a season that ended too soon. On the other side, Lake Travis enjoyed a four-quarter Mardi Gras, reveling in the 57-12 rout.

"The most fun football game I have ever played in my life," Brewer said. "It's not even close."

Lake Travis faced just one final, familiar, challenge. Longview, the exact same Longview squad from a year before, would meet the Cavaliers back at Baylor's Floyd Casey Stadium. The Lobos were older, wiser, just as talented, and hell bent on revenge.

By now, the order of things the week before a championship had become routine. The Monday media conference, the closed doors and laser focus leading up to the game. Looking back, it's clear now to Erickson which Longview game he had more confidence in winning.

"The second one. I was way more confident, we were used to them, and I don't think they were as good as they were the year before," he said. "And we were just on fire. No one was going to stop us."

Longview opened the game with the ball, but the Lake Travis defense quickly turned the Lobos around. Lake Travis' first snap came from its own 43-yard line. Brewer took the opening snap, rolled right and found nothing but Longview defenders closing in on him. He scrambled out of the scrum to his left and saw Erickson, who had run an out route and turned it up the field. On the television broadcast, cameras couldn't find a Lobo within 20 yards of Erickson.

"We had one of the normal pass plays called, I dropped back, and they had a great defense, and no one was open. My first, second, and third reads weren't there," Brewer said. "There was some leakage up front. I think I'm going to get out of this and try to get rid of the ball. I get flushed, make a move, roll to my left, and I see Andy streaking down the sidelines wide open. When I saw that, I just let go of the ball, and just hoped he'd catch. He did, and he went nuts."

"There's a picture of me screaming with my arms up after scoring that touchdown," Erickson said. "I was screaming out of shock and surprise. I couldn't keep it together."

Needless to say, the play looked a promising omen. Fyfe's extra point gave Lake Travis a 7-0 lead less than two minutes into the game.

Longview responded with a massive 16-play drive but walked away with only a field goal to show for its efforts after Lake Travis corralled Lobo quarterback Aaron Johnson for a one-yard loss on third-and-four at the Cavalier 13-yard line.

A big kick return by Erickson, improved by a Longview personal foul, put Lake Travis at the Lobo 45-yard line, and the Cavaliers scored in eight plays, the last a 10-yard strike from Brewer to Floyd.

Down 14-3, Longview needed a big drive to counter the Lake Travis momentum. The Lobos ate up time and yardage on an 11-play drive, but Lake Travis came up with another big stop, this time on fourth-and-six at the Cavalier 31-yard line, to maintain its command of the game.

By all rights, Lake Travis should have locked up the title before halftime, but an interception and a fumble ruined two golden opportunities deep in Longview territory, and the Cavaliers took a 14-3 lead into halftime.

"We had those turnovers, and that really concerned me because I didn't know how many chances we were going to get like that in the second half," Morris said.

Lake Travis opened up the second half with a nine-play drive that sputtered out at the Longview nine-yard line. Lake Travis settled for Fyfe's 26-yard field goal. But the drive proved costly. Starting left tackle Taylor Doyle suffered a broken leg just before the field goal.

Lying on the ground moments before the field goal, the massive lineman summoned his coach. After the game, Morris tried to recount it as he choked through the moment.

"[Doyle] called me over and just said, 'Coach, we've got to win this thing, tell the guys we've gotta go,'" Morris said. "To see that was unbelievable."

The big man, who would eventually play for the University of Texas, rode a cart off the field into a dark tunnel on the opposite side of the stadium. Lake Travis needed to hold on, and it would have to do it without one of the most important bookends to the offensive line in the program's history.

Longview pulled closer with a three-yard run by Da'Cedric Hunt with 7:04 left in the third quarter, and it appeared for a moment as if the Lobos would make a run back into the game. That notion grew stronger when they forced Lake Travis to punt on the ensuing possession.

The Cavalier defense put its stamp on the game throughout the night, but no play stood bigger than Trevor Gillette's forced fumble on a sack of Johnson on the Lobo 25-yard line on the next drive. Williams recovered the ball, and two plays later, the Cavaliers scored on Erickson's three-yard dive. Just like that, Lake Travis had breathing room again, up 24-10.

"The coaches do a really good job of giving us a game plan, and we just have to go out and execute," Gillette said following the game. "All of our hard work over the last year paid off tonight."

Lake Travis held the Lobos on the next two possessions, including a fourth-and-three at the Cavalier 30-yard line that fell short by inches. Time and again, the defense came through, stopping Longview twice on fourth down and forcing two turnovers.

"I couldn't be prouder of our defense – it's probably the most resilient bunch of guys I've worked with," Carter said afterward. "We've had a lot of injuries in the last week, and even had guys learning positions on the fly tonight. Our kids are winners, they know it and we know it."

Longview managed a last-gasp touchdown with 2:37 left in the game, but sent its onside kick out of bounds. Lake Travis took over, and three plays into the drive, with more than a minute left in the game, faced a fourth-and-three on the Longview 42-yard line. The Cavaliers needed to convert or risk giving Longview one more chance.

Brewer tried to draw the Lobos offside, and when they jumped, center Will Hawk snapped the ball. But no penalty flags flew. Tanner Gillette streaked down the Lake Travis sideline wide open and Brewer hit him. Gillette went down on the seven-yard line, and the Cavaliers began the celebration.

"That's just a gutsy play by those three kids," Morris said after the game. "Incredible way to finish that game."

The play has followed the players and coach involved in the years since.

"We won on a dummy call," Morris said. "Even to this day, when I'm working on this play at Clemson, I can say to our guys, 'This is how serious this play can be…it can win you a title.'"

In the midst of the celebration, Lazarus – the lone three-year starter during that span – relished not only the victory, but also his role in making the Lake Travis defense just as notable as its offense.

"To win my last game, in the third state championship I've played in, it's unbelievable," he said. "We've always wanted to make a name for ourselves on defense, and we did that. I couldn't be happier."

Another pillar of the team's success would be leaving after what would stack up as one of the greatest careers at the school. Few can boast the numbers and achievements that Lazarus can from his time in red and black, a run that spanned three titles and an unparalleled 47-1 record. Even without him, the defense would have a chance to extend its legacy, along with the offense, as the Cavaliers returned the majority of their starters for the 2010 season, extending their staying power even longer.

"We're going to be back, we've got a ton of kids coming back and we've had great senior leadership along the way," Morris said afterward. "This program is a force to be reckoned with."

Whether the coach would be around to see the legacy extended would be another matter.

Erickson earned the Central Texas Player of the Year award. He finished with 1,063 rushing yards, 1,325 receiving yards, and 38 touchdowns. Floyd had 1,316 yards and nine touchdowns through the air. Crow finished the year with 192 tackles. Brewer threw for 4,450 yards, 43 touchdowns and just seven interceptions.

And while the others celebrated, the quarterback couldn't stop crying. Some players well up, but the tears streamed and streamed down his face. Brewer had vanquished the proverbial monkey on his back. After a year of worrying, only sweet relief remained for the new quarterback. He didn't have to be Gilbert, he just had to be himself, and that would be good enough to lead Lake Travis. The question that opened the season had been answered, and the team stood poised to seamlessly march in to the next season and win a fourth title as easily as the second.

15: Tulsa Calling

After two perfect seasons with only a handful of close games, word had gotten out about Lake Travis' football program. New web sites that ranked high school programs had the Cavaliers ranked in the national top 50, and as the spread offense continued to grow in popularity, especially among the ranks of formerly run-first Texas High School football, football fans and writers descended upon the state to see how the shift had taken hold.

Sports Illustrated ran a story about starting NCAA Division I, now dubbed the Football Bowl Subdivision, quarterbacks who had played their high school football in Texas. With the success he'd had implementing Gus Malzahn's spread at Stephenville, Morris had sent Jevan Snead on to Texas before he transferred to Mississippi and transformed the Rebels from also-ran into bowl contender. Thanks to Snead's success at Ole Miss, coupled with Garrett Gilbert's dominance at Lake Travis – he'd earned Gatorade's National Player of the Year honors – the magazine paid Morris a visit. The article ran during the 2009 season, and it quoted Morris several times, including talking about the program he'd help grow and the line of quarterbacks he'd been coaching. Michael Brewer, he said of the then-junior quarterback, had emerged and had the ability to do what Gilbert did, if not more.

As Brewer quarterbacked the Cavaliers to their third straight state title, Morris began getting phone calls from colleges looking to upgrade their offenses. Even before the season they had been calling. Morris and his staff spent a week over the summer of 2009 in College Station showing then-Texas A&M coach Mike Sherman and his staff how to speed up their offense, and it worked. When the Aggies opened the 2009 season using Morris' tactics, they led the nation in offense and plays per game, getting off to an unbeaten start before fizzling late.

During the 2009 postseason, Morris recalled getting the first of many calls from a school and head coach interested in hiring him: Tulsa University and Todd Graham.

"I was contacted before Thanksgiving. I actually wound up telling Graham no on three occasions. He was persistent. Wouldn't let it die," Morris said. "We're getting ready to play Steele. He calls and says, 'We're looking at some of your players, and I want to fly down and look at them myself.'"

But that wasn't all. Graham wanted to meet with Morris at his Lake Travis office the Friday morning before the game.

"And presented the offer again to me that morning, but didn't want a yes or no, and that he'd call after the state championship," Morris said.

Morris and Carter had always planned for the day that the head coach might make the leap into the college ranks. Carter had played for Morris when he was in high school, and after joining his staff as an assistant had worked his way up into roles with more and more responsibility.

"He started giving me a lot more control at Stephenville of some of the things," Carter recalled. "He in a lot of ways was like an older brother or best friend to me, so I kind of had to make the transition from player-coach relationship with him since I played for him. When I got to Stephenville, I guess I kind of had to prove myself a little bit."

Morris didn't just oversee the program, he began to teach Carter the ins and outs of being the head coach. Seeing Carter's potential, he began imploring the young defensive coordinator to think like a head coach, to create a timeline for himself and a path that would get him ready to take that step.

"He started giving me more and more responsibility," Carter recalled, "and obviously he would talk to me about coming up with goals about, 'When you wanted to be a head coach and a timeline for that and how you wanted to do it.' But he also talked about you don't want your first head coaching job be your last, to be real careful. You watch the guys around you, and some of the guys who were with us in Bay City kind of jumped off the bandwagon early and taken some jobs and maybe …. I still talk to them. It didn't work out as well for them as it has worked out for some of us who stayed longer."

By the time the pair had reached Lake Travis, Morris had given Carter much of the responsibility that normally falls under the head coach's purview. The understanding was clear: if Morris left, he wanted Carter to succeed him.

"And he told me, 'I want you to be with me, be my assistant head coach until it's time for me to go to college, and then I want you to take over after me,'" Carter said. "So we always talked about that, obviously knowing that whenever he left he has zero control over who's going to be the next head coach once he's gone."

As Lake Travis' defensive coordinator, Carter did much more than make sure his defense could keep up with the offense that Morris and offensive coordinator Matt Green threw at him every day. By 2009, Carter said that much of the day-to-day football operation had become his responsibility, with Morris' blessing and encouragement.

"I kind of compared it to the king and the prime minister," Carter said. "He had to do a lot of the things with the boosters and with the parents and just meeting in all these different groups, dealing with all the things except running the program. He trusted me to handle the things about the everyday operation of the program, getting the off-season set up, dealing with the middle schools and getting them set up to make sure that they're doing the same things that we're doing at the high school level, taking care of the grades within the program, handling the discipline within the program, getting all that set up. Those were the things that I worked with. And then later on dealing with parents, if it wasn't a varsity offensive issue, then I pretty much dealt with it unless it needed to go to him. So all those things helped me get ready to be a head coach."

In a way, Carter even began practicing to hire assistant coaches when he and Morris first arrived from Stephenville.

"I can remember, too, when we were hiring coaches that first year, I spent a lot of time with Charlie Little, our principal, and I would always take over the candidates and do some of that," he said. "That was good experience too because Chad was doing tons of other things. Just having him trust me in that way and letting me get my feet wet, that was definitely very valuable for later on when I would be a head coach."

If he harbored any anxiety about taking over for his mentor, it came in an old sporting adage that rings true of coaches and superstars. When following someone exceptional, it is sometimes best to be one step removed.

"What's the old saying?" Carter joked. "You don't want to follow the guy who did it. You want to follow the guy who followed the guy that did it."

Examples are everywhere. Immediate success following a legend almost never comes easy. The Dallas Cowboys tried to replace Troy Aikman with Quincy Carter. Bill Cowher needed 15 years to win the Super Bowl following four-time winner Chuck Noll in Pittsburgh. The University of Texas needed five coaches, 35 years and Superman at quarterback to win a national championship after Darrell K. Royal retired.

But sometimes a better opportunity won't knock on your door, and that reality soon faced Carter. Morris took the opportunity to join Todd Graham's staff at Tulsa as co-offensive coordinator, running the passing attack. Tulsa's coach remembered his promise to call Morris. Graham called after the Cavaliers beat Longview.

"He calls after the state championship, and convinces me and Paula to at least come up and tell him no in person," Morris said.

But that's not the answer Graham got.

"I said yes," Morris paused. "It was tough. I loved my job, we loved Austin, and we had great friends."

But Graham's selling point to Morris had been clear: he had nothing left to accomplish in prep football. That did the trick.

"I needed to hear that," Morris said. "I'd achieved about all you could achieve at the high school level. I felt confident in the fact that the kids would be taken care of with Henry. I was able to rest easy on that alone. Would we have kept winning titles if I had stayed? I can't say we would. Henry was a good, new energy. The parameters were set, it was time to move on in my career, and they were in good hands."

Success would come quickly for Morris. He helped propel Tulsa into a top NCAA offense in one season, flirted with the vacated slot left by Graham when he moved on to Pittsburgh, and then deciding to move on to the Atlantic Coast Conference and Clemson as the Tigers' offensive coordinator, where he became one of the highest paid assistants in the country. Still, there had been uncertainty early on, late into those Oklahoma nights.

"I'll tell you this," Morris said. "Even after I took the Tulsa job, I was missing Lake Travis on some nights. There was just nothing like it."

Morris left behind a 32-0 record, a program at its peak, happy players and a content community. The last coach left in a hail of conflicted opinions and emotion. This one left on a wave of sad inevitability, saying good-bye to an appreciative community. Everyone understood, for all the right reasons, that the time had come for Morris to go.

In replacing Morris, Lake Travis did something it didn't do when Dicus left following the 2007 season: it looked within for its candidate. The chance to discuss the opportunity excited Carter, but he didn't allow himself to think beyond the interview.

"But I was excited about the opportunity to talk about being the next head coach here," he said. "In a lot of ways, I was fearful though because this had become such a high profile job. It was a pretty good secret in 2007 but it wasn't after 2009."

The opening, he felt, would draw the highest quality of candidates from across the state or beyond, and the school would certainly be within its rights to hire a coach with at least a little head coaching experience. But, no doubt based in part on Morris' recommendation along with what they'd seen in Carter in two years, the Lake Travis administration turned to Carter to keep the championship run going. The coach felt fortunate that the administration trusted him to keep the momentum going.

"So whenever they did name me to be the head coach, I remember being so excited and just so happy for entire staff too because there are so many things that go along with it," Carter said. "So many people are connected to the head coach. If they would have hired from the outside, it would affect a lot of families. I was excited about the opportunity to keep our staff together and kind of feel like we had a lot more good things to come."

Good things would come, but the 2010 season went from the frying pan to the fire in short measure for the new head coach.

16: One More Makes Four

For the second time, Lake Travis began defense of a state championship with a new head coach. But Lake Travis knew Hank Carter, and he knew the school, having coordinated the defense and built a strong rapport with the players under Chad Morris for the two previous championship seasons. The road to another – a fourth straight – title, wouldn't come easy, Carter knew, nor would he avoid growing pains as he followed his mentor as the school's head coach.

Just as he and Morris discovered while following Jeff Dicus in 2008, challenges abound in taking over a championship team. But inheriting a three-time state championship team proved more fun than taking over a Lake Travis program in the condition that Dicus had found it in 2003.

"At the end of the day, jobs like this one don't come open often," Carter had said. "There aren't a lot of jobs like this one. When you have an opportunity to come to a place like this, you have to take it and not worry about the timeline."

And so Carter moved into his mentor's office, beginning his head coaching career. Morris had trained Carter, advised him, and now the student had to take what he could from those experiences and develop his own identity. Carter wouldn't be another Morris. In fact, his expertise lay on the other side of the ball. He knew he wanted to continue the journey that he and Morris had started two years ago: to make Lake Travis known as a complete program, a team that could beat you any which way, not just an offensive juggernaut that outscored teams and won in spite of its defense.

The pair saw the potential when Morris first took the Lake Travis job, to take that first championship team and build it into a dynasty, much like Todd Dodge had done at Southlake Carroll in Dallas. The circumstances mirrored each other: single high school districts with a student population that trended toward affluent. Dodge's teams made their name on offense, sending quarterbacks Chase Daniel to Missouri and Greg McElroy to Alabama, respectively, and running back Tre Newton to Texas among the more prominent offensive standouts. Even Dodge's son Riley earned 5A

Offensive Player of the Year honors following the 2006 season that saw the Dragons win the state championship over Lake Travis' neighbor Westlake. But no one ever mentioned the Dragons' defense, and Carter noticed that. He wanted his dynasty to be different.

"What I think separates us from Southlake and some of those great other dynasties...I want people to say, 'They're not just a great offense,'" he said. "I want them to realize that these are great football players. They play both sides of the ball and special teams. That's my goal. I don't want to change anything about us being known for a high-powered offense. I want that. I want to win games and I don't care how we win them, but I would much rather win them 38-10 instead of 38-35 if I had my choices."

He reinforced that point quickly. While taking nothing away from the successful Katy High School teams, most recently the ones quarterbacked by future Cincinnati Bengal Andy Dalton, those Tigers emphasized defense, and the offenses couldn't be described as prolific by any stretch of the imagination.

"In hindsight, because I'm a defensive coach, I don't want people to think we're going to turn into Katy to where it's kind of all about defense and when they win it's 24-17," he said.

Toward the end of the 2009 season, the Cavaliers had begun to do just that. When opposing defenses slowed down Michael Brewer, Andy Erickson, Conner Floyd, Griffin Gilbert and Lake Travis' vaunted offense, Quinton Crow, Ian Lazarus and the defense flexed its collective muscle. Cibolo Steele saw that muscle first-hand in the regional championship game, when the defense stuffed University of Texas-bound running back Malcolm Brown in the waning moments of a 27-20 win. Carter said the defense's development showed up in the 24-17 win over Longview for the 2009 title.

"Even back in 2009, if you look at the Longview game," he said. "We didn't blow them out. We didn't score a lot of points, but to me the defense played a lot better than anyone would have given them credit for before that, and then going into 2010 most of the time we played well."

Armed with their new head coach, the Cavaliers took an experienced team into the 2010 season. They returned their quarterback (Brewer), top receivers (Floyd, an all-state selection as a junior, and Gilbert) and several key defensive players. Jonathan Roberts had become an anchor on the defensive line. Austin Williams stood ready to anchor the middle linebacker spot vacated by all-state selection Crow. Zach Streuling emerged as a heady junior whose older brother had started on the 2008 title team. And Colin Lagasse, who had earned all-state honors as a safety in 2009 after quarterbacking the freshman team in 2008, returned to give the Cavaliers a multi-dimensional threat. The new coach even had cause to joke with his predecessor about leaving him with a full cupboard.

"We really felt in 2010 we would have a chance to win it again," Carter said. "Most of our offensive skill players were coming back. We had our quarterback, we had Griffin [Gilbert] coming back, we had [Tanner] Gillette, we had [receiver Alex] Matthews, and some kids that have had some experience coming back. We had Taylor Doyle coming off of a leg injury in the state championship game. I felt good about it. I used to joke with Chad that if you're going to go, go when Michael is a senior so at least we'll have our quarterback. It just ended up working out that way."

***

The spring was virtually seamless, with everything on the field going largely to plan. Off the field, though, the program was rocked by tragedy.

Erickson's son, Brady Roy Erickson, was born January 25, 2010, a month after the state championship win over Longview. The spring was a whirlwind for the Rice University commit and his family, one that changed his life every single day.

"It changes everything, makes you think about everything differently," Erickson said. "It was amazing."

But Erickson lost his son in a tragic accident on May 9 that year, and a world of possibility seemed to come crashing down on him, Callie, and his entire family. A Christian, Erickson believes in the plan God has laid out for him, but still struggles with the lesson he was supposed to learn when his child was taken away.

"I still can't tell you. There's no one thing I think about," he said. "I've learned to appreciate life a lot more, to fulfill it and do the things I want to do. I think about it every day. It calmed me down a bit. I think I was a little wild before that, and it matured me a bit. If I had one good lesson it was to appreciate life more and know that not every day is promised to you."

The outpouring of support cemented Morris' idea of Lake Travis being a family, one that had been tested and responded.

"When he passed away, we just got smothered in love and support," Erickson said. "We had home cooked meals for two months straight."

And his coaches, now former, became much more than that.

"Coach Morris and his staff are so great. Coach Green was so great to me. All of the offensive coaches, I spent the most time with them, they all meant a lot to me. They were all there for me when it was tough, and I honestly don't think we could have won so much without them. They treated us like men."

The pain and shock united the community and revealed a support system that looked beyond its original hesitations with a teenage football star with

200

a son on the way.

"When he was actually born in January, the true colors really came out. Some people got closer to us and some people stayed away. You could just tell they felt awkward. But we still had so much support," Erickson said. "And when he was gone, everyone was there, regardless of how they felt before."

Football had become a great rallying point in Lake Travis, one that helped a family through a brutal hardship, less than a decade after the sport was all but an afterthought. It provided a somber spring atmosphere, but spirits on the football field couldn't have been stronger.

***

In looking for reasons to Lake Travis's success in recent years, injuries, specifically a lack thereof, proved key. Doyle's injury in the 2009 title game served as the first major injury the team had endured. The 2007 and 2008 teams had made it through their seasons without losing any key players, and the 2009 team had made it 15 games before facing a key injury. While Doyle, a Division I prospect who eventually accepted a scholarship offer from Texas, had worked hard throughout the spring and summer to rehab his leg after surgery, the Cavaliers developed some depth on the line in the spring. So when the fall arrived and Doyle returned healthy, the Cavaliers felt even better about their chances for another championship run.

Lake Travis entered the season riding a 46-game winning streak that dated back to the second week of the 2007 season. The early season schedule ranked among the state's toughest. Lake Travis would play 5A Westlake in a showdown at Royal-Memorial Stadium fresh off the Chaps' surprising run to the state 5A championship game and 4A district champions Hendrickson and Kerrville Tivy, which featured one of the state's most electric players in quarterback Johnny Manziel. The fourth non-district opponent, Aledo, entered the season as the defending 4A Division II champion. The Bearcats featured the state's most electric player, running back Johnathan Gray, who had earned player of the year honors as a sophomore in 2009.

"Going into the season, I was excited," Carter said. "I felt like we were going to do great things. I know we had a tough schedule. Westlake was a very good team like they always are, and we had some other teams on there: Aledo was very good, Tivy was very good, Hendrickson in the past has made some good runs."

Everything felt right. The Cavaliers were also coming off their first 7-on-7 state championship in July, edging out a talent-packed DeSoto team. Floyd earned tournament MVP honors and seemed to be on another level with Brewer. And the new coach was anything but new. With tons of momentum and familiarity, the tough schedule didn't seem nearly as daunting as it might have to any other team.

"I remember giving Coach Carter a pretty hard time because people would ask me if anything was different, but honestly it was the same," Brewer said. "Everything was the same. The only difference was practice ended on a good defensive play instead of a good offensive play."

After some solid preseason practices, the Cavaliers squared off with Westlake at Royal-Memorial Stadium. The game had generated tremendous buzz for a non-district football game on a warm Saturday night in August. The two schools from just west of Austin drew more than 30,000 fans to the stadium that night under the lights, and while the teams hadn't reached mid-season form, the game lived up to its billing.

The Chaps got off to a fast start and the Cavaliers appeared stuck in neutral. Receivers dropped balls and ran the wrong routes. The defense suffered uncharacteristic lapses against Westlake quarterback Lewis Guilbeau, who made his varsity debut that night. Lake Travis didn't remotely resemble the stream-rolling machine everyone expected to see. The game felt choppy, stagnant, and – most surprisingly of all – in doubt. Carter's head coaching debut had gotten off to a frustrating start, but a late first-half touchdown pass from Brewer to Gilbert sent Lake Travis into the locker room with some momentum, even if no one felt it trailing 15-10.

"Going into the season, we were probably overconfident. We'd just won the 7-on-7 tournament, beat a very talented DeSoto team. It gave us even more motivation," Brewer said. "Going into the Westlake game, everyone was excited. As soon as the game started, it was kind of like a reality check, you know?"

"That was one of those games where everything was going wrong for us," Carter said. "We couldn't catch a ball, we couldn't catch a punt. I can remember going in at halftime and just looking at our kids. They were probably wondering how I was going to react. I don't remember what the score was. We were down but we had a little momentum. They were probably thinking, 'What's he going to do here?' I just said, 'Are we okay now? Can we just go play football like we know how?' The kids were good. They were like, 'Yeah coach, we got 'em, we got 'em.'"

And then the second half kicked off and things went from bad to worse, so to speak. The Lake Travis defense had stiffened, but the offense still hadn't clicked on all cylinders. Finally, midway through the third quarter, Brewer and company kicked it into high gear. The Cavaliers were soon knocking on the door of the end zone, and they took the lead when Cameron Wrinkle scurried around the left end and dove into the end zone as Floyd blocked off the last potential tackler. The joy of the touchdown proved short-lived. Wrinkle landed on Floyd's leg as he held off the defender, and the star receiver's shin snapped.

"I can remember walking out – I couldn't see it because it was on the opposite side of the field – but I knew if he was laying down it was something pretty bad because he's such a tough kid," Carter recalled. "When I got out there [trainer] Ashley Bernard and Doc [Rick Schramm] just looked at me, and I knew it wasn't good. Didn't know exactly what it was, but I knew he was going to be out a while. I just thought, 'Are you kidding me, is this how we're going to start it all off?' We're losing, we just lost our best receiver and one of our emotional leaders for the whole team."

When key players get hurt, one of two things happen to teammates: they go into a shell and stop fighting, or they rally around their fallen leader. Though devastated by the injury, Carter couldn't have been more thrilled with how his team responded.

"But that kind of, in that game, gave us a spark," he said. "Teams are going to react one of two ways, it will either deflate them or they're going to get pissed and it will get them going and they'll go play. And that's what happened. Griffin played unbelievable. Michael played unbelievable. The defense figured it out and we came away with a win in that game, but still, losing Conner, that was tough. I wasn't as fired up about our chances of winning the state championship after we lost Conner Floyd."

"That was really hard, not just for me, but everybody," Brewer recalled. "Conner was a leader on the team, but also the go-to guy on offense. He'd emerged as that guy. But I remember, I looked at [the broken leg], didn't say anything, then jogged back to the sideline and signaled for the trainers. I yelled over to Conner, 'Don't worry, we got this.' And he just kind of rolled back over. He probably had the most pissed off look on his face I've ever seen. All of that happened, and then all this chatter started on the sideline about what we were going to do. But I just kept telling everyone we had to win this game without him, we still have to play this game. And the light switch went off. When he got hurt, you could see it in Westlake's eyes, like, 'Oh no, here they come.'"

And the receiving apprentice led the way. Gilbert, who had started as a sophomore for the 2009 championship team, wasted little time stepping into the leading role. His size – all 6-foot-5 and a half of him – made him virtually uncoverable, and time and time again he went over smaller Westlake defenders to make big catches. His height proved just one skill in his considerable arsenal. He showed surprising speed that allowed him to get deep into the secondary, and he also felt comfortable heading across the middle and absorbing contact from linebackers. Quiet by nature, a full glimpse of his potential hadn't really been seen. But he became a player possessed that night, celebrating loudly, and crying hard afterward for his fallen friend. As the season wore on, he'd emerge as the team's top threat while others developed into complimentary receivers who could also do damage. But as the team huddled around their fallen teammate on the turf of DKR, the junior understood what he needed to do.

"[Last year] when Conner went out it really set the tone for the rest of the season," Gilbert said. "It was such a struggle without him because he was such a big part of our offense. I knew that I had to step up as a player and try to replace him, and it's almost impossible to replace a player like Conner. That kind of set the tone for the rest of the season. The coaches said that I had to step up."

Gilbert earned MVP honors in the "Great Lake Showdown," collecting 10 receptions for 167 yards and a touchdown. The Cavaliers came back to win 32-21.

The path did not get easier. Lake Travis' other top receiver, Gillette, battled a nagging groin strain and couldn't play at 100 percent. The Cavaliers' depth at receiver helped ease the pain some as the team headed out to Hendrickson for week two. Again, the Cavaliers struggled against their own high standards, and Hendrickson's star running back Kenny Williams seemed to have his way with Carter's defense. For the second week in a row, nothing seemed to click the way it should.

"Our defense is playing awful against Hendrickson," he said. "We can't tackle. Every ball is bouncing. We cause a fumble and it bounces right to Kenny Williams and he takes it about 60 yards for a touchdown. We couldn't tackle the quarterback. We couldn't tackle the running back."

Yet through it all, including many moments of impending doom, the Cavaliers possessed a 34-24 lead in the closing minutes along with the ball and a chance to get one final first down to ice the game. Offensive coordinator Matt Green asked Brewer to run for it on fourth-and-short, trusting the senior to get the yards and avoid trouble. But trouble found Brewer.

"And Michael gets hit on his shoulder," Carter says. "He comes off with a horrible look on his face and I could tell he was really in pain. I'm thinking, 'Great, now what?' Trainers first told me it looked like he had a broken collar bone, and my heart just sunk. I was like, 'Are you kidding me?' It turned out that it wasn't a broken collar bone but it was a shoulder separation and it was his throwing arm. It was great news that he wasn't going to miss eight weeks but we knew he was going to miss several."

"The beginning of the season was tough. Conner goes down, then Tanner aggravates his groin. We play a talented Hendrickson team, a team we normally blow out, but they played us tough, and then I got hit," Brewer said. "They separated my AC joint, and I was immediately worried my collarbone was broken. I thought my season was over. I go to the hospital after the game and had to wait for three hours, and it was the longest three hours of my life. I thought my LT career might be over. But it was just a separated AC joint, out 4-6 weeks. For two weeks, I couldn't even throw a ball five yards. I rehabbed twice a day to try to get back."

If losing Floyd frustrated the team, seeing Brewer get hurt could have been devastating.

"Then you come back in the next game against Hendrickson, you lose Michael," Gilbert recalled. "Being the player that he is, it's almost impossible to replace him."

While the first two games hadn't been walks in the park, Carter knew that even with his team at full strength the next two against Aledo and Kerrville Tivy would be even tougher. And now he had to play those games short-handed.

"With Aledo and Tivy, those were going to be tough games without arguably your two best players on offense," he said.

As the Cavaliers prepped for Aledo, players struggled with the frustration of knowing they had to battle a reigning state champion without two major components.

"Just to know that you are missing two of your best players on offense, really two captains of the team, and you go into a game against another state championship caliber team, and you're not fully prepared and you're not facing a team healthy and you're going into the game wounded," Gilbert recalled.

While Carter knew Brewer wouldn't play, he held that news close to the vest leading up to the Aledo game. The Bearcats would be tough enough as defending state champions with the best offensive player in the state, and media attention had been through the roof. The Cavaliers were trying to protect a 48-game winning streak, and Carter didn't want to give the Bearcats any extra confidence heading into the game. Brewer dressed for the game took part in warm-ups before grabbing a seat behind the bench.

The Cavaliers faced a rather large dilemma. Throughout the injury-free run, the Cavaliers hadn't felt the need to ready a back-up quarterback for extended play, much less play against a championship-caliber team. The 2010 Cavaliers appeared so shallow at quarterback that Carter and Green had few options to get ready for Aledo in just one week. Senior Garrett Noak had quarterbacked the junior varsity in 2009 but hadn't taken a varsity snap. Sophomore Baker Mayfield was the junior varsity quarterback. But the Cavaliers had an ace in the hole, so to speak. Lagasse, who'd quarterbacked the freshman team in 2008 before becoming an all-state safety in 2009, had played a little offense. He took some snaps late in 2009 in a Wildcat package, and he still recalled some of the offense's base plays. He'd been promising enough as a freshman quarterback that Morris decided the previous year that he'd be the emergency quarterback should something serious happen to Brewer.

"Chad told him and told me that if anything happened to Michael, Colin would go in at quarterback," Dave Lagasse, Colin's father, said of the 2009 season. "Even if it was just to run Wildcat, he said they would want the ball in his hands."

Something serious had happened to Brewer, so Carter and Green looked back on Morris' emergency plan and decided to implement it. But as the team began prepping for Aledo, they decided to ease Lagasse into the role, as much as could be eased with so little time.

"I remember him coming home, I think on Tuesday, and he said they were working him a little at quarterback and he thought he'd run a little Wildcat," said Laurie Lagasse, Colin's mother. "And then Wednesday he came home and said they let him throw a little bit. And Thursday he came home and said, 'I'm starting in the game tomorrow, against Aledo.'"

Lagasse indeed started in the showdown of champions and took nearly all the snaps. Things could have been worse. Offensively, the Cavaliers looked like a team breaking in a new quarterback. With less than a week of practice at quarterback under his belt, the coaches kept the offensive plan simple.

"And so our play list was very small," the emergency quarterback said, looking back. "We did a lot hitches, nothing really. I think that kind of stopped us from doing a lot of things because it kind of became predictable."

Simple as the offense would be, Lagasse had to get himself on the field to run the plays. That proved more difficult that he originally thought. Nerves jumped up and grabbed him immediately prior to the opening possession.

"I almost threw up before the game," he recalled. "We were about to go out on the first series, and I had to take out my mouthpiece because I started choking on it. So I took a deep breath, and after the first and second play everything just kind of…the competitiveness kicked in and I kind of forgot about it."

While Lagasse and the offense gained confidence, the defense came out fired up to stop Aledo's Gray. For much of the first half, the Bearcats couldn't move the ball across a field left wet and a little soggy after an early week's rain.

Lake Travis fared slightly better. Lagasse engineered a drive that ended with a Stephen Pyle field goal for a lead, which grew when Lagasse scampered his way down the field to set up one of the Cavaliers' staple plays. Deep in Aledo territory, Lake Travis flexed the towering Gilbert wide and Lagasse threw him a lob in the corner of the end zone. Gilbert came down with it, and Lake Travis led 10-0.

Aledo's offense finally woke, and Matthew Bishop took the Bearcats down for a late touchdown to cut the Cavaliers' lead to 10-7. Late in the half, though, Lake Travis suffered another injury when starting center Casey Laney went down. Throughout the second half, the Cavaliers couldn't snap the ball back to Lagasse consistently, and possessions became two small steps forward and a large step back.

"We never really practiced another center so we moved our left tackle to center," Lagasse said. "So we had a new quarterback and a new center so pretty much everything went pretty bad."

The defense, though, kept plugging away, and Aledo didn't take the lead until Gray tried, tried and tried again to score from deep in Lake Travis territory. Late in the game, with Aledo needing a first down to run out the clock, the Cavaliers couldn't come up with a stop to get a final chance, though several players felt during the game they had chances to make key plays but didn't.

Lagasse recalled his frustration with one play in particular. Green had finally called a deep pass, one that Lagasse remembered from his time running the freshman team two years earlier. But the play broke down before it started.

"The one play me and Griffin always talk about...we did this freshman year all the time and it always worked every time for a touchdown," he said. "It was NCAA. It was where Griffin does a double move and goes deep down the middle and it worked every time. And it worked with Michael and Conner, they always did it. So this time they call it to me and Griffin, and that was the one play where the snap went between my legs 25 yards back. It's third down and I get a 20-something yard sack and it puts us in a bind. Our defense held them up, so all we needed was one score to really win that game, and it was just bad luck."

The score never came, and the Cavaliers saw their 48-game winning streak slip away.

"I think we still could have beaten them, just a couple of plays didn't go our way that would have made a stand," Lagasse said later. "I guess that kind of bothers me because I finally get a shot at quarterback and when I finally get a shot I lose the streak. Even with the guys we had, I still think we could have beaten Aledo to this day."

Lagasse's teammates felt the same way. Despite the injuries, they should have won the game. Streuling said he didn't play his best that night, and he pointed to one play in particular, when he jumped a pass route and had nothing but green grass in front of him for a touchdown, had he held on to the interception. He said recovering from that loss, which snapped the 48-game winning streak, proved to be one of the toughest things he endured at Lake Travis.

"There was one play that I felt might have changed the outcome," he said. "I personally felt that if I had played my best, we would have won, but everyone felt the same way."

Frustrated with the outcome, the Cavaliers reconciled themselves that they came together and fought until the end, shorthanded as they had been.

"The Aledo game was so frustrating," Brewer said. "The winning streak was coming to an end, we lost to a team at home that we were better than, everyone was hurt, and when we got in the locker room, everyone was so down. I was down, too, but I was a leader and I knew I had to say something. I said they didn't hand out trophies for winning streaks. They hand it out for championships. We can still do that."

And they'd found that they indeed had a quarterback who could step in while Brewer recovered.

"Colin did such a great job stepping up and playing his first game as a varsity quarterback," Gilbert recalled. "It just didn't pan out well for us. Things weren't going our way and Aledo is a team you can never look past."

The thing Carter remembers most about the game remains how the players and the fans responded in the moment.

"We lost that game to Aledo," he said. "I thought our kids played admirably well. They always exceed our expectations but they went out there and played their tails off, and we had a chance to win. We just couldn't make a couple of plays. Our defense had a chance to stop them and we didn't stop them. The thing I'll never forget is after that game, so many kids coming up to me saying, 'Coach, I'm so sorry.' Zach Streuling: 'I dropped an interception that would have been for a touchdown.' Griffin telling me he dropped a ball and he was upset. Linemen telling me they're sorry for this snap or this or that. I just tried to tell the kids that it's all right. We did our best and that was a heck of a team and we just didn't get them today. We're all right. I told them after it was all done that they had nothing to hang their head about. The sun will come up in the morning, we'll be just fine and we still have a lot of football to play."

Following every game, win or lose, the team gathers in front of the stands, players hold their helmets high and players, coaches and fans all join in as the band plays the school song. Carter said that occurrence proved more memorable than any other he's been a part of.

"I also remember after we broke, one of our traditions is when they play the school song to hold our helmets up to the crowd," he said. "Nobody had left. They gave our kids a standing ovation. It was incredible. I got a letter from one of our school board members the next Monday. It said he had never been more proud to be a Lake Travis Cavalier watching our kids compete against Aledo in a losing effort. That made me feel so good about the place where we are and how supportive everyone is."

Lake Travis' non-district gauntlet left the team no time to wallow in any misery at the demise of the 48-game winning streak. Kerrville Tivy, ranked fourth in the state, wanted nothing more than to get Lake Travis started on a losing streak. And as the game kicked off, that's exactly the direction the Cavaliers started heading.

"We started off terrible and ended up getting down 19-0," Carter recalled. "In the back of my mind I was just thinking how this [head coaching] isn't going exactly how I planned."

Losing his first game as quarterback and falling behind 19-0 in his second hadn't been Lagasse's dream scenario, either.

"I think that was a big thing for our whole season," Lagasse said. "Those three guys were gone and Tanner Gillette was out too. And following that loss, we were down by 19 in the first or second quarter, and so all odds just go against us. I would think that everyone would say, 'Well, we're just not the same, we'll just have to wait until we get our players back and then hopefully build up from there,' but then the fact that we just kept fighting."

The Cavaliers did indeed fight, and they clawed their way back into the game. Lagasse connected with Wrinkle and then Dannon Cavil on touchdown passes to close the gap to 19-16 at the half. After the fill-in quarterback scored on a short run, he found Gilbert twice for second half scores to erase a 33-23 deficit and give his team its first lead of the game in the fourth quarter at 37-33. And for all he did offensively, it turned out to be Lagasse's play on defense that clinched the come-from-behind win.

Coaches hurried Lagasse onto the field late in the game. Tivy quarterback Manziel, dubbed "Brett Favre on a motorcycle" by Carter, had passed for 215 yards and rushed for an astonishing 273 when he came to the line for a fourth down play deep in Lake Travis territory that would clearly decide the outcome. He dropped back to pass, scrambled a bit to his right, and running out of time, threw a prayer into the end zone. There to make the play stood none other than Lagasse, who intercepted it to preserve the win.

"That was fun, though," Lagasse recalled. "They told me and I just kind of ran on the field so I'm just reacting as it goes. I didn't really think about it until after the game. Really, I wasn't even the one doing all the work on defense. They were doing it, stopping Manziel. And I get in there and the ball goes right to me and I intercept it. I almost feel sorry because someone else should have gotten that, someone like Zach Streuling, who'd been fighting the whole game for it. But the second half started off with me throwing an interception on the first drive, and then we came back from that."

Lagasse's play, and the confidence the team gained from winning the tight game, proved to be a spark.

"But we found a way to win it," Carter said. "Colin intercepts the ball in the end zone down there while they're trying to come back and beat us and we got on a roll for a while."

Roll they did. Lake Travis won its first five district games, getting Brewer back and healthy in the process, by an average score of 49-4. Twice the Cavaliers topped the 60-point mark and the defense shut out Dripping Springs, Marble Falls and Vista Ridge. Heading into the regular-season finale, at home against a tough Cedar Park team, Lake Travis looked more like, well, Lake Travis.

Until kickoff.

"You want to talk about another frustrating game, talk about Cedar Park," Brewer said. "I was sick as a dog before that game, getting IV's all day before it because I was so dehydrated. And we just did everything wrong. Bad News Bears. Fumbles, penalties, interceptions."

Playing on television on a Thursday night instead of Friday, the Cavaliers never got rolling. They mostly idled in the mud and watched an inspired Timberwolves team run circles around them. Led by district MVP Brian Hogan and a quartet of offensive linemen who'd earn scholarships to FBS schools, Cedar Park started quickly. And if the Timberwolves needed help, Lake Travis obliged. The Cavaliers suffered four first-half turnovers and spotted Cedar Park an unthinkable 28-0 lead.

"It was a short week, which is tough anytime but [especially] when you're preparing for Cedar Park and all the things they do offensively and defensively," Carter said, without making excuses. "They took it to us. I think we turned the ball over five times. Defense did not do a good job stopping them. I mean it was a team effort of bad football. They whipped our tails no matter how you look at it."

The players agreed with Carter's assessment.

"Last year we picked a bad time to have a bad game for all of us, but that was last year," Gilbert said following the 2011 season.

Despite their early trouble, when Brewer connected with Gilbert in the third quarter, the Cavaliers had climbed within 28-21 and had then had the ball again, looking to score. But an underthrown pass led to an interception in the end zone, and Cedar Park eventually left Lake Travis with a 35-21 win, an undefeated record and the District 25-4A championship. Like the Aledo loss earlier in the season, the loss snapped a 48-game district winning streak as well as a six-year streak of district titles.

"And we came back and almost won, but didn't," Brewer said. "We'd already bought district championship shirts, and had to throw them away. But again, it was about a different trophy. We could still win that one."

Streuling said the two losses marked the toughest moments in his Lake Travis career.

"I was here when the streak snapped," he said of the Aledo loss. "That was a rough week I guess. It was tough knowing that all of the guys before you had worked so hard to build something, and it all comes crashing down. You had to change your mindset completely. We had to realize that it didn't really matter in the long run. And then the second game, against Cedar Park, it wasn't fun at all. At our own place, again, and losing the district championship for the first time in seven years or something."

The loss forced Streuling and his teammates into a new mindset. Refocusing following such a thorough defeat proved difficult.

"The week that followed that was probably the toughest time in my coaching career," Carter said. "We're getting ready to play McCallum and McCallum on film was not very impressive. Our juniors and our seniors were butting heads a little bit. Obviously everyone was upset because we'd lost and we're just not used to losing. We had a terrible practice week for McCallum, and I can't remember us having another bad practice week but we did that week."

Coaches often say teams play like they practice, and unfortunately for Lake Travis, the Cavaliers played liked they practiced against McCallum. The Knights jumped out to a 10-0 lead behind surprising running from quarterback Colton Lusson.

Offensively, the Cavaliers struggled. Lagasse had moved primarily to offense upon Brewer's return following the emergence of safety Dane Balasz. The new receiver/running back noticed that the Knights chose to mimic Cedar Park's defensive philosophy and play man-to-man coverage on the Cavalier receivers rather than a softer zone. The high risk defense had worked early.

"McCallum went man on us, and most teams don't do that," Lagasse said. "We're used to zones opening up, finding the holes and we just pick everyone apart. This time, all the DBs were just lined up on our receivers and our receivers weren't getting off of it and Michael was throwing too tight to where they were just knocking things down."

Brewer struggled to find consistent accuracy, but he hit his spots enough to find Gilbert and Turney Maurer for second quarter touchdowns to give his team a 14-10 halftime lead. The Cavaliers gave the lead back in the third quarter when the Knights intercepted Brewer twice, converting one into a Michael Sorrells touchdown run. Trailing 17-14, Brewer responded with his legs, breaking off a 41-yard run and a six-yard scamper to reclaim the lead. Following another McCallum field goal, the Cavaliers extended the lead to 28-20 when Brewer found Gillette for a 12-yard score.

McCallum didn't go quietly into the November night, though. Playing on their home field at historic House Park in downtown Austin, the Knights marched 70 yards, reaching the Lake Travis three-yard line. But on fourth-and-goal from that spot, Sorrells ran right, got strung out and then wrestled down by Omar Duke-Tinson and Roberts for a one-yard loss. Brewer took a knee twice to kill the clock and Lake Travis escaped an upset of epic proportions. Brewer led the Cavaliers with his rushing rather than his passing, gaining 126 yards with his legs while completing just five passes for just 34 yards – both career lows – but three touchdowns.

"We nearly lose the ball game," Carter said. "Our defensive tackle Jonathan Roberts gets hurt. We played most of the game without two of our starting defensive players. We fumbled the first snap, threw three interceptions I think. We found a way to win that even though we had played terrible. And it seemed like after that, we calmed down."

Looking back, Lagasse said the back-to-back games with Cedar Park and McCallum helped steel the Cavaliers' resolve.

"It was good that we played those two teams early on," he said. "They were the two teams who were most physical against our offense. They played hard and were athletic, so it was kind of a wake-up call to show that we weren't just going to get by teams. Once we get into the playoffs, that's when the real good teams come out and they are going for us every week. I was glad to get out of it, but because it was that close it definitely taught us something and I think from then on everyone took things a lot more seriously and gave it all they had."

The Cavaliers could hardly breathe easy after vanquishing the Knights. Kerrville Tivy had won seven straight games following its lone loss at Lake Travis in the season's fourth week, and the Antlers wanted revenge. The fact that Brewer and Manziel, two of the best quarterback recruits in the 2011 class, would finally square off only added to the hype.

Carter remained wary, given that the Antlers remained ranked in the state's top 10 and took the field angry. Add to that the old football adage that it's hard to beat the same team twice in a season. In fact, Carter's past experience didn't give him loads of confidence facing that scenario.

"We played Tivy again, which I wasn't looking forward to," he said. "It's so hard to beat somebody twice. In my past experience at Stephenville, we had not done well [in that situation]. We had played Wichita Falls Rider, twice we had played them in the regular season and beaten them and twice we played them again in the playoffs and they beat us, so I'm trying to shake that."

The Cavaliers also wanted to shake the slow start they managed in the first meeting. With a healthy Brewer motivated from the previous week's sub-par performance, the Cavaliers didn't struggle. Facing a dual-threat quarterback who had produced more than 400 yards in the first meeting, Brewer threw down the gauntlet at Manziel, and by all rights out-Manzieled him.

When all was said and done following a 48-42 win, Brewer had put together his best game of the season, and perhaps of his career. He rushed for 192 yards and two scores on 26 carries and passed for another 249 yards and two scores without an interception after throwing six in his two previous games.

"There was all this talk, and Johnny and I are friends so there were no hard feelings, but it was just about how lucky we were against Tivy the first time. We weren't clicking, this was Tivy's time, and they've got the most exciting player in the state, he does it all. We all heard it," Brewer said. "That whole week of practice was the first time the coaches were really OK with me running around and unhinging and throwing. I ran around a lot in the first game against McCallum. In the second game, I had the mindset that I had to do anything I could. It was time to run the offense like I never had before. It was pick your poison because we were clicking on all cylinders. Everyone played well."

Lake Travis led by two touchdowns throughout the first half, but when Tivy scored in the final minute of the half, the lead shrunk to 35-28. But on the ensuing kickoff, the Cavaliers showed their versatility when Wrinkle fielded the ball in his end zone and returned it 100 yards for a touchdown to stretch the lead back to 42-28. One former player in the stands said the ways Lake Travis could beat teams amazed him.

"I went to the playoff game at Tivy, when they played Manziel," said Greg Wiggins, who graduated in 2000. "They ran back two kickoffs – one was nullified, but they ran back a second kickoff, and these are white kids that are athletic, fast, but it just seemed like everyone was on the same page. It's a totally different world."

With the win, the Cavaliers stood only one-third of the way toward their goal of the fourth straight title, but they'd gotten over one of the biggest roadblocks. Games against teams from District 27-4A have been the tougher playoff games over the years. The Cavaliers have had to go to the wire to beat Cibolo Steele twice, Alamo Heights and now Tivy. Games against teams from the Rio Grande Valley or Corpus Christi have proven much easier. And that proved true again with a regional semifinal win over Victoria East. The Cavaliers started fast and cruised to a 59-28 win, leading 35-7 at the half and 49-14 after three quarters.

The highlight of the game, though, had been Floyd's incredible return from the broken leg he suffered just 12 weeks before. And he and Brewer connected on the first pass they could, moments after Floyd stepped onto the field again for the first time – to a standing ovation that echoed throughout the Alamodome. He had fought tears before the district finale, a game he

213

thought he could make it back for. He had dressed out before the Tivy game, knowing he'd never see the field in the shootout. But his moment finally came in San Antonio, and there was still time left for him to make an impact.

"I was just extremely happy for him. Everything he'd been through, for him to finally get back out there. It was just awesome," Brewer said. "I was hoping they'd give us a chance to get it to him, it was a roll-out to a right, and he ran a corner route, and I saw the cornerback sitting on Tanner, so I knew Conner was open, but I couldn't see him because I was about to get the crap knocked out of me. But it goes back to knowing where he is because he's been my friend and teammate for so long. I got smacked, but he went down and made a diving catch and the crowd went crazy. It showed how hard work paid off. Nobody thought he'd be back ever at one point, and he was back that season."

The easy and inspired win, coupled with Cedar Park's easy win over Weslaco East, set up a rematch with more at stake than the previous month's battle for the district title. Cedar Park entered the Region IV championship game ranked third in the state having beaten Lake Travis already. Many considered them the favorite not only to win again but to go on and win the state title. And maybe most impressive of all: they'd found a way to get inside the Cavaliers' heads.

"They did things on defense that no team has ever done to us before," Brewer said. "They were extremely talented and well-coached. It's extremely hard to play against. Throw in that offensive line and you knew you were in trouble because they could run the heck out of the ball."

But it wasn't the same Cedar Park team that had defeated Lake Travis four weeks earlier. In their second-round playoff win over Smithson Valley, Hogan injured his knee and missed the rest of the season. The Timberwolves, like Lake Travis, dominated a team from the valley to advance, but Hogan's absence loomed large in the showdown of District 25-4A rivals on a glorious Saturday afternoon at Royal-Memorial Stadium.

"Cedar Park was without their quarterback, which was a tough break for them," Carter recalled.

The Timberwolves definitely missed their dynamic leader. Without him, the run-first Wolves became run-at-all-costs, and early on, behind their massive offensive line, the strategy worked. They ground their way to a 10-0 lead, and their defense continued to give Lake Travis' offense fits. Later, Carter detailed what exactly gives his team trouble with Cedar Park.

"They are very physical on their defensive and offensive lines," he said. "They give us problems when we're on offense because they've been more physical than us up front, and they play tight man coverage."

To beat the tight coverage, Carter said, the quarterback must throw into some tight spots and receivers must make plays. The Timberwolves bet that, more often than not, a high school quarterback won't be able to hit his spots consistently, and they pounce on mistakes, as they did in the teams' first match-up that season.

"When we played them in 2009 they were running that same defense and we beat the dog out of them," Carter recalled. "We made some tough catches in some tight windows which is what you have to do against man coverage. And since then we haven't done a lot of that."

The Cavaliers' struggles with the Timberwolves continued early on, but they somehow found a spark thanks to a win in the field-position battle. After a drive stalled, the Cavaliers punted and pinned the Timberwolves deep. The defense stepped up and forced Cedar Park to punt from its own end zone. Wrinkle fielded the punt on the Cedar Park side of midfield, broke a tackle, made a cut and finally broke free for a touchdown. Two plays into Cedar Park's next possession, the Lake Travis defense forced a fumble, and Michael Pojman swept around right end for a touchdown on the ensuing snap, giving the Cavaliers a 14-10 lead at the break.

"We didn't play well in the quarterfinal game against them offensively but got the special teams touchdown by Cameron Wrinkle again," Carter recalled.

In the second half, Cedar Park continued to make life tough on Brewer, forcing two more interceptions. After driving for a touchdown to take a 17-14 lead, Cedar Park had a chance for some separation after intercepting Brewer. The Timberwolves marched methodically down field and reached the Lake Travis six-yard line when coach Chris Ross tried something uncharacteristic. Having run the ball with success, the coach felt deception would work, so he had backup quarterback Alex Curl fake a run and try to throw for an insurance touchdown midway through the third quarter. The deception didn't work, though. Streuling, who 11 weeks earlier blamed himself for dropping an interception that could have been a touchdown against Aledo, came up big, intercepting Curl's pass at the goal line and bringing it all the way back.

A penalty nullified the touchdown return, but the offense made the penalty moot. Brewer connected with Gilbert for a long gain and then carried the ball for the final three yards and a touchdown on a quick, four-play drive. Leading 21-17, the Cavaliers watched Cedar Park mount another third quarter drive, but the defense again stiffened and allowed only a field goal and clung to a 21-20 lead entering the fourth quarter.

The teams battled back and forth as if the state title lay in the balance throughout the final quarter, with Cedar Park delivering heavy blows and Lake Travis covering up, holding on for dear life. The Cavaliers survived another Brewer interception. The Timberwolves breathed a sigh of relief when safety Ryan Roberts not only caught Colin Lagasse after he'd broken free but forced a fumble that a teammate recovered. With four minutes left, Cedar Park had a chance, and began a march into the wind against a Lake Travis defense that had spent most of the day on the field.

The Timberwolves marched from deep within their territory across midfield methodically. Lake Travis' defense made a key stop, and finally Cedar Park faced a tough decision on fourth down from the Cavaliers' 30-yard line. They needed eight yards for a first down, and a field goal into the wind from 47 yards would be no gimme. Faced with the same choice that Highland Park coach Randy Allen had to make three Decembers earlier on a windy championship Saturday in Waco, Ross made the only real choice he could, to try for the first down. Curl dropped back to pass, and Dylan Bittles got away from his blocker, working a stunt with teammate Shaq Marable, to make the biggest sack of his life.

"We ended up beating them, but offensively we didn't play well," Carter said later. "Defensively I was proud of how we played. We played pretty good considering they had the ball on our side of the field a lot. We came up with the big play, Dylan Bittles getting the sack on fourth and eight. Coach Ross decided to go for it instead of kicking a really long field goal into the wind."

Streuling, looking back on the game a year later, said the moment the defense sealed that win is something he'll never forget.

"That was the best feeling ever with the one point win," he said. "Sitting on the sideline, our defense had over 80 plays that game, so we were exhausted. Knowing that we'd come out and done everything that we could to win, that was one of the best feelings ever."

Lagasse had played plenty of offense and defense that afternoon.

"I don't think anyone really started breathing until that last play went off and Dylan Bittles came up with the sack in the backfield," he said. "I think that's when everyone could just relax. There was not one point in that game where people weren't totally focused. It was intense the entire time, very nerve-wracking. They had beaten us once – killed us – so not everyone has that same confidence heading in, that, 'We're Lake Travis, we're going to get out of this one,' because we didn't get out of the last Cedar Park one. Everyone was trying as hard as they could."

Like many others around the state, Carter believed that the Cavaliers wouldn't face a tougher test than the one they'd just survived as they continued on their championship quest.

"I really felt like if we beat Cedar Park we were going to win the state championship," he said. "I knew the teams that were left, and even though they were very good teams I thought the way we matched up, we matched up better with the rest of those teams than we did with Cedar Park."

His players agreed. Getting over the Cedar Park hurdle, avenging the loss a month earlier, proved a huge confidence booster.

"We knew that Cedar Park was a state championship caliber football team, and we knew that if we lost that game, Cedar Park was going to go on and win the state championship," Gilbert said. "There was really no team that was going to stop them unless it was us. Being a rival team that they are, we've always had grudge matches with them, and they took our district championship from us. All these stats, these thoughts, just piled up. Knowing that this was really the game of the century, knowing that we have to take care of business or we're not going to accomplish our goal which is winning the state championship. So going out and beating them by one point was really an amazing feeling because we knew if we could win that game we'd go on and win state because there wasn't another team that could stop us. It was real satisfying in a way, and we were relieved to know that we could accomplish our goal if we just kept taking care of business."

"It's so hard to not turn the ball over, not shoot yourself in the foot when you play a team like that," Brewer said later. "Both teams played a little sloppy, but the better team won. And we went on to prove it in the state championship game."

But Cedar Park had left a lasting mark on Brewer that went beyond impressions. He had dinged his shoulder again, and heading into the state semifinal, he feared the damage might be serious.

"In the Cedar Park game, we ran a stretch play where I shuffled and handed it off to the left, and the exchange fumbled and I dove for it on my right arm and someone jumped right on my shoulder where it had separated. Two hours after the game, I could hardly pick my arm up," Brewer said. "I didn't lift over the weekend. I came in for practice on Monday, and started throwing. After about 10, I just turned to Coach Carter and told him something was wrong with my shoulder. I just couldn't throw. I thought it was bad. I thought I'd torn my labrum because my symptoms were similar to what Garrett went through. But I had bruised my rotator cuff and popped my bursa sac and had a partially separated shoulder. I didn't throw one pass all week. We went out in the Friendswood game and it did not go super well, our offense was average, but the defense was amazing. So we were fine."

After stopping the Timberwolves, the Cavaliers' defense exuded confidence, and that carried over into the next week. In the state semifinals at Kyle Field, Lake Travis' defense decimated traditionally powerful Friendswood in a 24-3 win. The Cavaliers intercepted Mustangs' quarterback Pete Maetzold four times, two by Bryan Kribbs. Brewer connected with Floyd, getting stronger since his return, for the go-ahead touchdown.

"It was awesome. I'm so happy for Conner," Brewer said after the game.

"He worked his tail off just to get back in the mix and play again. For him to do what he's doing now, and give us mismatches, it's really incredible. It's a credit to him, our trainers and everyone involved. There were some big smiles on our faces after that touchdown."

"Defense, boy, we played lights out, we played great," Carter recalled. "I think we held them to three points, and that probably hadn't happened [to them] in five years because Friendswood's always been good on offense."

That set the stage for another trip to the title game. Lake Travis had been a creature of habit: all four state semifinal games had been played at Texas A&M's Kyle Field, and all three title games had been played at Baylor's Floyd Casey Stadium, but something would have to give in 2010, though, as the UIL had consolidated all title games at Cowboys Stadium in Arlington. Superstition, though, became the furthest thing from anyone's mind as Lake Travis began planning for powerful Denton Ryan.

Carter recalls looking at film of Denton Ryan and its standout defense led by state MVP Mario Edwards and all-state linebacker Alex De La Torre. Carter also remembered his familiarity with Ryan coach Joey Florence, who had lost to Carter when he was Morris' defensive coordinator at Bay City in the 2002 state championship game.

"We had a chance to face Coach Florence when I was in Bay City my second year in coaching and we beat them in the state championship game," he recalled. "Looking on tape, looking at what Denton Ryan did defensively, I felt like if we played them we would have a chance to score some points because of how we'd match up with them. Offensively, they'd lost a great quarterback and a great receiver the year before, so they really hung their hat on defense. We felt like if we could score early and we could hold their offense, we could try to tire them out by using some tempo and things like that and we'd have a great chance to win the game. And it worked out."

There were a few moments again in the week leading up to the championship game when Brewer's arm put a scare into him and the rest of the team, but when game day arrived, his shoulder cooperated, avoiding the need for an unhealthy medical decision.

"There was a point where I thought I was going to play no matter what, I was going to shoot it up if it hurt, but that was the last thing we wanted to do," Brewer said. "Coach Carter and my dad were saying no way are you shooting up, but I wanted the final say, and I didn't want to miss the game. But it felt good enough where I didn't need anything. At the same time, I felt like if I had just gotten hit the wrong way, it would be over. When the game started, though, I didn't hold back. It was the last game I was ever going to play as a Cavalier and I was going to make the most of it, hurt shoulder or not."

The Cavaliers nearly scored on the opening kickoff. Cavil fielded the kick and broke free but somehow fumbled the ball at the Ryan 30-yard line. The mistake ensured that he wouldn't see the field again, but the Cavalier defense rose to the immediate challenge and forced the first of many Ryan punts.

With the ball, the Cavaliers went to work. Offensively, the Cavaliers wanted to do two things: attack the perimeter to get Ryan's big defenders moving on every play, and they wanted to send a message to Edwards that his size, his ability and his reputation didn't intimidate them. The Cavaliers rarely script their plays, but all week the plan for the first play called for Gilbert, a wide receiver in Lake Travis' scheme who projected as a college tight end, to crack down and throw a wham block on Edwards. The block would free up a lane for Lagasse, who'd be headed that way on a speed sweep.

"To do something unexpected and surprise Mario Edwards, we had Griffin motion in from outside and try to hit him from the side, kind of crack-back on him so he'd be hesitant off the line and be looking for Griffin," Lagasse said of the opening call.

Sometimes, though, plays don't come off as called. Gilbert admitted, reluctantly, that he never got a clean shot at Edwards on the play.

"I had to go block Mario Edwards," Gilbert said later. "Heck, during the whole week I was pumped up about it. I knew that I had to motion down and try to knock him out, but unfortunately he had a different assignment on his play. He was gutting and so he ran away from me, so I didn't get to hit him hard at all. I just kind of pushed him in the back."

The little push turned out to be enough. Lagasse popped outside and gained 17 yards, and the Cavaliers began their opening march. Brewer ran for a pair of first-half touchdowns, including one where he somersaulted over a tackler, captured in an award-winning photo by freelance photographer Erich Schlegel, who was shooting the game for the *Lake Travis View*, and into the end zone for the game's first score. At the half, Lake Travis led 17-0 and had not surrendered a first down.

Later, Gilbert reflected on the importance of Brewer's acrobatic score.

"Michael always talks about – and any high school kid will tell you – that it's an absolute dream to go dive into the end zone in the state championship," Gilbert said. "And especially the way that he did, going in on a somersault. It was a sight to see and there was so much excitement, being on the first drive of the game, to go in and score against Denton Ryan, such a hard defense, obviously. But it was such a memorable play because he just makes plays and set the tone for the rest of the game. It shows the type of players that we have, the type of leadership he had on the field and off the field."

With the early lead and a defense that completely dominated Ryan's offense, the Cavaliers worked their offensive plan to perfection. They lined up quickly and ran plays from sideline to sideline. By the third quarter, the Raiders appeared gassed, Edwards especially.

"We kind of owe that to our coaches and having the high-tempo offense that we do," Gilbert said. "That's always and advantage for us to go into each game with the high-tempo offense and just getting teams worn out. Ryan wasn't used to having each play going back-to-back-to-back-to-back. They were used to having some rest between plays, but we knew if we could keep that going that we'd wear out their good players and big plays would happen. And that's exactly what did. We kind of neutralized their players and set the tone for the rest of the game by having the high-tempo offense that we did."

Gilbert did get his chance to line up against Edwards during the game, and even as a junior he knew enough to rely on help from tackles Taylor Doyle and Nick Magnella. Though Edwards eventually got a sack, the Cavaliers minimized his impact.

"There were a couple of plays where I got to line up at tight end and I got to block him," Gilbert recalled. "Heck, I had help from the offensive linemen. I told them, 'I've got this guy, you've got to help me out a little.' He's a load. I had all the confidence in the world that I could take care of my job, and the coaches have coached us well enough that if we just take care of our jobs, they know we can get the job done."

For his part, Magnella made himself a championship hero for a second year in a row. He had filled in when Doyle went down in the 2009 title game, and now he held Edwards at bay with the most important assignment on the offensive line.

"He's one of the most amazing defensive ends I've ever played against," Magnella said after the game. "The week's preparation was about finding the biggest guy and having him come full force at me. I watched tons of film, studied all his moves and I think it helped me."

Ryan made things interesting briefly in the third quarter. Going for it early in the quarter on fourth down at their own 28, Kaylon Alexander broke free and scored on a 72-yard touchdown run, and the Raiders recovered the ensuing onside kick. They embarked on their first and only extended drive of the game but stalled in field goal range. The try missed, and the Cavaliers allowed nothing else defensively.

The Cavaliers sacked Ryan quarterback Nash Knight six times, two from Marable and one each by Bittles, Roberts, Jude Jeffress and Corbin Crow. Streuling, Bittles and defensive MVP Williams each made 11 tackles and the defense allowed only six first downs and 210 yards, 72 coming on one play.

When Lagasse scored in the fourth quarter, the countdown to the school's fourth straight title – and Carter's first – began.

"There was some relief there," Carter said as he looked back on the win more than a year later. "One thing we dealt with in Stephenville was the old Art Briles jinx. After he left, they haven't won a state championship. So we got that off our backs [here]. It was gratifying for the coaches, but it's about the kids, and we just want to make sure that we repay them for all their hard work and make sure we did our job to the best of our abilities. So we were overjoyed and relieved."

Gilbert echoed his coach's sentiments about relief.

"A state championship is so much relief that you actually accomplished your goal, that you did what you were supposed to do," he said later.

If the Cavaliers didn't appear elated following the win over Ryan, they point back to the emotional, grueling win over Cedar Park. That win, they said, brought them more joy than the title win, which served more as an affirmation of their success.

"I definitely think [beating Cedar Park] felt better [than beating Ryan for the title] because we didn't even know if we were going to make it to the next round," Lagasse said later. "Against Ryan, we were winning at the half and we kind of knew we were going to win state."

"As a junior, winning [the Cedar Park] game felt better than winning the state title," Streuling said.

Defensively, the leaders looked back at the game as merely the continuation of a journey that began following the school's first title in 2007, when defense took a back seat to the offense.

"I think over the last few years...I remember when my brother [Michael] was a senior he was always complaining that the defense didn't get any recognition," Streuling said following the 2011 season. "His senior year was the second year they won. They didn't get anything. But it's been five years now, so every year we've gotten a little more recognition. We've all played better. Offensively, the first year they scored so many points, but last year they struggled – not this year but in 2010 – they struggled a little because of injuries. I think our defense has always been kind of good, except the focus hasn't been on it since the offense has been amazing. But now our defense has stepped up and I think we'll continue to."

Immediately following the game, Brewer said things didn't get to feel any better, especially given what the Cavaliers had to overcome throughout the season.

"I don't think you could ask for anything more," Brewer, the game's offensive MVP, said. "For us to be right here with another state championship, after all the adversity we've had to come through, it's awesome. It seemed like every single week a new player would step up. We've been a big family that relies on each other. I'll never forget any of this."

Brewer, despite missing the four games with the shoulder injury, still led the team in rushing with 743 yards on 135 tries including 12 touchdowns. He also threw for 2,865 yards and 26 touchdowns, impressive on their own, but not compared to the 4,450 yards and 43 touchdowns he amassed as a junior.

His favorite and most reliable target proved to be Gilbert, who doubled his production from 2009. He caught 74 passes for 1,199 yards and 12 touchdowns, up from 522 yards and six touchdowns as a sophomore. After a 1,300-yard season as a junior, Floyd overcame the devastating injury in the opener to catch 10 balls, all but three of them in the postseason. He'd earned a scholarship to Tulsa University before the season, and Todd Graham honored it despite the early injury.

And Lagasse, the ultimate team player, picked up the pieces and carried the team along the way when he had to, when no one else could.

"He was great. The thing about him is we could put him at any position. He did it all," Brewer said of the versatile junior. "And it made him smarter and smarter as time went on."

With the title win, Lake Travis became the first team at the 4A classification or higher to win four straight state titles. The win was also the Cavaliers' 24th consecutive in the postseason, one shy of a record held by Celina. Celina (2A) and Sealy (3A) are the only other schools to win four consecutive state 11-man titles. Fort Hancock won four straight 6-man championships.

While Carter felt relief following the win, he also realized that the relief didn't come from the actual winning of the game. It came at the end of a process where Carter and his staff got the ultimate validation for themselves and the players.

"I want to make sure our coaching staff is doing everything we can for our kids to give them the best chance to succeed," he said. "And so, I felt like we had a team good enough to win a state championship, so after we won it I was relieved because I felt like we did our job as coaches. We put our kids in position where they could go play and go do it, to fulfill their potential. That's what I've told the coaches all the time. Hey, we're going to have different kinds of kids. Our job is to teach them how to be a man. Their parents do a great job, but boy, we've got them a lot so let's see if we can continue on that line. And let's make sure we put them in position to succeed because we've got great kids that do what we ask them to do."

With title number four behind them, both Carter and the returning players started on the next chapter: accomplishing something no team had ever done. And so the "Drive for Five" took shape.

17: Drive for Five

As Lake Travis began preparing for its "Drive for Five" following a surprisingly difficult, injury-marred 2010 season, Hank Carter and his fellow coaches must have thought seasons couldn't get any tougher than the one they'd just survived. In Carter's first year at the helm, Lake Travis overcame early season injuries to the star receiver, the star quarterback and the starting center in successive weeks to gut out a record-tying fourth consecutive championship. They'd have some expected holes to fill in 2011: who would replace the star receiver, the star quarterback and the starting center, not to mention three other offensive linemen and a handful of key defenders including middle linebacker Austin Williams, who'd earned MVP honors in the state championship game.

But if defense wins championships, offense still drives ticket sales, and the Cavaliers had two key offensive questions to answer before spring practice began. First, who would replace the graduated Michael Brewer at quarterback? Second, who would replace Matt Green, the offensive coordinator who resigned after the season? Green had come to Lake Travis from Stephenville with Carter under Chad Morris as offensive coordinator and had taken over the play-calling responsibility when Morris left for Tulsa following the 2009 season.

Entering his second season as head coach, Carter began looking across the state for someone who could not only keep Lake Travis' offensive momentum going, but expand on it. His search brought him to a familiar albeit unexpected face. David Collins had just completed a successful season calling plays at Garland High School, and he came across Lake Travis' posting for an offensive coordinator. So Collins called Carter.

"We worked at the same little bar and grill Mexican food restaurant in college there on Cedar Creek Lake [in Tyler]," Carter recalled. "He actually married a girl from my hometown, so I had known him. That being said, we didn't keep in touch much over the course of the years. I'd see him at convention every now and then."

Carter didn't know what to think. He hoped that this long-time acquaintance hadn't hoped to use his alumni connection to get an inside track on the job.

"When he called me after the job was posted, I kinda thought, 'Are you kidding me? This guy thinks I'm gonna give him the job just because we used to serve rice and beans together.'"

Any concerns, though, vanished as soon as the formal interview took place. Just as many of Lake Travis' recent football games have been no contest, Carter said by the time he had finished interviewing Collins, no one else stood a chance.

"He was by far the most qualified that I interviewed, and I interviewed guys from Allen, Colleyville Heritage, guys from all across the state at some of your best places, and he was the guy for the job," Carter said.

While Carter found Collins, the returning players began looking at the team as it started to shape up for spring practice. They could see that the defense, which had become more and more prominent over the years, would again be solid with a chance to dominate. Offensively, players realized they weren't just looking for a quarterback. Other key positions needed some new faces as well.

Colin Lagasse, who'd become as versatile and valuable as any player in the state, saw it clearly.

"We thought our defense was going to be really good and it turns out we were right," Lagasse said following the season. "They were amazing. Our offense, everyone was saying we're losing Michael. This was going to the first year our quarterback was going to be a new guy who didn't have all the experience. Michael had two years. Garrett [Gilbert] had three years. Todd [Reesing] was before that. I guess that was a really big question, and then also receivers. We had Griffin [Gilbert] coming back, but we didn't have anyone else. And also, we lost all our o-linemen except for one, so pretty much the real question was our offense. But we also knew there were a lot of athletic guys coming up. It was just the experience was bad."

After settling in, Collins took a quick look at the offense as a whole, then went about putting his own subtle tweaks to the offense Lake Travis had been using to dismantle opposing defenses for four years. He quickly began to evaluate his options at quarterback. Carter wanted to know early on if the decision could be made in the spring or if there would be a continued competition in the fall.

When spring practice began, three candidates battled for the job. Lagasse, the senior jack of all trades, wanted a shot at the job. Lagasse, athletic, muscular and 5-foot-10, had last been a full-time quarterback while on the freshman team in 2008. He joined the varsity lineup on defense in 2009 and earned all-state honors as a safety. He was slated to start at safety again in 2010 as well as make odd appearances as a running back, receiver or kick returner, but he had filled in admirably at quarterback when Brewer missed four games with a shoulder injury. Baker Mayfield, a playful, unassuming 6-foot junior with a mop of curly black hair and broad shoulders showed promise running the junior varsity team. Sophomore-to-be Bear Fenimore had the prototypical size at 6-foot-4 and flashed enough potential to be included in the competition as well, Carter said.

"Coach Collins had a tough job of trying to figure out a way to distribute the reps fairly so that we could make sure after spring we had a solid answer on who our guy was going to be going into the season or did we need to have a two-headed monster?" Carter said.

In sizing up the three candidates, Carter saw ways each would succeed if they won the job.

"Colin had expressed that he wanted to try to be the quarterback, and obviously he had shown that he can do it," Carter recalled. "He beat Kerrville Tivy playing quarterback for us, and if not for losing our center, we would have beat Aledo [with him at quarterback]. We were ahead until we lost our center and that was just too much. We couldn't overcome all that. We also had a kid named Baker Mayfield coming off the JV that everybody just described as a gamer because he'd always been one of the smaller kids coming through. I remember him battling for the freshman job with another kid. He always had such a great attitude and he always had a bounce in his step and was a great leader but he was so small and pretty slow but he could throw the ball pretty good. I can remember that. And then we had another kid named Bear Fenimore who was trying for the job."

The only definite decision Carter and Collins made prior to practice concerned Fenimore.

"I had pretty much made the decision that if the sophomore didn't win the job that he would be our JV quarterback because I didn't want to punish him," Carter said. "I wanted him to be able to take the reins on that JV and go with it."

Before the competition began, Carter shared a different insight with Lagasse, not trying to impact what would happen but more to help the player see the big picture. Carter saw the Cavaliers as a stronger overall team with Lagasse not playing quarterback.

"Part of the reasoning, and I told Colin this from the beginning, was I will not root for or against kids in this battle, but in my heart I would wish that someone else would play quarterback well enough where we didn't have to use him there," Carter explained. "I felt like we would be a better team overall, because it's kind of like a boat with four or five holes in it and sinking. If we plug Colin in at quarterback, he'll plug one hole and he'll fix that one, but then we've got three or four other leaks. If we plug in Baker or Bear at quarterback, then Colin can fill a special teams void, defense and offensive skill positions."

Lagasse understood what his coach told him, but he saw the opportunity to play quarterback as a chance to get back to his roots. For two years he'd played where coaches needed him. He'd excelled on defense, and he'd gotten to play in spots on offense. In 2009 he ran some Wildcat packages with Andy Erickson as a change-up to Brewer. In 2010 he saw time at receiver and running back in addition to subbing for Brewer. But in the end, he still saw the majority of his snaps on defense.

"I wasn't really upset with it because I knew I could help the team wherever, but I knew in the back of my mind me being the best I could be on the field was going to be on offense," he said. "That's what I always wanted to play, not that I didn't like to play safety."

Throughout the spring, each player got the same amount of snaps, and coaches documented every play. As things shaped out, Lagasse forged ahead with Mayfield running a close second. Then, the spring game arrived, and Lagasse put on a show. Defensive players can't tackle the quarterback in practice, and during the live scrimmage Lagasse showed a dimension with his legs that set him apart. Carter's defense, which had ended the 2010 season as one of the stingiest in the state, couldn't contain Lagasse.

"The first couple of weeks I think they all competed well and all did some good things," Carter said. "Really in the spring game, Colin kind of gave us a glimpse of what he could do when it was full contact. He made some good plays throwing the ball. He made some good plays running."

Carter remembered what he had told the player before the practices began, and regardless of his personal feelings, he did exactly that the competition told him to do.

"We felt like [Colin] had earned the right to start the season as our quarterback," he said.

Though he'd start the season as the backup, Mayfield would still get plenty of reps with the first team in practice. While he didn't possess Lagasse's overall athletic ability, both Carter and Collins saw him as a weapon in the passing game and wanted him ready for more than mop-up duty when the season opened. Fenimore, having battled for the varsity quarterback position, wanted nothing to do with the junior varsity and moved out of the district. He enrolled at nearby Westwood and played the season as the Warriors' varsity back-up quarterback.

When the team reconvened for practice in August, it took the Cavaliers a while to resemble what the coaches had come to expect of Lake Travis football players, or even what they glimpsed during the spring game. A scrimmage against Bastrop didn't go well, and entering the season's first week, Carter didn't quite know how things would play out. The team followed the shaky scrimmage with a solid week of practice, and Carter could hardly wait for the season to begin.

"I was a little concerned," Carter said. "We actually lost the scrimmage to Bastrop. They scored two touchdowns and we only scored a touchdown and a field goal. We went into Westlake and had a great practice week. I was ready for the lights to turn on and us to go back to being Lake Travis. We definitely didn't play like that against Bastrop."

When the lights came on, Lake Travis had indeed returned to normal. Playing Westlake for the second straight year at Darrell K. Royal-Texas Memorial Stadium, the Cavaliers received the opening kickoff and Lagasse hit the ground running. Six snaps into his season as the starting quarterback, he had already amassed 53 yards of offense on three runs and two completions. But on the sixth play, Lagasse landed awkwardly after a quarterback keeper and came off with an injured shoulder.

"We get the ball and here we go, rocking and rolling," Carter remembered. "Colin breaks a long run down the sideline and goes down on his shoulder. I thought he went down pretty hard, and sure enough he was injured."

Usually upbeat, Lagasse couldn't believe it when the doctors shut him down for the night.

"They took away my pads, and that's when I got emotional," he said. "I mean, the game was just getting started. I was kind of in shock, like, 'What just happened?' Within two plays, I'm out. And this is the year I wanted to be the leader of the team and help out the best I could. It was senior year, and I didn't really like it too much."

Carter didn't like it either. For the second straight year, he'd lost a key player in the season opener, this time his quarterback. But unlike the year before, when Brewer had gotten hurt against Hendrickson, Carter felt like the team had someone they could turn to without missing a beat. The competition for the starting spot in the spring and continued reps for Mayfield in the fall served the team well.

"I didn't gasp, though, like I did when Michael Brewer went down the first time because I felt like we had several guys trained and ready to go," Carter said. "And here comes Baker."

Here comes Baker, indeed.

Though he had gotten plenty of reps at practice and he believed he would get his share of playing time because of his passing ability, Mayfield hadn't expected the call to come as early as it did. But the suddenness to it all also served as a blessing.

"At the time, I was kind of scared a little bit, but after the first play, I calmed down and I handled the situation and stuff," Mayfield said. "I was ready for it because during the meetings, Coach Collins had stressed about how we both had to be prepared no matter who wins the job. We were both going to get playing time, so I was ready for it. It's just a whole different situation when you're just thrown in there instead of knowing that you're going to be the starter. I guess it was just kind of nervous for me."

The nerves lasted all of one play. After misfiring on his first pass, Mayfield connected on 14 straight. He even showed he could make plays with his feet, a surprise to both himself and his head coach.

Looking back after the season, Carter recalled that he felt Lagasse would be the right choice to start the season at quarterback because of uncertainty on the offensive line. The Cavaliers were plugging in new pieces, and Carter didn't know how long it would take for the unit to gel. While they did, he wanted someone he knew could get himself out of trouble should it arise. In that scenario, all signs pointed to Lagasse.

"We were really young on the offensive line, and we really weren't sure how long it was going to take to get that group playing well together," Carter said. "One thing was I didn't want Baker to go in and cut his teeth and us to kind of force that and we lose to Westlake and we lose to Aledo, which wouldn't have been the end of the world. We've already proven if we lost a game in pre-season we could still win a state championship. But I didn't want that to define the type of quarterback Baker was going to be going through the rest of his high school days. We would much rather start with Colin. He's the experienced guy and he can do a little more with his feet and we may need that if we're not protecting real well, and that was kind of the plan. We knew that Colin and Baker would both play quarterback and that Baker would start getting a lot of reps as we moved into the season. Based on what we knew at the time, we thought it would be better for Colin to start it out and get us through that tough run and if it looked like we needed to make a change later, we could. But, Baker jumped in there and never looked back."

Mayfield knew the coaches saw him as the passer of the pair. His ability to run came out of nowhere.

"The running part, my ability to get out of the pocket and stuff, that kind of surprised me," Mayfield admitted.

Watching his teammate from the sideline, Lagasse could only smile as the rest of the world met the player Lake Travis had seen develop in practice.

"I think it was a surprise to the fans, but I think everyone on our team knew he was…we had been going back and forth all spring," Lagasse said. "It was good that that had happened because he was prepared for it. Me and Baker, going head to head [in the spring] we both learned everything, we were both side-by-side doing everything. He was a different style of quarterback, more of the passer and I was more athletic and scrambling around and making plays. Once he went in, I think Coach Collins and Coach Carter, they were the ones who were thinking this would be too big of a deal. But I don't think anyone thought he'd do that. He showed a lot, he looked experienced. He looked like he'd been playing."

He finished the game with 278 yards passing, 94 yards rushing and aced the postgame interviews with a silly grin on his face. Lagasse the quarterback became Wally Pipp, which turned out to be a blessing for the Cavaliers. While it hadn't been by design, Carter could now, once Lagasse returned healthy, play him wherever he needed to, plugging all of those other holes while Mayfield held down the quarterback position. Looking back following the season, Carter said he was confident Mayfield would do well. He just didn't know how good he'd be that soon.

"I don't want to sound like a know-it-all," he said later. "We thought Baker would be a heck of a quarterback. He probably did more with his feet early on than we thought he was capable of. That's one thing: we don't tackle our quarterbacks at practice. It's just a philosophical thing we believe in, and so you don't get a lot of live shots. In the Westlake game he got out of trouble quick and that was one of the things we were worried about with him, his feet compared to Colin's. We knew he could throw the ball. We knew he had the great field presence and attitude and would be a great leader. We just had to find out a lot quicker than we had planned."

While he played well against Westlake, many wanted to see if Mayfield could duplicate his success against Hendrickson the following week. A growing program, Hendrickson had been in the playoffs and featured a breakaway threat in Daje Johnson and his blazing speed, and the Cavaliers couldn't afford to look past the Hawks with Aledo on the horizon.

Mayfield needed to adjust to being the full-time starter, which could have been more nerve-wracking than being thrown into the fray like he was against Westlake. But circumstances favored him, and he responded.

"I think [knowing I was starting] would have been harder, but the fact that it was a home game, my first home game, kind of calmed me down," he said. "I knew all of my friends and family would be there to support me no matter what happens. So that made it easy."

And Mayfield continued to make the game look easy. He ran for a touchdown and passed for five more to lead the Cavaliers to a 43-14 win. Junior receiver Zach Austin, who had quickly emerged as a playmaker opposite Griffin Gilbert, and Cameron Wrinkle caught six passes each with five touchdowns between them. Lake Travis led 36-6 at the half and Hendrickson never threatened.

From there, the Cavaliers got down to brass tacks, prepping for Aledo, the two-time defending 4A Division II champions. Many around the state, both Lake Travis supporters and football fans in general had been looking toward the game ever since the Bearcats came into Lakeway and defeated the injury-riddled Cavaliers 14-10 in 2010. The game had plenty of other sub-plots, none bigger than the showdown between Lake Travis' defense and Aledo's quick-strike offense featuring the nation's top-rated running back, Texas-bound Johnathan Gray.

Mayfield had been on the sidelines for the previous year's game. He couldn't wait to take part in the big game for the first time, and after the season said the Cavaliers had a simple game plan.

"That was a lot of fun," he said. "We knew we had to get revenge for them, that we were a different team from the year before. Our goal was to get up on them early and just stay ahead."

While Lagasse had missed the Hendrickson game following the early shoulder injury against Westlake, he planned on playing against Aledo though he didn't quite know how his body would respond. He just knew he couldn't miss the game.

"I went back in for the Aledo game," he recalled. "I was fine, it was sore. In the beginning I was kind of nervous because I hadn't been playing much. I'd only played four plays so I was wondering how my body was going to hold up. I was nervous. But also, I knew I had two years under my belt, and Aledo was the first team to beat us when I got the chance to play quarterback so I wanted to get back at them."

The key to defending Aledo demanded that teams keep Gray from breaking loose on long runs, something the Cavaliers excelled at in 2010, "holding" Gray to 140 yards on 30 carries. Though Gray scored the winning touchdown that night, he had worked for every yard he gained, and Carter and the Cavalier defenders would have been happy to allow Gray another 150 or so yards if it took him another 30 carries to get there.

As it turned out, Gray broke loose, but it didn't matter. When he broke free on an 82-yarder in the second quarter, he tied the game at 14. The Cavaliers had gotten off to a quick start thanks to a healthy Lagasse, who returned to the offense as running back, Mayfield's accuracy and Aledo's inability to cover Gilbert. Lagasse gave Lake Travis a quick lead with a 26-yard touchdown run and Mayfield and Gilbert connected for the first of four touchdown passes to the big receiver for a 14-0 lead. Aledo rallied with consecutive scoring drives, but the Bearcats still couldn't stop the Cavaliers. Mayfield hit Austin for a 41-yard score, and Aledo answered with a field goal. Mayfield and Gilbert connected twice more for scores, sandwiched around Gray's third score, and Lake Travis took a 35-25 lead into the locker room.

In the second half, Gray broke loose on another highlight reel run, a 68-yarder in which he crisscrossed the field before scoring. By that time the Cavaliers had opened up a 55-28 lead after Aledo had pulled within 35-28 early in the third quarter thanks to a Lake Travis turnover. After the turnover that led to Aledo's field goal, the Lake Travis defense stiffened. But the Aledo defense had no answer for Mayfield, who went on to throw for 464 yards and six touchdowns. He threw scoring strikes to Gilbert and Austin, and Lagasse added another touchdown run to grow the lead to 55-28 before Gray used up whatever energy his side had left with his 68-yard run.

In the end, Lake Travis avenged its 2010 loss with a 62-35 win. Mayfield had the most prolific day of his budding career, and Lagasse rushed for 100 yards. Gray got his yards and set the state touchdown scoring record in the process, but his 263 yards didn't impact the outcome.

"We got on them, scored 62 points, so it was a fun offensive game," Mayfield said. "I know defense, going up against a guy like Johnathan Gray, that's a tough challenge, but we scored a lot of points and had fun with it."

Later, Gilbert reflected on his big game.

"Baker did such a great job that game," Gilbert said. "Heck, he threw six touchdown passes or something like that. I really had the easy job. He would just throw it in spots that only I could catch it. I'd just go up there and try to use my height to my advantage, and that's what I did most of the game. I happened to have a mismatch on a corner – he was a little bit shorter than me. Throughout the years I've always kind of been the taller guy, so that helps out. Baker and the rest of the offense did such a great job letting those opportunities come to hand. The coaches gave me great opportunities, calling plays for me and I just tried to the best of my abilities to go up and make a play. Scoring four touchdowns was kind of unheard of for me. Before that I hadn't even scored three touchdowns in a game on varsity, so it was obviously an unbelievable experience to get back at them the way we did. It really was a team effort and everyone really did their part."

The following week Lake Travis continued its roll with a 56-14 dismantling of seventh-ranked Kerrville Tivy, an annual playoff team that had tested Lake Travis twice in 2010. While the offense continued to flourish, the Lake Travis defense dominated play. The Cavaliers sacked Tivy quarterback

Parks McNeil six times led by two from Tyler Paulsen and intercepted him four more times, twice each by Zach Streuling and Dane Balasz. Tivy's offense managed just one touchdown, a long drive in the third quarter. The Antlers had tied the game early when Mayfield suffered a pick-six. But that gaffe seemed to energize the Cavaliers rather than the Antlers. Following the interception, Mayfield's first of the season, the Cavaliers reeled off four straight touchdowns and took control. Mayfield would finish with 290 yards and three touchdowns through the air and another 116 yards and two scores on the ground.

With the explosive start and the bevy of points, Collins had more than proven himself an exceptional replacement as Lake Travis' offensive coordinator. After being hired in the spring, he spent more than a week with Morris at Clemson, learning the details of Morris' system to complement his play-calling style. The marriage became seamless, and it continued to gain momentum as the Cavaliers ran their non-district gauntlet.

As District 25-4A play began, the Cavaliers continued to roll. In the five wins that followed over Dripping Springs, Vandegrift, Vista Ridge, Rouse and Marble Falls, the Cavaliers outscored their opponents by an average of 53-13. They trailed just once, after an early safety in the district opener against Dripping Springs. Games were decided early, giving coaches the chance to improve depth and injured Cavaliers the chance to rest, Lagasse chief among them.

"In the Kerrville Tivy game I landed on it again and that made it worse, so I was out for four or five games," Lagasse recalled. "The bye week was in there and that got me a chance to heal up and then I came back for the last three games."

In the interim, the Cavaliers brought running back Varshaun Nixon into a more prominent role. The promising sophomore looked to lock up the main running back role in the spring and fall preseasons, but an early season injury limited him. Against non-district opponents, Nixon carried the ball just 21 times for 91 yards and two scores and caught it five times for 61 yards. In the team's first district game against Dripping Springs, Nixon rushed eight times for 81 yards and a score and caught five passes for 101 yards. He rushed for more than 100 yards in four of the six district games and scored eight touchdowns, and he got his yards in bunches. Prior to the district finale at Cedar Park, Nixon torched the opposing defenses for 618 yards on just 53 carries, an average of more than 11 per rush. He also returned a kickoff against Marble Falls 90 yards for a score.

Having avenged one of their 2010 losses already and cruised through District 25-4A play, the Cavaliers couldn't wait for Nov. 4, which brought them face-to-face with the other team to defeat them: Cedar Park. In 2010 the Timberwolves and Cavaliers met twice, and Lake Travis played far from perfectly either time. In the regular season finale, Lake Travis turned the ball over five times and Cedar Park won the district title with a 35-21 win at Lake Travis. In the Region IV-4A final, the Cavaliers outlasted the Timberwolves, who were without star quarterback Brian Hogan, 21-20 to advance in the playoffs. Cedar Park had been unbeaten heading into the playoff game, and the Timberwolves could only watch as Lake Travis claimed a state title that many felt Cedar Park would have won easily had their junior quarterback been available.

Both teams, to their delight, entered the 2011 district finale with their full complement of offensive stars. Hogan came back healthy and had led the Timberwolves to the brink of their second straight district title, and Lagasse had been cleared for full contact earlier, though coaches had eased him back onto the field, saving him for the Cedar Park game. In the wins over Rouse and Marble Falls, he carried the ball just eight times and caught three passes, which left him feeling fresh heading into the showdown with Cedar Park.

Lake Travis had gotten off to an awful start in the 2010 district finale, falling behind 28-0 thanks to a quartet of turnovers and Hogan's running. Thanks to Lagasse, the 2011 district meeting saw Lake Travis jump out to the early lead. He scored on a short run midway through the first quarter to open the scoring. When he scored on a short pass from Mayfield in the second quarter, Lake Travis led 17-0. When he broke free for an 85-yard touchdown run early in the third quarter, the Cavaliers appeared in control, up 24-0.

"That felt good for me to finally be able to help out the team because I'd been sitting out," he said. "This whole season I'd been feeling like I'm going along with it, not really in it like I was the last two years. That game, to finally be a part of the team and make an impact, was great."

Following Lagasse's long touchdown, Lake Travis' coaches tried to use the clock as an ally, running the ball as much as they could to limit Cedar Park's chances. But Cedar Park wouldn't let the Cavaliers execute. Their defense began making plays, and pushed against the wall, Cedar Park's offense began to click.

"We were trying to run the ball to let the clock keep going, and they were going to let the clock run so it would be a whole bunch of time going by and they wouldn't have as much time to win," Lagasse recalled. "But the problem was their D line and linebackers, that whole front, was just destroying our front, so we couldn't really run anything anywhere and we were going three-and-out really fast instead of running the clock out. Before we know it, they're coming back. Our defense made a great stand."

Hogan rallied the Timberwolves but ran out of time. Despite the Cavaliers' controlling possession for much of the game, the Timberwolves rallied late and closed the gap. The final touchdown came with just seconds remaining and never gave the Timberwolves a chance at a final possession to threaten the lead. In the end, Lake Travis walked away with a 24-21 win and a perfect regular season.

"Considering last year we lost to them we just wanted redemption really bad to get the district championship," senior linebacker Blake Burdette said following the game. "Even though we've got the state championship, it still feels really good."

Burdette and Streuling led Lake Travis' defensive effort. They each made 25 tackles and helped keep Hogan, who had rushed for more than 1,000 yards coming into the game, in check. Cedar Park's vaunted offense managed less than 50 yards in the first half and dug too big a hole to escape.

Having won the district title, Lake Travis began its playoff run by flexing its substantial muscle against McCallum. The Knights, who might have seen Lake Travis at its worst in the 2010 playoff opener, got an up-close look at a sharp, focused and brutally efficient Lake Travis team. The Cavaliers scored early and often. The first eight possessions all resulted in touchdowns, and by halftime the game was so out of hand that officials decided to play the second half with a running clock to minimize the carnage in a 58-7 win. Lagasse and Nixon combined to rush for 245 yards on just 15 carries with five scores. In all, the Cavaliers amassed 436 yards of offense while running just 46 plays.

The win sent Lake Travis on to the Area playoffs in San Antonio against Smithson Valley, one of the more successful teams from the greater San Antonio area. The Rangers have been consistent winners over the years, whether the school's enrollment has placed it in Conference 5A or Conference 4A. Smithson Valley played for the 5A, Division II championship in both 2002 and 2004, falling both times to Southlake Carroll. They also played in the 4A Division II championship game in 2001, losing in overtime to Denton Ryan and becoming one of the only teams in Texas history to play in state championship games in different classifications in successive years. According to *Texas Football*, Celina is the only other team to play in title games in different classifications in back-to-back seasons. Celina won the 2A, Division II title in 2005 and lost in the 3A, Division II final the following year.

The Cavaliers and Rangers met in San Antonio's Alamodome. While much closer to Smithson Valley than Lake Travis, the Cavaliers feel quite at home in the dome, where they had not lost since 2004. Lake Travis had won eight straight games there, where the elements will never work in the favor of teams trying to contain Lake Travis' hurry-up, no-huddle spread attack. In a set-up where coaches can contest every option of a playoff match-up, why teams agree to play Lake Travis in the dome remains a mystery.

Smithson Valley scored first thanks to back-breaking work from running back Lawrence Mattison. The Rangers controlled the pace of play early, using their big running back to grind out yards and keep the Cavalier offense waiting in the wings. The Cavaliers failed to convert a fourth down try on their opening possession and didn't see the ball again until Mattison scored on a 25-yard run with 1:51 left in the quarter. Mattison would be the Rangers' workhorse throughout the night, gaining 182 yards on 35 carries, but the work took its toll. Worn out and banged up, he'd be on the sidelines by the fourth quarter.

Lake Travis kicked it into high gear and evened the game early in the second quarter. With a mix of Mayfield's short passing and quick-burst runs from Nixon and Lagasse, the Cavaliers marched into Smithson Valley territory. A 33-yard catch and run from Wrinkle set up Lagasse's one-yard run, and the Cavaliers drew even.

Needing to answer, the Rangers couldn't and punted after driving to midfield. Following a touchback, Lake Travis quickly crossed midfield and took the lead when Mayfield scrambled away from pressure and lofted a strike to Austin, who had come free in the back of the end zone for a 14-7 lead. The Rangers tried to answer and drove to the Lake Travis 26 before Paulsen sacked Parker McKenzie on third down. Not wanting to give up field position, the Rangers went for it on fourth down, but Paulsen got to McKenzie again and forced a fumble that Corbin Crow returned 50 yards to the Smithson Valley 23-yard line. Mayfield scored on the next play and the Cavaliers took a 21-7 lead into the locker room.

The Cavaliers kept charging ahead in the second half, driving 74 yards in less than three minutes, scoring on another Lagasse one-yard run to lead 28-7. The teams traded fourth quarter touchdowns – Mayfield connected with Gilbert twice on fades, each time answering touchdown passes from McKenzie to Baron Hill, including an 80 yarder. The Cavaliers used some late rushing from Lagasse to eat up time. The senior finished with 132 yards and two scores on just 13 carries. Mayfield completed 17 of 21 passes for 225 yards and three touchdowns in the 42-21 win.

The Cavaliers returned to San Antonio to take on Corpus Christi Flour Bluff. Playing on a perfect Thanksgiving Friday afternoon outside at Heroes Stadium, the Cavaliers wasted no time stinging the Hornets. Lake Travis scored on all eight of its first half possessions and for the second time in three weeks played a playoff game with a running clock after halftime. The Cavaliers led 58-0 before the Hornets scored twice in the fourth quarter against reserves that included a number of Lake Travis junior varsity players who dressed with the varsity. Nixon ran for 100 yards on just a few touches, including three scores, and Mayfield completed 10 of 13 passes for 213 yards and four scores, two to Gilbert.

The blowout win sent the Cavaliers into the Region IV championship game against a familiar foe in a familiar place. While the Cavaliers were beating Flour Bluff, Cedar Park also enjoyed an easy Friday in San Antonio, shutting out Weslaco East 49-0 to earn another rematch with Lake Travis. The teams would collide again at Royal-Memorial Stadium, this time at night in a rematch of epic proportions.

Given that two of the teams predicted to be the favorites to win Region I and II lost in the third round – Denton Ryan to Waco Midway 19-7 in Region I and Highland Park to Tyler John Tyler 42-39 in Region II, most felt that the Lake Travis-Cedar Park game would be the de facto state championship game, as it had been in 2010.

The Timberwolves spent the entire off-season bristling at the thought that they had been the better team in 2010 only to lose without Hogan and watch as Lake Travis continued on and hoisted their fourth straight trophy. Just three weeks removed from Lake Travis' district-title clinching win over the Timberwolves, Cedar Park was determined to return the 2010 favor and advance on what it hoped would be a title-winning run of its own.

Playing at Royal-Memorial Stadium on a cool night following a day of rain, the teams battled back and forth in a battle befitting a regional championship. The Cavaliers drew first blood, scoring on a Mayfield pass to Gilbert. The Timberwolves, who didn't throw a pass until midway through the second quarter, made the most of the pass they threw. Hogan dropped back, caught the Cavaliers in a corner blitz and lofted a beautiful strike to Ethan Fry streaking up the sideline into the end zone. The Cavaliers blocked Austin Randa's extra point and clung briefly to a 7-6 lead. Cedar Park took a 9-7 lead later in the second quarter when Randa connected on a 33-yard field goal. Lake Travis didn't like playing from behind and responded with haste. Less than 40 seconds later, the Cavaliers had crossed midfield and Nixon got around the left end and scored from 44 yards out, returning the Cavaliers to the lead, 14-9.

The defenses took over after halftime, keeping both offenses firmly in check. Lagasse credited the Cedar Park defense's relentlessness for the struggles Lake Travis had offensively.

"Their defense, they play so aggressively and fly to the ball," he explained. "I think they are a lot like our defense where everyone always asks, 'Where does it come from?' On every play, someone is just flying around and that's how they play. Once you get the ball, it's not just one person in open space. They are just flying to the ball. As a player, that's what I notice. I never get something free. I may break one tackle, but right after that there's [another] guy on me and they just dive in there."

Cedar Park's best chance to take the lead came when the Cavaliers nearly suffered a colossal special teams' miscue in the third quarter. Punting from their own 40, the snap should have sailed over Paulsen's head. But the defensive end/punter timed his leap perfectly and grabbed the ball before it got past him. He couldn't get off a punt, though, and Cedar Park took over in Lake Travis territory at the 37-yard line. But on the first play, Balasz picked off Hogan's pass, and the Cavaliers avoided disaster.

The Cavaliers' offense couldn't put the game away, and it once again came down to the defense late. Cedar Park marched into Lake Travis territory and had two long gains negated by holding penalties. With less than a minute left, Hogan tried to get a chunk of yardage back and lofted a pass up the right sideline. Brock Kenyon saw the play develop and the Lake Travis safety jumped and reached above a pair of Cedar Park receivers to intercept the pass and seal the game for the Cavaliers.

Mayfield gave the credit to the defense, deservedly so. He said the two games against the district rival, but especially the second game, remained the biggest challenges the team faced.

"We know them just like the back of our hands and they know us the same," Mayfield said of the Timberwolves. "When you get two teams that are that good, it's a huge obstacle that you have to overcome and you realize it's all the little things that are going to decide the winner. We just had to grind it out. We realized we had to be more physical, especially through all of the fourth quarter and especially in that second game. We didn't get any yards, so I'm going to give all the credit to our defense and how they just stuck it out the whole game and only let up nine points. All the little things, like gaining two or three yards at a time was okay for us because they had a great defense."

Gilbert concurred.

"That game couldn't have been any better," he said. "Obviously it was a low scoring game because you had two hard defenses playing against each other. We just came out on top. We knew we'd prevail but we knew it would be a grudge match like it was. For the defense to make plays like they did, it was just unbelievable. We owe it all to them because they really pushed us through that game."

The win sent the Cavaliers into the semifinals, and back to the Alamodome to face Pearland Dawson, which had won its region by outlasting Angleton. Dawson and Lake Travis had infamously met before in the semifinals, with the Cavaliers crushing the Eagles 57-12 in 2009 after much pre-game taunting by the Eagles. Dawson had only been open three years at that meeting and looked to do better against the Cavaliers this time around.

Lake Travis fired the opening salvo. Penalties on Dawson's first two plays, a precursor to the theme of the night, left them deep in their own territory and a punt gave the Cavaliers the ball at the Eagles' 44-yard line. Nixon ripped off a 26-yard run, and three plays later Lagasse stretched the ball across the goal line to cap a five-yard run. The Eagles wasted no time in responding. Tre Oliver returned the kickoff 35 yards, and Garry Kimble scrambled for another 25 into Lake Travis territory. After another false start pushed the Eagles back, Kimble connected with Tony Upchurch for a 40-yard score to tie the game.

Buoyed with enthusiasm after the score and a stop from its defense, the Eagle offense picked its defense up. Mixing runs from James White and keepers and designed draws from Kimble, Dawson went on a 16-play, 84-yard march that took nearly seven minutes off the clock. The Cavaliers gave the Eagles plenty of help with penalties that twice extended the drive, including pass interference in the end zone on third-and-18. Kimble was happy to take advantage, connecting with Isaac Jordan on a four-yard score, giving the Eagles a 14-10 lead.

As had been the case throughout the playoffs, Lake Travis didn't trail for long. Dawson enjoyed the lead for 3:25. Mixing keepers and short passes, Mayfield moved the Cavaliers down the field efficiently, and Lagasse capped a 60-yard drive with a three-yard run. The lead grew to 24-14 after Streuling intercepted Kimble's ill-advised deep pass. Three plays later, Austin out-jumped a Dawson defender for a Mayfield pass and then outran him down the sideline for a 61-yard score.

Trailing 24-14 at the half, and having watched Lake Travis score on four of its five opening-half possessions – the fifth possession ended when time ran out in the half, the Eagles knew they needed to force the issue, so they tried an onside kick to open the second half. Lagasse recovered it for the Cavaliers, who then took the reward for the Eagles' risk. Nixon carried three times to get the Cavaliers to the Dawson 21, and on fourth down Mayfield scrambled for an apparent touchdown that a holding penalty erased. No problem. Backed up 10 yards, Mayfield found Gilbert wide open down the middle for an easy 31-yard score.

With a 31-14 lead, the Cavalier defense took over, holding Dawson without a first down in the third quarter. By the time Kimble connected with Upchurch for a 24-yard gain and a first down on the first play of the final quarter, the Cavaliers had taken total control, with Mayfield having capped a 57-yard drive with an 11-yard pass to Lagasse, who was the beneficiary of coverage bust and found himself alone at the goal line to accept the gift. He later hauled in a long pass, shook off a defender and coasted in for the final score, a 72-yard Mayfield pass, in the 45-14 win.

"It took us time to adjust to their speed, and they were strong kids too," Carter said later. "We missed some tackles. Offensively, I thought we played pretty well, even in the first half, but defensively we didn't play as well as we could. But credit to our kids, we made some adjustments and they did what we asked them to do and didn't allow them to score any more."

Mayfield completed 14 of 22 passes for 279 yards and four touchdowns. Lagasse caught six passes for 107 yards and two scores to go along with his two rushing touchdowns. Austin had 99 yards receiving on four catches. Nixon rushed for 134 yards on 18 carries.

Defensively, the Cavaliers limited the Eagles to just 285 yards of offense, much of which came in the first half. The Eagles gained just five yards in the third quarter and 83 in the fourth quarter. Penalties plagued both teams, especially Dawson, which was flagged a whopping 23 times for 169 yards. Lake Travis' 16 penalties for 122 yards seemed reasonable by comparison.

Three days after the game, Carter laughed about the penalty festival, but that night, with his team gathered around him following the win, he offered a simple, congratulatory message.

"There are only two left, and we're off to Jerryworld on Friday night," he said. "I'm proud of you guys. I love you guys. It doesn't matter who we play. It's all about us at this point."

Leading up to the championship game, the Cavaliers all embraced the opportunity they now had to make history – to become the first Texas team to win five consecutive state championships. The Cavaliers thumbed their nose at superstition and talked about it. To a player, they realized what their "Drive for Five" meant and, while they couldn't guess at how they'd feel should they complete the task, they weren't afraid of the moment.

"We've talked about it," Carter said. "Some people say you're not supposed to talk about it, but we don't get into that whole jinx thing. We plan on winning a state championship. That doesn't mean it's going to happen, but that's what we're setting our goal for."

The fact that the Cavaliers had a chance to make some history the year before helped, Carter said.

"I told the kids that we had a chance to make history last year because no team had ever won four that was a 4A or 5A school," he said. "Now, we want to rewrite history. We want to stand alone and we have a chance to do that. Obviously we have a great team to play in Midway, and I know that it will be a challenge for us, but I think that our kids are going to rise to the occasion and we are going to go out there and play our tails off."

It took much more than the week preceding the game to get the Cavaliers ready for the task that faced them. The recent tradition, the five years of success and the four years of work under the system Carter and former head coach Chad Morris had installed each played a part in getting the Cavaliers ready to battle for their fifth-straight title.

"These kids have all been with us since they were freshmen, so they've all been learning the same defense," Carter said. "The biggest thing is, to play defense, we kind of want to have a moxie about us. I don't want the kids to be cocky. That's not how I coach them and that's not how I want them to play, but I want them to think that it doesn't matter what you do, we're going to figure out a way to stop you and we're going to give the ball back to our offense, they're going to go score and we're going to do it again. That's how we're going to get you."

As the Cavaliers prepped for the title game, Carter knew Midway's potent offense would test his defense. He also expected his defense would rise to the occasion and keep the Lions in check. Midway entered the championship game after topping the 50-point mark in wins over Wichita Falls Rider in the quarterfinals and Tyler John Tyler in the semifinals. The Cavaliers understood that, given the opportunity, Midway's offense could do some damage.

"I felt like Midway had it figured out on offense," Carter recalled. "They had been scoring a lot of points and they had been playing their best football. That being said, I knew that our kids knew how to prepare for a big game like that because we've done it and we've had the same guys who have done it over and over and over. So we got in and we laid it out to them about what we were going to do. We got in and we watched film and we learned them and we learned them, and then Monday's practice was, ehhhh."

Translation: not great.

The Cavaliers shook off that manic Monday and practiced well defensively on Tuesday and Wednesday. By the time the team boarded the buses and rode up to Arlington, Carter sensed his team just wanted to play. When kickoff rolled around late Friday night, Lake Travis' defense showed up. Carter grew even more encouraged when the Lions couldn't block Lake Travis' front seven early. All told, the Cavaliers sacked Midway quarterbacks six times, including starter Kramer Robertson five times.

"We got into the game and when they didn't protect against us, I was thinking if offense got us one or two scores, we'll take care of business," he said.

Easier said than done, however. Midway's defense proved ready for Lake Travis as well. Looking back, Mayfield said the combination of the moment and Midway's defense made things difficult for the Cavaliers to gain any offensive momentum.

"When you have athletes on the defensive side like Waco Midway had, it's just hard to get the ball moving and get into a rhythm," he said. "I mean, you know it's the state championship game and there's that much more on the line, so there's that much more pressure on you. In Cowboys Stadium like that, with 32,000 people, it's just all on the line, and so it was kind of hard to settle in. But the few drives we had that we got points on, it was like eight or 10 plays where we actually moved down the field consistently."

For the most part, Midway's defensive front bested Lake Travis' offensive line. Normally a quick-starting, quicker-strike offense, the Cavaliers sputtered early. Midway's defense forced a three-and-out on the opening possession, and Lake Travis' defense followed suit.

The Cavaliers soon began to move the ball, though. Mayfield settled in, connecting on several short passes to move the chains. He converted an early third-and-seven with a swing pass to senior running back Cameron Wrinkle for 11 yards. After another completion, this to Gilbert, netted a first down, he found Lagasse on a catch-and-run that went for 31 yards into Midway territory. A fumbled snap lost 10 yards, but Mayfield got that back on successive completions Austin, and Lake Travis appeared in business at the Midway 16-yard line. After Nixon gained four yards, Mayfield misfired twice, and Midway avoided an early deficit when Orion Stewart blocked Kevin Marcotte's 29-yard field goal try.

"We started off pretty bad," Lagasse recalled. "They were shutting us down. The first series they stopped us. The second series they blocked a field goal. After those first two drives, as an offense we came off looking at each other. The defense was getting stops right away. They were holding their own ground. We were looking at each other saying we need to relax. Coach was looking at us, telling us we can do this, 'Let's let the defense get a rest and let's actually make some kind of drive.' And we happened to score."

Midway gained the upper hand following a Mayfield fumble late in the first quarter and drove to the Cavaliers' 40-yard line before punting. Hunter Jarmon's punt pinned the Cavaliers deep in their own territory when Wrinkle fair-caught it at his own four-yard line. Two plays later, facing a third-and-nine, the Cavaliers appeared to be going nowhere fast. But Mayfield dropped back, eluded the pressure and managed to gain just enough for a first down at his own 15-yard line.

With breathing room, the Cavaliers kicked the offense into high gear, hurrying their way along. Mayfield found Lagasse for 23 yards and then again for 12 to reach midfield. Then he found Austin for 18 yards and Gilbert for nine. Lagasse took a Wildcat snap and bulled his way for a first down on third-and-one, then took a 12-yard pass to the Midway 15. On third down, Mayfield used his legs to buy time and lofted a high pass toward the back corner of the end zone, where Gilbert used every bit of his 6-foot-5-and-a-half frame to leap, snag the ball and get a foot down for the game's first score, capping a 96-yard, 13-play march that took 3:36 off the clock. Call it Lake Travis' version of "The Catch," authored more than 30 years earlier by Joe Montana and Dwight Clark.

"It felt like it was an eternity before that ball came down," Gilbert recalled. "Really, we had called a play that wasn't even designed to me. It was designed to go to the other side of the field, but Baker had some pressure coming into him. Their defensive linemen made some good moves and put pressure on him."

The senior receiver, bound for Texas Christian, gave his quarterback the credit for making the proper play after Midway's defense stepped up.

"Baker did a great job scrambling out of the pocket, heck we work on it every single day on our scramble drill," he said. "We know what positions we need to go to, and Baker was looking at me and I was just standing in the back of the end zone. I just pointed up to tell him to throw it up to me. I just have to go up and make a play if he's going to throw it up to me, and that's exactly what he did. He put it in a perfect spot to where no one else could get it except me. He used my height to my advantage. I just went up there and got it and kept my feet in."

The score came early in the game, but the receiver won't soon forget it.

"I had never scored a touchdown in a state championship before, so obviously that was a special moment for me, but to have the first touchdown of the game and really get the tone going for the rest of the team," he said later.

As Lake Travis' defense repeatedly stuffed the Panthers' running attack, Robertson tried a different tact on the next possession, lofting a long pass for Dustin Vasek. The Cavaliers weren't fooled, and Streuling intercepted the pass, giving Lake Travis more momentum. A long run from Lagasse and a completion to Wrinkle brought the Cavaliers back across midfield, but the Panthers foiled the Cavaliers' fourth down try when Shaki Randolph and Justin Richter dropped Lagasse a yard short.

Midway's ensuing possession proved its best drive of the half. Robertson found Jarmon for 19 yards on third down, and the Panthers moved quickly into Lake Travis territory at the 36. But Lake Travis' defense stepped up. Burdette sacked Robertson on first down to put the Panthers behind the chains. Facing a fourth-and-six, the Panthers decided to go for it from the Cavaliers' 32-yard line. Robertson dropped back, but pressure forced him to run. Junior defensive back Hunter Streuling brought him down short of the first down, and Lake Travis took over.

With little more than two minutes left in the half, the Cavaliers went back to work. Nixon broke off his best run of the night, an 18-yarder to midfield.

Mayfield found Lagasse twice to convert back-to-back third downs, the second of which covered 33 yards and took the Cavaliers to the Midway 12-yard line. Midway's defense stepped up, and after a short run and two incomplete passes, the Cavaliers settled for Marcotte's 26-yard field goal.

Lake Travis led 10-0, though no one in the stadium would describe the lead as comfortable. The second half plan, with Midway set to receive the kick, called upon the defense to continue its stellar play and the offense to pick things up. Looking back, Lagasse said he didn't recall much about the halftime discussion. He only said the team had to overcome some early fatigue issues and settle down.

"I know in the first half, a lot of us were getting real winded for some reason," he said. "We'd come off to the bench just really tired and we didn't know what it was. I honestly don't know. It could have been [nerves about trying for fifth title]. It just took us a little time to break in.

"In the second half, that's when everyone was just fine and we all had energy and just kept going," he said.

Gilbert said much of halftime revolved around offensive players thanking their defensive counterparts, almost apologizing for what many considered a sub-standard performance, Midway's defense notwithstanding. The offense wanted to do its part, and the defense had confidence that it could.

"We actually thanked our defense for stopping them so many times and doing such a great job stopping their dangerous offense," Gilbert recalled. "We knew as our offense that we needed to step it up and take care of business and help out our defense. Our offense needed to step it up because our defense was playing so well, and the defense was really supporting us. They knew we would take care of business and they would just keep stopping them. "

It turns out that the Cavalier players would need all the energy they could muster. The Panthers wasted little time in reminding the Cavaliers that a fifth straight title wouldn't come easy. Stewart fielded Marcotte's kickoff, broke several tackles and outraced the rest of the coverage team for a 90-yard touchdown.

"Then we have a big letdown on special teams and that kind of changed things for a while," Carter said.

Lagasse said any level of comfort he and his teammates had taken into the locker room vanished with that kickoff return.

"Going into half, I think we felt pretty comfortable so we just wanted to keep doing what we were doing, but of course it's the first half and anything can happen in the second half," he said. "Once they ran the kickoff back, that made us get edgy a bit."

Gilbert agreed.

"Definitely that kickoff return took our breath away," he said. "We knew we really had to step it up. They were there to play and they weren't quitting on us, and they weren't just going to roll over for us. Offense said we needed to go take care of business."

You can't force momentum, or at least Lake Travis couldn't force it that night. Still, those on the Lake Travis sideline kept the faith.

"We didn't really start it off too well, but our coaches knew that we'd get rolling and start playing LT football eventually," Gilbert said. "The coaches told us to pick it up because the defense couldn't keep doing everything for us."

With momentum on their side, the Panthers forced a quick, short Lake Travis punt and then drove into Lake Travis territory. The Lake Travis defense stiffened, and the Cavaliers took advantage of a bad snap on Midway's punt to get the ball on Midway's side of midfield.

Lagasse rushed twice, including a 15-yarder around left end to move the ball to the Midway 23, but he couldn't convert a third-down swing pass into a first down, and the Cavaliers settled on Marcotte's short field goal to get a bit more cushion at 13-7 with 7:10 left in the third quarter.

The teams exchanged punts before Midway used quarterback Robertson's running to get into field goal range of its own, but Drew Owen hooked his 41-yarder wide left, and Lake Travis' defense took a collective breath. The offense mounted its best offensive drive of the half on the ensuing possession, moving from its own 24 across midfield before a false start set them back and Mayfield got sacked back at his 48. Paulsen's punt bounced at the 13, and for some reason Midway's Gary Goode tried to pick the ball up amid a crowd of Cavaliers. Junior defensive lineman Spencer Staples hit him as he grabbed the ball and jarred it loose. Senior safety Jacob Standard fell on it for the Cavaliers. The Cavaliers lost two yards in three plays, but Marcotte connected on his third field goal to give the Cavaliers a two-score lead.

"Marcotte had made two field goals to put us up 16-7, and the way our defense was playing we were all just, 'Keep it up and last a little longer and we'll have this,'" Lagasse recalled.

"I was looking up on the big screen and saw that play," Gilbert said. "I started laughing to myself because I knew we'd go in and score points, whether it was a touchdown or a field goal because we had a good enough kicker to put points up on the board. All credit goes to Kevin Marcotte for having the game that he did. Just kicking two long field goals in such an environment is amazing for a first year varsity player. I started laughing to myself because I knew if our defense keeps taking care of business, we've got another championship."

Midway shook off the blunder and went back to work, moving near midfield before the Lake Travis defense rose up again. In a five-play stretch, Lake Travis' defense sacked Robertson three times, the final time by Burdette for a 12-yard loss. With little more than half the final quarter to play, the Panthers needed a big play, and Robertson went for it on fourth down from his team's own 34-yard line. His long pass never found its target. Standard came up with his second turnover, returning the interception back across midfield.

After Midway dropped Nixon for a loss on first down, Mayfield found Gilbert for 18 yards to the 24. Lagasse broke off an 11-yard run, and when the Panthers interfered with Gilbert as he tried to make a catch in the end zone, the Cavaliers stood just two yards from the potential game-sealing score.

Gilbert could all but sense that the Cavaliers were on the verge of putting the nails in Midway's coffin.

"Whenever I felt comfortable was when we were on their one-yard line and we knew Colin was getting the ball," he said. "Heck, I was like a kid on Christmas Day, knowing that he was about to run in for a touchdown and we were about to win our fifth championship in a row. It was an unbelievable feeling, so much happiness around. We were all kind of jumping up and down like little kids. It was a sight to see and an unbelievable feeling."

The Cavaliers shifted into the Wildcat formation, and Lagasse found the end zone on the second snap. When he emerged from the crowd, he did so with five fingers raised – the first celebratory act from a player known by his coaches and other fans to never show emotion as the "Drive For Five" drew ever closer to reality.

"A lot of our guys did celebrate [touchdowns] – nothing really cocky or anything – and I never did that," he said. "I guess I knew it was going to be the last touchdown so I felt there was a need for it. I never wanted to [score a touchdown] and celebrate and do that because I'm still focused on the game, but because I knew if we scored, that was going to be it and this was history. It felt like a really big deal to me."

That Lagasse led the celebration didn't get lost on the fans or the coaches. In the stands, a fan sitting next to Dave and Laurie Lagasse noticed and felt compelled to tell Colin's parents.

"When Colin put up that five," Laurie Lagasse recalled, "I had a dad turn to me and say, 'I've watched your kid play and I've never seen him ever do anything. He walks over and he hands the ball to the [ref], he never shows excitement.' So for him to do it was something special. After the game Coach Carter walked up to Colin and said, 'Hey, I think I saw a little excitement in you tonight!'"

Later, the player acknowledged that he rarely, if ever, showed emotion on the field.

"Coaches always gave me grief," he said through a smile well after the season. "They thought I was too serious during the game. Even Eric, the guy who prays with us before the game, said he'd never seen me smile on the field before. I don't mean to do that, I guess, but I guess I'm always focused. I guess that was the one time the coaches saw that I was excited about something. I'm always excited, but I'm just always focused on something."

Like their leader, the Cavaliers maintained their focus until the end.

Midway made one final drive, but sophomore linebacker Luke Hutton intercepted Jordan Darling's fourth-down pass, and the Cavaliers ran out the clock and stepped into history with the school's fifth straight state championship, a feat unparalleled in Texas' storied football tradition. Mayfield didn't relax until the call came in from Collins to get in the Wildcat formation with Lagasse taking the direct snap from center on the final possession.

"That's how we ran out the clock against Cedar Park, so I knew that was the same game plan for Midway in the end," he said. "It just kind of set in when I was out there lined up at receiver that we had finally done it and our goal had come true."

And it had come true in front of thousands from their community, which had witnessed the incredible transformation in just a few short years. They did it with their old coach and program architect, Jeff Dicus and Jack Moss, in the building.

"As the clock ran down I was just very proud to be a small spoke in the big wheel that LT has become," Dicus said later. "To see the support that fans displayed was great. [I'm] very happy and proud for everyone involved with LT."

They did it with Garrett Gilbert and Michael Brewer watching side-by-side from the sideline. So many people that gave the dream a chance, and so many that kept it going, witnessed its culmination in person.

In the end, Lagasse became the game's offensive MVP, rushing for 80 yards on 17 carries and catching 11 passes for 130 yards. His 210 yards of offense out-gained all of Midway, which managed just 165 yards against Lake Travis' tenacious defense. Mayfield passed for 276 yards and a touchdown, completing 24 of 39 passes without an interception. Defensively, Standard took home game MVP honors with his fumble recovery, interception and trio of tackles. Burdette had six stops, including four behind the line of scrimmage and two of the team's six sacks. Junior defensive end Connor Shannon added seven stops including a sack and a half.

On the field following the game, players and coaches alike had no answers for how the accomplishment made them feel. For historic accomplishments, it takes time for the meaning to set in. For some, it's the end of an era. Many won't play football again.

"I never really get to play that any more, never get to hang out with my friends [on the field]," said Balasz, who earned defensive player of the year honors from one group of state sportswriters. "But it was a great accomplishment and something that we'll all share in common and never forget about it. I guess no one will forget about it either, since we're the first ones to do it."

For Lagasse and Gilbert, teaming together for three consecutive titles and being integral parts of the run of five titles, the win becomes a final high school memory that they'll take on to college careers at Southern Methodist University and Texas Christian University, respectively.

Lagasse believed the win did much more than validate the 2011 team's success. It brought back into focus the championship teams that preceded this one.

"Winning it, of course we think for ourselves – let's win it for us – but also winning history, it makes everyone else's that much more special – the state champs – because all of it goes in [the record books]," he said. "It's not just that year, it's five years that makes the history. I think it helps everyone out and I'd hope that everyone was rooting for us so it would make the whole thing that much more special."

Gilbert has been on the sidelines for all five championship teams. As an eighth-grader, he stood on the field when his brother quarterbacked the 2007 team to the school's improbable first title. In 2008 he was one of a few freshmen who got to dress with the varsity for the playoff run, and he became a starting receiver on the next three teams.

"Obviously you have to owe it to the past years who won it before us because you wouldn't have five state championships without them," he said. "It was breathtaking just knowing that we were the only team to do it and we could possibly be the only team to ever do it. To be that team is just an honor and you kind of feel like you're more a part of the Texas high school history because we kind of wrote it ourselves. In setting history in Texas football, being such a prolific state, it's really an unbelievable feeling."

From the sidelines, the two former quarterbacks tried to put the journey into words.

"With the coaches and players we had, we built a winning tradition. We passed it on to very capable and talented players, and the coaches kept everyone on the same page," Garrett Gilbert said. "But honestly, I can't say I ever expected anything like this. I'm so proud of these guys and my little brother."

Brewer added, "It's a special thing we've got here. We're family."

Streuling, who also won his third ring in 2011, hadn't stopped thinking about the accomplishment months after the game and doesn't want to stop thinking about it.

"It's awesome," the strong safety said. "I pretty much think about it every day, especially walking around my house. We've got pictures up on the wall. I go up in my room and see the medals. I think every day about how cool it was to do something that no one else had ever done before."

Much later, Carter smiled knowing that his players and fellow coaches finally had a chance to let the accomplishment soak in.

"What I've tried to let sink in is just we've done something that no one else can ever take away from us," he said. "And how proud I am for the kids and the coaches and the parents and everyone who's been involved in it. This is something that will never go away. It will always be talked about. It's pretty rare that you get to be a part of that, and I'm proud that I've been a small part of it. It's overwhelming to think about."

In today's high school football world, the off-season doesn't last too long. Just a handful of weeks following the historic win, the Cavaliers' winter conditioning program began. When it did, the focus had shifted to 2012.

"The one thing is, we just started off-season," he said only a month removed from the historic win. "You don't get to enjoy the wins as much as you agonize over the losses. We're in the rare air in the fact that I want us to be proud of what we accomplished, and at the same time our kids are working their tails off right now in off-season and after-school. If you walk in that weight room in 20 minutes there will be 150 kids in there working their tails off. The turf room will probably be full of kids throwing the football. I want to relish what we've had a chance to do and let the kids be proud of that. But at the same time, we're making plans for next year and this spring and what's going to happen. It seems like the good moments last [snaps his fingers] that long. The bad moments last forever. I want us to enjoy this, be proud of it, hold our heads high."

18: Repeat the three-peat?

Once the celebrations from the fifth straight title died down, Lake Travis got back to work. Though spring practice didn't officially begin until April 30, the Cavaliers returned to the weight room in mid-January with new goals and a completely new challenge.

Through its biannual realignment, the University Interscholastic League guaranteed that the Cavaliers would not win a sixth consecutive championship at the 4A level. Based on enrollment figures the Cavaliers became a member of the state's largest classification, Conference 5A, and the debate began almost immediately. How would Lake Travis fare against the state's largest schools?

The Cavaliers themselves leave any such debate to those outside the program. They see the move simply as the next step to the next season, one in which each player, both returning and graduating, expects to end in a giant stadium in mid-December holding a large trophy. Pundits agree. In its post-2011 wrap-up, *Dave Campbell's Texas Football* immediately installed Lake Travis as the third ranked team in 5A, behind Dallas Skyline and reigning Division I champion Southlake Carroll. In their annual summer season preview, they ranked the Cavaliers second and predicted that they'd win the 5A, Division II championship.

"Anyone who doesn't think Lake Travis will win [the 5A title in 2012] is just being a hater," said *Austin American-Statesman* preps writer Danny Davis, who's covered his share of Lake Travis games since joining the paper in 2007. "There are all kinds of examples of Lake Travis beating 5A teams."

The Cavaliers haven't lost to a 5A team since 2007, when new district rival Westlake beat the Cavaliers 28-21 in the season's second week. Since then, the Cavaliers have beaten Westlake four consecutive times. Lake Travis has also beaten Westwood, Louisiana power Evangel Christian and other top Texas teams such as Longview and Cibolo Steele, who have since moved up in classification to find success. Free of Lake Travis with the 2010, Steele won the 5A, Division II title in 2010 and lost in the championship game in 2011.

Lake Travis coach Hank Carter began looking at the 2012 season shortly after the 2011 ended. He knew the numbers and saw that Lake Travis would almost certainly move up. Once official notification came, he didn't miss a beat. The Cavaliers moved into District 15-5A with Westlake. Austin High, Bowie, Anderson, Del Valle, and Akins rounded out the district, and all early signs pointed to a week 10 meeting with the Chaparrals as a championship showdown.

"In the regular season, I think moving up to 5A hurts them because the district they are going into isn't as strong as the one they left," Davis said, a nod to the recent battles with Cedar Park, both for district and regional supremacy.

If the district schedule appears weaker, the non-district contests will again keep Lake Travis on its toes. As he'd done in previous years, Carter scheduled the toughest teams he could find. The non-district gauntlet includes traditional playoff qualifiers A&M Consolidated, Westwood and New Braunfels Canyon. And though the Converse Judson Rockets haven't won a state title since 2002, they remain one of the most storied programs around, having reached the state championship game a Texas-best 11 times, winning six. Both coach and players understand the landscape into which Lake Travis stepped and expectations, they point out, remain the same.

"It will be a new set of challenges, but if we continue to have a great run of kids....in my four years I would have faced us up against any 5A and thought we'd do fine," Carter said. "I don't know that we'd beat them all, but I can't imagine lining up against someone and felt like, 'Boy, we can't beat these guys.'

"If you look at it Division II, 5A: Steele played for [the title] twice, Longview's been to the semifinals, [Denton] Guyer last year played for it. We beat Longview twice, we beat Steele twice. Guyer got beat by Longview once and beat Longview once," Carter said.

That attitude rubs off on the players, the quarterback included.

"We're not too worried about the 5A thing," Baker Mayfield said. "It's a new district, but we've played Westlake so many times before, so it's not that big of a deal switching into that. The playoffs are the harder challenge."

Carter understands the team won't have Colin Lagasse, Zach Streuling or Griffin Gilbert to lean on, but Lake Travis has developed the inherent belief that new players will step up the way Mayfield, sophomore running back Shaun Nixon and junior receiver Zach Austin developed in 2011. When they emerge, either in the spring or later in the fall, Carter knows his team will be able to compete with anyone they line up against.

"I think that when you're good, you're good, whether you're in 4A or 5A," he said. "You should be able to play with anyone. That being said, we just lost one of the best senior classes ever to come through the school, so there's a lot of big shoes to fill."

The biggest difference won't be in moving from 4A to 5A. It may come in moving from Region IV, where the Cavaliers' road to championship games sent them to San Antonio and the Rio Grande Valley, to Region II, where the team will face new challenges from Round Rock or the greater Houston area.

"That first round game, against the Round Rock schools, will be tougher," Davis said. "The third round game will be tougher without the pushover from Corpus Christi."

Carter knows as well.

"It will be different," he surmised. "We'd play Round Rock [ISD] in the first round of the playoffs and in the next round we'd probably go to the Houston area, Cy-Fair, Cy-Falls, that bunch. Then you get someone like Belton or Copperas Cove or Garland or someone like that."

Even before the UIL announced realignment, the Cavaliers had started focusing on overcoming any challenge the new season would present.

"We're just going to have to stay healthy throughout the regular season, take it one game at a time and try to be perfect district champs again," Mayfield said. "Then the playoffs will definitely be a harder challenge in the first and third rounds. Region II is a lot harder. It's just going to be more focused and more determination will help us win."

One thing remains clear: the Cavaliers will not be intimidated by the 5A world.

"I don't think 5A will make that big of a difference," Lagasse said. "Maybe as they go later in the playoffs because there will be a lot more, better teams but Cedar Park last year, that's the best the competition gets. As long as the players keep buying in. You know, we've won five in a row so it's hard to doubt that we'd win six, 5A or not, so I think a lot of people think that there's a good chance of winning."

Gilbert had the same perspective. What separates 5A football from 4A football is the number of quality teams.

"I really don't see it as a difference, and people try to make it out that 5A is so much better than 4A," he said. "But the way I see it – yes, 5A has some very, very good teams – there are more good teams but not necessarily better teams. It's more dense. There are more good teams because there are more players, more students."

As the playoffs progress, should Lake Travis extend its state-record post-season winning streak, the Cavaliers (enrollment roughly 2,200 for the 2012-13 school year) will no doubt face off against a school with twice its numbers, a football team with more players to plug in at each spot.

One former coach with very personal, Lake Travis experience in moving from 4A up to 5A says the difference will mainly come in the speed the Cavaliers will see in their opponents.

"They have played talented teams where they've had one, two, maybe three very fast, very quick guys at times," said Jeff Dicus, who jumped from Lake Travis to 5A Duncanville in 2008. "At this level, they'll see teams with a lot more speed and quickness per position. At least that's the biggest thing I've seen moving from 4A to 5A, especially up here where I am. They have some tough teams on their schedule, but once they get deeper in the playoffs, that will be very evident."

Former Cavalier Austin Pollard said the Cavaliers might find themselves outnumbered on the sidelines, but only 11 can play at a time, and how those 11 execute will make all the difference.

"It's not about how much talent you have, it's about how disciplined you are and how close you are and how much you can trust your coaches and your teammates," he said. "That's something that Lake Travis has built. They have a system there where it's proven the last five years. Just because they are going up to 5A, it shouldn't be a problem."

Motivation won't be a problem either. The Cavaliers want to continue winning for a number of reasons: tradition, expectation, and validity chief among them.

Gilbert and Lagasse think the most recent title simply adds to the motivation those leading the 2012 team will feel. Not only will the team be motivated to succeed, it will be motivated not to fail. After all, the recently graduated players have felt that pressure for three years.

"I felt it," Gilbert said. "My brother [Garrett] felt it. Now these guys get to feel it. You always do want to be the team that doesn't end it. You want to be the team that keeps going out on top and you never really want it to end. Those losses that we've had in the past – to Cedar Park and Aledo – really kind of helped us out because it was a lesson for us, that we never want to have that feeling again. We never want to go out and lose a game because that was hurtful to our entire program. We have to have the leadership to go out on top, to go out and win a state championship."

Dave Lagasse, whose sons Bryant and Colin have four championships between them, sees the same thing in the area's younger players.

"The young players now, there's such a legacy to it, that 12-year-olds are doing everything they can to be ready to play when it's their turn," he said.

The expectation of success starts early, and it only grows as the young players see team after team continue the winning tradition. No one, as Gilbert explained, wants to be on the first team that doesn't win the state title.

"It definitely was a relief for the seniors because we'd always say we didn't want to be the class to mess it up, even though maybe we'd be remembered the most because it wasn't part of the consistency," Colin Lagasse said.

Players can remember when they didn't win, before they got to the high school. Streuling remembers his introduction to football at Lake Travis after moving to the area from Louisiana. His older brother, Michael, was headed into high school, but he and younger brother Hunter, also a member of the 2011 team, looked for spots on Pop Warner teams and then at Hudson Bend Middle School.

"My first three years here, I think I won one game, by forfeit," Streuling said. "Those were the worst three years of football in my life in, ever."

Dane Balasz, another senior on the 2011 team, enjoyed playing football from his early years. He first took the field as a first-grader at the youngest Pop Warner level. Like Streuling, he also remembers not finding much success on the field at the middle school level.

"In eighth grade, we didn't win until after football season was over," he said. "No one expected this at all."

Maybe they didn't expect to win as middle schoolers, but by the time Balasz and Streuling had enrolled at high school, Lake Travis had already won its first title and seemed poised for more, which made the desire to continue winning grow even stronger throughout the program. Four years after the first title, the winning has continued, and no one wants to be part of the class that doesn't continue the streak.

"All the seniors, we didn't want to be the class that ruined it," Balasz said. "We wanted to keep it going because we know the kids before us set the tradition and we just wanted to keep it going."

Though the Cavaliers all say that little difference exists between the top 4A and 5A programs, each is aware that the 2012 season brings added pressure to win the title. They won't say that a sixth straight title, and first at the 5A level, legitimizes the record streak, but deep down they feel it, even if they joke about it.

"That's what Colin teases the younger class about, saying, 'You guys better go win so they can't say we only did what we've done because it was 4A,'" said Dave Lagasse.

Lake Travis parents, even those with extensive football backgrounds such as Gale Gilbert, Griffin and Garrett's father, believe Lake Travis would have succeeded similarly had the move up taken place years ago.

"I would venture to say that they probably would have won four or five in 5A," he surmised. "The year they beat Longview, didn't Longview beat the 5A winner? [Longview lost the 2008 season opener to eventual 5A champion Allen 21-7. The Lobos beat Allen 28-25 to open the 2009 season.] I know who beats who on any given day doesn't matter but... That Highland Park team was probably the strongest school in the state, 4A or 5A, when we beat them."

Streuling, for his part, wishes the move had already taken place so those who question Lake Travis' dynastic success would have no argument to minimize it.

"I wish I would have gotten to move up just to prove what we've done," Streuling said. "Some people doubt us, that we couldn't do this in 5A. But there's no doubt in my mind that we could have."

Doubters or not, the Cavaliers will get their chance to prove themselves at the 5A level. Each of the 2011 team's key leaders echo Streuling's confidence that the level of competition doesn't matter, which goes back to the philosophy that Chad Morris brought with him from Stephenville in 2008, one that Carter still espouses.

"I think they can do it," Griffin Gilbert said. "I have all the faith in the world in them. They definitely have enough talent to do it, but you owe it to the coaches to coach us up to be the players that we are today. It really depends on the coaches also because they do such a great job of teaching our offense, teaching our defense and helping us become the players that we are. They help us out in the way we build the program and to go out and win games."

Even the players who played on the first and second championship teams believe the championship success will continue.

"They are going to do their thing," Pollard said. "They won't change anything. It's not that they are playing 5A teams that is worrisome. We dominated 5A teams and they have dominated 5A teams since we left. It's the fact that they are losing talent. They've got people coming up, so if they can get those young guys to buy into the program and fill the shoes of the big guys like Colin Lagasse and Griffin, they are going to be fine. Baker Mayfield is going to be a senior and he's got a lot of experience now. He's going to be good."

Griffin Gilbert agreed.

"I don't think it will be too much more of a challenge for them because I have all the faith in the world in Baker, for Zach Austin, for being the players that they are," he said. "They can easily step up like they did this past year. They can step us as seniors and do an even better job. They can lead their team to another state championship and try to go out and win a 5A state championship."

"It's going to be more of a challenge week by week, but I definitely feel like it's something they can handle," Pollard said. "Coach Carter is without a doubt the best defensive coordinator that I've ever seen. No matter how big of a hole they get into or how good of athletes they have to play that week, he's fantastic at being able to game plan and put his men in the right position to stop those athletes. It doesn't worry me too much when they have the coaches and they're sticking to the system that has worked the last five years."

The newness of 5A after a decade and a half playing 4A opponents will make things exciting even if the games remain lopsided. And make no mistake. No matter the score, no matter the players, Lake Travis' fans will continue to come out.

"We're excited about 5A because we get to go to different stadiums this year," said Laurie Lagasse, Colin and Bryant's mother. "People ask if we're still going to go to the games, and how can we not? I mean, these boys – Baker, Shaun [Nixon], Luke [Hutton] – they're always at our house. Of course we're going to go. Colin won't be there and Bryant won't, but we'll be there. It's just that tradition."

"I really believe they've got a shot to do six," said Glenn Pollard, Austin's father. "Great parents, great kids still. We don't miss anything. I mean, what else are you going to do on Friday night but go to football games?"

It says a lot about how far football has come in the lake town. They'll expect success, because that's just the tradition now, too.

"In our second year Jeff [Dicus] won the district title, and we knew that we would be pretty good, and I thought that we would be pretty good from now on," former athletic director Jack Moss said as the fifth title game approached. "When I mean good, I mean whenever you pitch the ball out there, you have a chance. We will be in the playoffs every year. How far you go, who knows? You need some luck because one call can change the whole thing in a flash. But the big thing is attitude."

Fans believe the winning, and titles, will continue.

"Five years in a row, I guess there's no reason to stop now," said Todd Reesing, the quarterback from 2004-05. "From what I hear, their team was pretty full of underclassmen so they have a lot of guys coming back this year to a defense that I think was their strength last year. They were pretty tough on defense last year. I don't see any reason why they couldn't do it. I don't think moving up to 5A really has anything to do with it at this point. I think 4A and 5A are probably pretty similar at the bigger school level, so they might as well go ahead and six-peat at this point, which is a funny term to hear myself say."

Six-peat. That's something Guy Clayton, a lifelong Lake Travis resident and school board member, vowed he'd never say. He has a different motto in mind.

"I like, 'Repeat the three-peat.'"

That quest begins, as it always does, when summer officially ends and a new season with a new promise begins with the first practice.

19: Secret to their Success

One question about Lake Travis' record championship run remains unanswered. Why? What makes Lake Travis so special?

Those closest to the program speak to the process, the selflessness, the never-ending desire to improve. Hank Carter, the head coach who will attempt to guide the Cavaliers toward their sixth straight title, his third, says many reasons exist for the Cavaliers' success. Those reasons stretch across coaching to community and back.

Lake Travis, through all its early history of failure on the football field, couldn't wait to taste success. When Jeff Dicus and his staff turned the tide following the 2003 season, the success whet the community's collective appetite, and now there's no quenching it. Part of that credit, Carter said, goes to the administration as well.

"This community was hungry," he said. "I think it was a community that was sick and tired of hearing about Westlake and was ready and was hungry for something like that to come to Lake Travis. I think that our administration understands and has understood how important athletics can be to a community and to a school, and so they've set us up to be successful with facilities and allowing us to hire coaches and doing things to let us be successful."

To assuage that hunger, the community eventually came together and, the majority at least, officially voted to make athletics a priority. The Lake Travis ISD administration twice asked voters to approve the sale of bonds to fund district progress. A 2003 election approved the sale of $36 million in bonds to fund work primarily done at the district's elementary schools. Two years later, voters approved nearly $127 million in bonds that included a new elementary school, expansion of the district's three upper level campuses, and improvements to extracurricular program facilities. That bond program included the construction of the multi-purpose Cavalier Activity Center, which houses the football offices and a 40-yard covered turf field. Other athletic facilities including basketball courts and the district's weight room, located in the field house adjoining the football stadium, also benefited during that bond election. As a whole, Lake Travis High School has some of the best athletic facilities, practice especially, in all of Texas.

Glenn Pollard, whose sons Justin and Austin played football at Lake Travis, served as chairman of the bond advisory committee in 2005.

"We did all of that because of what the kids needed and what the community asked for, what was good for the school district," he said. "Not just for football, but for all sports to use that turf room."

Other sports have enjoyed state-level success, as well. The volleyball team won the 4A state championship in 2010 and 2011. The boys golf team won state championships in 2011 and 2012. The baseball (2011) and boys basketball (2010) teams both advanced to the state semifinals for the first time. The swimming and tennis teams have also enjoyed unparalleled success.

And they accomplished it without compromising any of the school district's academic values or successes. The district's academic reputation, Carter said, remains a huge part of the football program's success.

"The academics at our school are incredible," he said. "People get on line and they start looking because they're going to move to the Austin area, they look up at Lake Travis as an exemplary district. Your best and your brightest want to come here. Our enrollment has grown because of that and it's only going to help us in the future."

The coaches represent another unique aspect to the championship run. Dynasties traditionally come with stability, and change at the top rarely happens. But Lake Travis broke that mold. Carter is the third head coach to lead the team to glory, continuing in the school's tradition of short head coaching stays. He recognizes that his situation may be unique, but he also said the right kind of change can be healthy for a football program.

"I think that we've had a little bit of turnover but not much," he said. "When I say little bit, it's enough to keep things fresh and you don't get stagnant. It's not the same 15 guys doing the same things. We've had a couple of changes here, a couple of changes there, just enough where the kids are learning some new things, learning some new faces and the coaches are learning some new guys, just enough to where it doesn't set you back because it's the whole staff change but just enough to keep from getting old hat."

And the coaches who stay mesh well with the coaches who arrive. They understand the one thing that the entire staff must do to succeed: sacrifice the one to lead the many.

"We've had coaches that have put their egos in their pocket," Carter said. "They come here and they want to do what's right for these kids, and it's not about who gets the credit and who's getting to call the plays or who's getting to coach this. We have a group of guys who love these kids and who want to do everything they can for these kids."

Part of that involves continually learning about their craft. Lake Travis' coaches don't sit idly by over the summer, playing golf and going to the beach. They attend camps, visit other schools – especially colleges – to see if they can find something that will improve things even further. Carter himself enjoys hitting the road and visiting with college coaches.

"I'd like to say that we have been on the cutting edge of trying to go out and learn what's the best way to do things offensively, defensively and on special teams," he explained. "I think that our relationships with college coaches and going and visiting them and picking their brains and studying with them [has helped]. I know for a fact offensively and defensively [that has helped]. Defensively we are totally different now because of what we have learned from the colleges, especially TCU. Offensively, it started with Coach Morris and whenever he went up and visited with Coach Malzahn and installed that offense."

The offense has been Lake Travis' calling card, though Carter and the defensive staff have worked long and hard to make sure the Cavaliers don't become one-dimensional. That work has paid off in droves. Offensive players proudly proclaim how the defense carried the team to hard-fought wins in the 2010 and 2011 quarterfinal rounds, making late stands to beat title-worthy Cedar Park in back-to-back years. No matter. Even if defense wins championships, offense remains what brings people to the stadium to watch, and Carter says Lake Travis has always, and will continue to, put a top-notch offense on the field.

"We've had excellent quarterback play," he admits modestly. "We've been able to throw the football effectively."

Counting Todd Reesing before the run of state championships began, Lake Travis sent three straight quarterbacks to play Big XII football: Reesing to Kansas, Garrett Gilbert to Texas and Michael Brewer to Texas Tech. Baker Mayfield, who stepped in as a junior to lead the 2011 championship drive, will become the school's fourth straight Division I quarterback when he decides where he'd like to play following his Lake Travis career. As he entered the summer between his junior and senior seasons, Mayfield had already received scholarship offers from Washington State and Rice with more to surely follow.

But quarterback play alone hasn't defined Lake Travis. Carter also points out that the Cavaliers have enjoyed some success on special teams, not just with the kickers and punters but with long snappers as well, a unique run for a high school.

"We've had really good kickers and long-snappers, probably better than anybody else," Carter said. "We've sent kickers and punters and long snappers to Division I. That's a rare skill and we've been fortunate to have those."

Ryan Erxleben and Kramer Fyfe punt and kick, respectively, at Texas Tech. Fyfe's successor Stephen Pyle earned first team all-state honors in 2010 and left Lake Travis to play soccer and football at Cal Poly San Luis Obispo. Trevor Gillette went to Rice as a tight end and long snapper.

Talented players at any position help, but talent alone doesn't win championships. Gale Gilbert, Garrett and Griffin Gilbert's father and a former NFL quarterback, pointed out that other high schools have had multiple major college quarterbacks but didn't have the same success Lake Travis has had. He returns to the relationships the coaches have built with the players, not just the quarterbacks, as the driving force for the success.

"Other programs have had Division I quarterbacks back-to-back-to-back-to back years, and other programs have had multiple linemen, multiple receivers, running backs go through their system," Gilbert said. "So what made this all so special was the combination of the coaches working with the kids, coaches working with the parents, the community support, but it goes back to its 12 coaches working with 60 kids and how they maintain their work ethic. No way do you play at a high level every week. You're just not going to play perfectly every week, and they've done a fabulous job of motivating. You can't tell them the same story every week. They've just done a fabulous job with the kids. When's the right time to chew their butts, when's the right time to be a little loose with them."

Players throughout the championship era agree with those sentiments. Lake Travis' coaches seem to have the Midas touch when it comes to molding individuals into a selfless, motivated, championship team. Austin Pollard played for both Dicus and Morris. He saw the benefits that both coaches brought to the program but said that players really blossomed under Morris.

"I can't speak for the guys in the locker room the last few years," he said. "For us, we were a family. More so than normal high school teams are like. I think some people claim they are a close team, but until you are in that locker room with that team, you have no idea how close we were. We were very close. We all trusted each other. We didn't make mistakes."

The trust and pursuit of perfection have come to define Lake Travis, Pollard went on to say.

"Ever since we graduated and when I was there, we weren't the biggest, fastest or strongest, but we did our jobs," he said. "That comes down to coaching and the will to win by the group. I think for us being bad for so long, for me I refused to be like that. That was my mentality. I saw how the program was so I wanted to be a perfectionist on the field, and I thought everybody felt like that. It's just a big family. Everyone trusts each other; they trust the coaches and you can't really teach that. It just has to come naturally through time. It's something that Lake Travis has developed and it's been amazing."

Pollard's father Glenn remembers talking with former athletic director Jack Moss about the size, or lack thereof, of Lake Travis' football players.

"The kids were your size and my size," Glenn Pollard, who stands about 5-foot-8, recalled. "Jack Moss was standing with me one day looking at the kids. He said, 'People see these kids standing around like that, and they said there's no way these kids can win a state championship. Look at the size of our kids, there's no muscles on them, but they're just fast and strong. They've got heart.'"

Through the years, the Cavaliers have gotten bigger. Colin Lagasse bristles at the description that the Cavaliers are smaller, slower and weaker than the teams they face week in and week out.

"I watched the video of the 2007 team, and they have the long white socks on," he said, throwing a slight barb at his older brother Bryant, a captain on that team. "And everyone looks like a twig. People say we're not the strongest, but I think we've really gotten a lot stronger as a team. Our defense has gotten a lot more physical."

No matter the reality, the Cavaliers still don't scare people, at least physically, when they step off the bus or take the field to go through their pregame routine. Most times, especially in big games, the Cavaliers fail the eyeball test. Fortunately for Lake Travis, the eyeball test doesn't count for much. Perhaps when lesser teams see a team of big, strong players taking the field, they may quake a little in their cleats. But while opponents may not quake from Lake Travis' appearance, the reputation the Cavaliers have developed – earned – over their five championship years may be worth something tangible on the field.

"They just don't think they're going to lose," Moss said. "It's like Odessa Permian and Brownwood. When they took the field, they had seven [points] before they kicked off. I think it's like that with Lake Travis now."

"When you see Lake Travis warming up on the field [in a big game], you think they're going to get rolled," said the *Austin American-Statesman's* Danny Davis. "They just don't have the great athlete. But they have good athletes in a great system."

The system. So what defines Lake Travis' system? Literally speaking, the Cavaliers employ a hurry-up, no-huddle offense that looks to identify and attack the soft spots in an opposing defense while running plays at breakneck speed. Defensively, the Cavaliers attack as well, coming at any time from any angle to try and disrupt timing and create turnovers. As Austin Pollard explained, the Cavaliers expect perfection from themselves and spend nearly all of their practice time perfecting their craft.

But the scheme doesn't define Lake Travis' dominance by itself. Other teams have tried to spread the defenses out and throw the ball into open spaces. Other teams have played hurry-up, no-huddle styles. But for some reason, they haven't been able to mirror Lake Travis' success on either side. So maybe the style isn't everything that defines Lake Travis.

"The style of play is the base," Davis said. "That's been their identity, but at the same time I would assume people have tried to mimic what they do. There are other teams that throw without as much success, so it goes back to the coaching and the players."

Coaches coach, but the players have to execute, and at Lake Travis that willingness to execute exactly what the coaches want without regard for individual recognition or glory sets the program apart.

"It's the coaches, but then also for the coaches – for what they say to come out on the field – you have to have a team that's willing to do it, that has that connection and is smart enough to play as a team and not be all about yourself," Lagasse said. "To just do your role. Every person wants to do their role because in the past that's been successful. Once that first year started, no one's going to put any doubt in it because it's like, 'Oh, we did it last year so let's just keep doing [things] the same way.' Once you start it, everyone just listens and goes with it."

They know that listening and buying in brings desired results, so no one dares to step outside the line.

"I feel like it's a lot of that. It's a lot of coming together and not being selfish," Griffin Gilbert said. "We have players who just want to win. They don't care about their own accomplishments. They want to go out and do their individual assignments well because that helps the team more than it does themselves. They go out and put themselves on the line for the team and try to win football games, because that's what we're here to do. We're here to go out and try to win state championships and be a high school that is unstoppable in winning football games."

Another aspect of the success has been the success itself. The regular season is 10 games. Roughly half of the schools in Texas don't make the playoffs, so their seasons, and practices, end after that tenth game. Its five championship seasons – six playoff games each – have amounted to three extra seasons for the Cavaliers, and that extra practice time helped the Cavaliers continue on their quest for perfection.

"And when we started making the playoffs, those extra weeks of practice really helped," said Moss. "It's one of the reasons we're still winning. Playing 16 weeks is a major difference than playing just 10."

While Lake Travis' rapid rise caught the state's football community off guard, now that the Cavaliers stand atop the mountain, something surprises their supporters. Some Lake Travis fans are shocked that other high school coaches haven't made it their off-season mission to park themselves at Carter's office door begging to learn what he and his staff do that separates Lake Travis from the rest of the pack.

"The game of football is such a copy-cat game," Gale Gilbert said. "Who's doing well, who's hottest at the time, everybody is going to follow suit. Why aren't people doing exactly that at this level? Here's the question: Why aren't there more teams doing what Lake Travis does? And not just on the field itself but from the way the program runs, from their voluntary weight lifting prior to school to first period athletics, where you can do some work on game plan, and then after school where you can actually do your real football practice."

Through his work with the school's summer 7-on-7 competition, coaches thought his NFL experience would benefit the Cavaliers while they couldn't work with the group, Gilbert's become closer to other high schools and their programs than most parents. What's glaring, he said, is what he doesn't see.

"What is it that other people aren't mimicking?" he asks, only somewhat rhetorically. "I've asked Hardee [McCrary, a former assistant coach at the University of Texas] that before. Why isn't it going on? He didn't have an answer for it either. I mean, if I was a new coach and I was going to get a head coaching job, I would be quizzing [Jeff] Dicus, I'd be quizzing [Chad] Morris, I'd be quizzing Hank [Carter]. What are you guys doing different here?"

For Gilbert, the reasons for Lake Travis' success start with the coaches. While it has been Morris and Carter who have gotten the lion's share of the credit for winning the most recent titles, Gilbert quickly points out that no one has forgotten what Dicus did to turn the program around and lead it to the very first championship.

"But I think, and it goes back to Dicus and it carried over to Chad obviously," he said. "They both demanded a lot of the kids. It's how you praise them or scold them. With Dicus in turning the program around, the kids and the parents bought in to what he was trying to do. And Chad [Morris] and Hank have taken it the next step further."

To some, Lake Travis no longer looks or operates like a high school program. Sure, the Cavaliers look like Texas Tech on the field both with uniforms and the once wide-open but surprisingly balanced attack, but there's more to the program's college feel than that. Part of that can be attributed to the level Texas high school football has reached, yet Lake Travis transcends that as well.

"Lake Travis is a college level football program, the way that kids are brought up from eight years old running the same system," said former all-district quarterback Greg Wiggins. "The strength, the speed, the conditioning. Just look at the size of the kids who play football now, it's totally different. But that's what Texas high school football has become, not just Texas but nationwide. Lake Travis is that shining star on the hill. They are Texas high school football now."

How long they remain the face of Texas high school football, no one can tell. One year, championship Saturday will come and go, and the last team standing won't be Lake Travis. While no one in red and black will admit it, they will be ready for it.

"Now that they've kept it up, it's very special to me," said Austin Pollard. "I'm still very close to a lot of the guys who still play. Griffin, I've been very close to him ever since we were little. The people who still play, I'm very close to Baker Mayfield and Zach Austin. I still have connections there. It's not just that I played there. I still have friends playing there. I couldn't be more proud of Coach Carter taking over and all he's done. I still talk to him on a regular basis and see him whenever I'm in town. It's very special how I've been around to see how bad it was, then every year getting better until where we are today. It means a lot. I'll be one of the saddest people if the day comes when they don't win one even though I won't be playing."

They'll think back on the record streak of five – or whatever the number climbs to before it ends – and remember what it meant to take part in it, to be a part of a football family that found unprecedented success.

"I think when you look at the history of Texas high school football and sports in general, every year that they win it, the odds of winning it again become slimmer and slimmer," Morris said. "The streak will end. What you hope is that the community hasn't become so spoiled that it's taken for granted. You hope the community has embraced and savored the last five years – and I think they have – while doing something that may never happen again in our lifetime. It's inevitable, but enjoy it while it's lasting."

Appendix: Photos

Above, Coach Jim
Shewmake celebrates
Lake Travis' 21-14
Bi-District win over
Pflugerville Connally
in the 2000 season.

Right, quarterback
Todd Reesing became
Lake Travis' first state
player of the year in
2004.

Above, Fred Robinson became Lake Travis' first all-state receiver, starting from 2003-2005 and finishing his career as the fifth all-time receiving yardage leader in state history.

Left, Jared Quick hauls in a touchdown pass during Lake Travis' first playoff-qualifying season in 2000.

Clockwise from top left: Jack Moss joined Lake Travis as athletic director in early 2003 and began implementing his strategy to make the school relevant in athletics. His first hire was Jeff Dicus, who took Lake Travis from a winless team in 2002 to a state championship in 2007. Hank Carter, talking to his players following a 2010 loss to Aledo, followed his mentor, Chad Morris, who guided the Cavaliers to 32 consecutive wins and titles in 2008 and 2009.

Jason Bird set a state record with 153 catches in the 2007 season. He averaged better than 10 catches and 150 yards per game.

Bryant Lagasse pressures Highland Park's Dutch Crews in the 2007 title game.

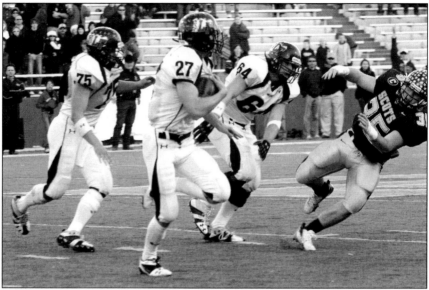

Jay Plotkin

Chris Aydam follows blocks from Zach Peckover (75) and Dusty Williams (64) in the 2007 championship game against Highland Park.

Jay Plotkin

Part of the Lake Travis crowd painted their school spirit on for the 2007 state championship game.

Jay Plotkin

With quick linemen, Garrett Gilbert had plenty of room in the pocket against Highland Park.

Jay Plotkin

Lake Travis defenders Garrett Culwell (1), Bryant Lagasse (16) and Sean Robinson (31) begin to celebrate after Highland Park's Austin Mai couldn't handle Winston Gamso's fourth-down pass late in the 2007 championship game. The Scots' sideline, including legendary coach Randy Allen (in hat, back turned), can't believe what it's just seen.

Jay Plotkin

Above, Cohl Walla's touchdown catch late in the first half helped Lake Travis hold on to a precarious lead against Highland Park. Right, Sean Robinson's touchdown-saving tackle on Chase Davis typified the Cavaliers' effort in their first championship game.

Jay Plotkin

Receiver Cade McCrary hauls in a touchdown pass at DKR-Texas Memorial Stadium in Lake Travis' 2008 regional final win over Killeen. McCrary earned all-state honors following the season.

Bob Cooper, Courtesy of Lake Travis View

Defensive standout Harry Hatch makes a leaping interception in the Cavaliers' win over storied Evangel Christian. Hatch helped anchor Lake Travis' much-improved defense in 2008.

Bob Cooper, Courtesy of Lake Travis View

Jay Plotkin

Receiver Austin Pollard scores in an early-season win over future rival Cedar Park in 2008. Pollard amassed more than 1,500 all-purpose yards as a senior and had his two biggest games in the state semifinals and final.

A three-year starter, Paden Kelley (70) anchored Lake Travis' offensive line during its first two championship seasons. As a senior, he didn't allow anyone he blocked to sack Garrett Gilbert.

Jay Plotkin

Jay Plotkin

Above, Chris Aydam has plenty of room to run against Alice High School in Lake Travis' 2008 regional semifinal win, thanks to blocking from Will Hawk (53) and Andy Erickson (13). Left, defensive line stalwart Todd Perry makes a sack against Dripping Springs.

Bob Cooper, Courtesy of Lake Travis View

Quarterback Garrett Gilbert finished his Lake Travis career a two-time state champion, Class 4A player of the year in 2008, Gatorade/USA Today National Player of the Year and the all-time leading passer in Texas high school history. Below, freshman Griffin Gilbert hauls in a pass from older brother Garrett late in the Cavaliers' thrashing of Killeen in the regional championship game. The younger Gilbert thanked head coach Chad Morris for the opportunity to catch a pass from his brother.

Left, quarterback Michael Brewer took over for Garrett Gilbert and passed for more than 4,400 yards in a perfect 2009 season. Gilbert, above, scoring against Longview in the 2008 title game, finished his career as Texas' all-time leader in completions and passing yards.

Jay Plotkin

Above, Quentin Crow (42), Ian Lazarus (6) and Shaquille Marable (9) led Lake Travis' attacking defense in 2009. Right, Conner Floyd emerged as an all-state receiver and Michael Brewer's favorite target.

Bob Cooper, Courtesy of Lake Travis View

Bob Cooper, Courtesy of Lake Travis View

Above, Andy Erickson celebrates a surprisingly easy touchdown in the 2009 championship game against Longview. Below, linebacker Austin Williams leaps to apply pressure against Alamo Heights in the 2009 Region IV championship game.

Jay Plotkin

279

Above, Ian Lazarus lunges to make a tackle against Longview. Below, Trevor Gillette stretches to recover a fumble he caused after sacking Longview's Aron Johnson in the title game.

Bob Cooper, Courtesy of Lake Travis View

Above, Will Hawk (53) started at center for two years and proved another vital cog in Lake Travis' offensive line. Below, Taylor Wrinkle played defensive back and returned kicks for the first three championship teams. He is the middle brother of a trio who played at Lake Travis, including Austin (2005-06) and Cameron (2010-11). All wore No. 2.

Bob Cooper, Courtesy of Lake Travis View

281

Jay Plotkin

Michael Brewer, with protection from Nick Magnella, gets set to throw a pass in the 2010 season opener against Westlake at DKR.

Bob Cooper, Courtesy of Lake Travis View

Taylor Doyle (77), blocking for Andy Erickson in a 2009 playoff game, started for three years and overcame a broken leg in the 2009 state championship game to earn a scholarship to Texas following the 2010 season.

Nick Magnella (62) locks up 2010 state player of the year Mario Edwards in the title game against Denton Ryan. Magnella kept Edwards at bay, playing a key role for a second straight year in the title game. In 2009 he stepped in when Taylor Doyle got hurt against Longview.

Jonathan Roberts, sacking Marble Falls' Zed Woerner, anchored the Lake Travis defensive line in 2009 and 2010.

Above, Cameron Wrinkle breaks free for a crucial punt return touchdown in the 21-20 win over Cedar Park. Below, Zach Streuling's interception stopped a potential Cedar Park touchdown and led to Michael Brewer's go-ahead score.

Erich Schlegel, Courtesy of Lake Travis View

Michael Brewer hurdles a Ryan defender into the end zone for the first score in the 2010 title game.

Shaquille Marable leaps to Dylan Bittles (47) after Bittles' last minute sack of Ethan Fry sealed the Cavaliers' grueling win over Cedar Park.

Bob Cooper, Courtesy of Lake Travis View

Jay Plotkin

Above, Baker Mayfield burst on the scene in the season opener against West-lake, stepping in when Colin Lagasse left injured. Mayfield threw for 3,788 yards with 45 touchdowns and only five interceptions and rushed for 754 yards and 10 touchdowns. One of his favorite targets was Zach Austin (below), who caught 72 passes for 1,340 yards and 16 touchdowns.

Jay Plotkin

Jay Plotkin

Above, Griffin Gilbert celebrates following his touchdown in the 2011 championship game. Between Griffin and older brother Garrett, the Gilberts have played on all five championship teams. Below, running back Varshaun Nixon emerged as an offensive force in his sophomore season.

Jay Plotkin

Jay Plotkin

Above, defenders Brock Kenyon, Jacob Standard (16) and Corbin Crow celebrate Standard's interception in the 2011 championship game. Standard earned defensive MVP honors in the game.

Right, Corbin Crow applies pressure to Smithson Valley's Lawrence Mattison. Crow is another younger sibling (older brother Quentin) to win a pair of titles.

Jay Plotkin

Jay Plotkin

Above, Cavaliers begin the 2011 celebration after Colin Lagasse scored the clinching touchdown and help up five fingers. Right, Lagasse being presented the championship game offensive MVP award.

Jay Plotkin

2007 Lake Travis High School Varsity Football
Conference 4A, Division II State Champions

Jay Plotkin

No.	Name	Grade	Pos
1	Garrett Culwell	12	DB
2	Taylor Wrinkle	10	RB
3	Marcus Dunn	12	QB
4	Cade McCrary	11	WR
5	Cohl Walla	11	WR
6	David Foley	12	WR
7	Garrett Gilbert	11	QB
8	Jack Hourin	11	QB
10	Hunter Akers	10	SS
11	Zach Dixon	11	FS
12	Jason Bird	12	WR
13	Andy Erickson	10	WR/RB
14	Ryan Erxleben	11	DE/P
15	Tim Spohrer	12	DB
16	Bryant LaGasse	12	DB
18	Thomas Rebold	12	K
20	Ryan Adams	11	FS
21	Colton Volpe	11	RB
22	M.J. Mann	10	SS
23	Austin Pollard	11	WR
24	Jacob Kennon	12	DB
27	Chris Aydam	11	RB
28	Ian Lazarus	10	FS
30	Harry Hatch	11	CB
31	Sean Robinson	12	DB
33	Marcus Pate	11	DB
34	Jon-Michael Paul	11	LB
35	Kyle Brady	11	LB
40	Andrew Naylor	11	LB
42	Mike DeWitt	12	LB
43	Jeff Markim	12	DB
44	Trevor Gillette	10	TE
45	Tanner Kyle	12	DE
46	Logan Harvill	12	DE
47	Sean Kelley	12	LB
48	Mike Adams	11	LB
51	Derik Harding	11	DE
53	Norman Gutierrez	12	LB
54	Nick Whitehair	11	DE
55	Matt Kuenstler	12	DL
56	Mike Morstad	12	OL
58	Michael McIntyre	11	OL
59	Ian Kelso	10	OL
62	Michael Scotty	12	LB
64	Dusty Williams	11	OL
65	Tyler James	11	OL
70	Paden Kelley	11	OL
73	Todd Perry	11	DT
74	Michael Walsh	11	DE
75	Zach Peckover	12	OL
76	Austin Jauregui	11	OL
77	Josh Clark	12	OL
81	Sam Rodriguez	11	DE
82	Michael Benson	12	WR
83	Ethan Willinger	10	WR
84	Jackson Deen	12	WR
85	Steve Blackwell	12	WR
86	Philip Bouza	12	DB
88	Tim Dash	10	TE
90	Logan Davis	11	DL

Head coach: Jeff Dicus
Assistant coaches: Dave Nelson (DC), Jerry Bird (OC), Roy Hudson, Duston Culpepper, Jerry Kantor, Kenneth Gilchrist, Kevin Halfmann, George Oakes, Jason Jaynes, Donnie Funderburg, Roy Kinnan, Michael Wall
Trainers: Brandy Gothard, Ashley Bernard
Superintendent: Rocky Kirk
Principal: Charlie Little
Athletic Director: Jack Moss

2008 Lake Travis High School Varsity Football
Conference 4A, Division I State Champions

Jay Plotkin

No.	Name	Grade	Pos
1	Luis Barrientos	12	K
2	Taylor Wrinkle	11	RB/DB
3	Kramer Fyfe	11	K
4	Cade McCrary	12	WR
6	Ian Lazarus	11	DB
7	Garrett Gilbert	12	QB
8	Ethan Willinger	11	DB
9	Jack Hourin	12	DB
10	Hunter Akers	11	DB
11	Clay Faust	11	DB
13	Andy Erickson	11	RB
14	Ryan Erxleben	12	P/DE
15	Michael Streuling	12	DB
16	Michael Brewer	10	QB/WR
18	Mark Hoy	12	WR
19	Brent Garrett	12	WR
20	Ryan Adams	12	DB
21	Colton Volpe	12	RB
22	Collin Chalmers	12	DB
23	Austin Pollard	12	WR
24	Trent Shumate	12	DB
27	Chris Aydam	12	RB
28	Drake Screws	11	FB
31	Harry Hatch	12	DB
32	Jagger Ramsey	12	FB
33	Marcus Pate	12	DB
34	Jon-Michael Paul	12	DL
35	Kyle Brady	12	LB
40	Drew Naylor	12	LB
42	Quinton Crow	11	LB
43	Bailey Metcalfe	12	DB
44	Trevor Gillette	11	LB
45	Alex Matthews	10	WR
48	Mike Adams	12	FB/LB

No.	Name	Grade	Pos
53	Will Hawk	11	OL
54	Nick Whitehair	12	DL
55	Frank Contreras	11	DL
56	Rodrigo Sanchez	12	DL
58	Mike McIntyre	12	OL
59	Ian Kelso	11	OL
64	Dustin Williams	12	OL
65	Ryan Nuckolls	12	OL
67	Scott Morris	11	OL
68	Starrett Hicks	12	OL
69	Doug DeSpain	12	OL
70	Paden Kelley	12	OL
73	Todd Perry	12	DL
74	Michael Walsh	12	LB
75	John Amberger	12	DL
76	Austin Jauregui	12	OL
77	Taylor Doyle	10	OL
81	Sam Rodriguez	12	DL
82	AJ Neeld	12	WR
85	Tanner Gillette	10	WR
86	LaMarquis Thomas	12	DE
88	Conner Floyd	10	WR

Head coach: Chad Morris
Assistant Coaches: Hank Carter (DC), Matt Green (OC), Jonathan Coats, Robbie Coplin, Kevin Dydalewicz, Randall Edwards, Kevin Halfmann, Jason Jaynes, Roy Kinnan, Jess Loepp, George Oaks, Kyle Spano, Michael Wall
Trainers: Brandy Gothard, Ashley Bernard
Superintendent: Rocky Kirk
Principal: Kim Brents
Director Extra-Curricular Programs: Gary Briley

2009 Lake Travis High School Varsity Football
Conference 4A, Division I State Champions

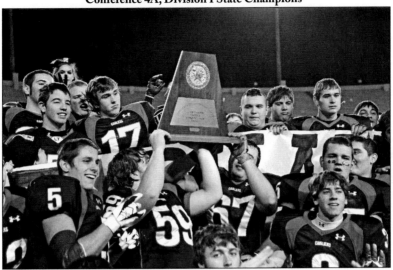

Bob Cooper, Courtesy of Lake Travis View

No.	Name	Grade	Pos
1	Michael Pojman	11	RB
2	Taylor Wrinkle	12	DB
3	Kramer Fyfe	12	K/WR
4	Colin Lagasse	10	DB
5	Jack Patton	12	FB
6	Ian Lazarus	12	DB
8	Ethan Willinger	12	DB
9	Shaquille Marable	11	DE
10	Cole Purswell	12	WR
11	Tanner Gillette	11	WR
12	Hunter Akers	12	DB
13	Andy Erickson	12	RB
15	Regan Strickland	12	WR
16	Michael Brewer	11	QB
17	Tommy Voos	12	QB/WR
18	Omar Duke-Tinson	11	DB
19	Jonathan Bird	11	DB
20	Mark Kelly	12	DB
24	Blage Magee	12	DB
22	Clay Flinn	11	DB
23	Griffin Gilbert	10	WR
25	Alex Matthews	11	WR
27	Steve Peacock	12	DB
28	Drake Screws	12	FB
30	Hayden Garrett	12	DB
31	Tyler Listz	12	DB
32	Turney Maurer	11	FB
42	Quinton Crow	12	ILB
44	Trevor Gillette	12	DE
45	Bret Plymire	12	ILB
46	Anthony Nelson	12	ILB
47	Dylan Bittles	11	DE

No.	Name	Grade	Pos
51	Austin Williams	11	ILB
53	Will Hawk	12	OL
54	Drew Patterson	12	DT
56	Frank Contreras	12	DT
57	Regan Womack	11	OL
59	Ian Kelso	12	OL
62	Nick Magnella	11	OL
64	Anthony Carchi	11	OL
65	Casey Laney	11	DL
67	Scott Morris	12	OL
68	Jonathan Roberts	11	DT
71	Kyle Connell	11	DE/OL
72	Jonathan Briones	11	OL
73	Michael Schappel	12	OL
74	Zach Watts	12	DT
76	Nick Ribera	12	DT
77	Taylor Doyle	11	OL
84	Alex Calloway	12	WR
88	Conner Floyd	11	WR

Head Coach: Chad Morris
Assistant Coaches: Hank Carter (DC), Matt Green (OC), Randall Edwards, Ryan Luedecke, Mike Wall, Kevin Halfmann, George Oakes, Kyle Spano, Robbie Coplin, Kevin Dydalewicz, Johnathan Coats, Roy Kinnan, Ryan Priem
Trainers: Brandy Gothard, Ashley Bernard
Superintendent: Rocky Kirk
Principal: Kim Brents
Director Extra-Curricular Programs: Gary Briley

2010 Lake Travis High School Varsity Football
Conference 4A, Division I State Champions

No.	Name	Grade	Pos
1	Stephen Pyle	12	K
2	Cameron Wrinkle	11	RB
3	Michael Pojman	12	RB
4	Colin Lagasse	11	DB
5	Blake Burdette	11	LB
6	Axel Gomez	12	DB
8	Tyler Paulsen	11	DE
9	Shaquille Marable	12	DE
10	Paul Heinen	11	DB
11	Tanner Gillette	12	WR
12	Brock Kenyon	10	DB
13	Zach Streuling	11	DB
15	Bryan Kribbs	12	DB
16	Michael Brewer	12	QB
17	Garrett Noak	12	QB
18	Omar Duke-Tinson	12	DB
19	Jonathan Bird	12	DB
20	Alex Smelcer	12	DB
21	Jake Kotalik	12	RB
22	Clay Flinn	12	DB
23	Griffin Gilbert	11	WR
24	Garrett Faber	12	WR
25	Alex Matthews	12	WR
26	Dane Balasz	11	DB
27	Andreas Soto	12	RB
29	Cody Alexander	12	DB
30	Will Jones	12	DE
32	Turney Maurer	12	FB
33	Sean Craig	12	DB
34	Alex Chapman	12	DB
35	Connor Nelson	12	DB
42	Corbin Crow	11	LB
43	Gokmen Tireng	12	RB
47	Dylan Bittles	12	DE
48	Jacob Garner	11	LB
50	Cullen Richardson	12	OL
51	Austin Williams	12	LB
52	Adam Jemmott	12	OL
53	Danny McIntyre	11	OL
54	Evan Faust	12	OL
55	Jude Jeffress	11	DL
57	Reagan Womack	12	OL
58	Kevin Quinn	11	OL
59	Luis Godinez	12	DL
62	Nick Magnella	12	OL
64	Anthony Carchi	12	OL
65	Casey Laney	12	OL
68	Jonathan Roberts	12	DT
70	Josh Leyva	12	DE
71	Kyle Connell	12	DE
72	Johnathan Briones	12	OL
73	Sam Schlanger	12	DL
77	Taylor Doyle	12	OL
81	Alex Walsh	12	WR
82	Dannon Cavil	10	WR
83	Zach Austin	10	WR
84	Justin Alexander	12	WR
85	Austin Lee	12	WR
88	Conner Floyd	12	WR
90	Jeremy Amberger	12	DL

Head coach: Hank Carter

Assistant Coaches: Matt Green (OC), Randall Edwards (DC), Ryan Luedecke, Judd Thrash, Kevin Halfmann, George Oakes, Kyle Spano, Robbie Coplin, Jarrett Lambert, Jonathan Coats, Ryan Priem, Robert Rayos, Ian Dillon, Roy Kinnan

Trainers: Brandy Gothard, Ashley Bernard

Superintendent: Rocky Kirk

Principal: Kim Brents

Director Extra-Curricular Programs: Gary Briley

2011 Lake Travis High School Varsity Football
Conference 4A, Division I State Champions

Erich Schlegel, Courtesy of Lake Travis View

No.	Name	Grade	Pos
1	Zach Joiner	11	WR
2	Cameron Wrinkle	12	RB
3	Varshaun Nixon	10	RB
4	Colin Lagasse	12	QB
5	Blake Burdette	12	LB
6	Travis Schoonmaker	12	WR
7	Griffin Gilbert	12	WR
8	Tyler Paulsen	12	DE
9	Zach Austin	11	WR
10	Paul Heinen	12	DB
11	Baker Mayfield	11	QB
12	Brock Kenyon	11	DB
13	Zach Streuling	12	DB
15	Skylar Strickland	12	WR
16	Jacob Standard	12	DB
17	Michael Mayes	12	K
18	Dean Young	11	DB
19	Blake Harvey	12	WR
20	Kevin Marcotte	11	K
21	Hunter Sundbeck	12	RB
22	Hunter Streuling	11	DB
23	Nico Escalante	11	LB
24	Luke Hutton	10	DB
25	Vincent Villagomez	11	DB
26	Dane Balasz	12	DB
27	Austin Cluck	12	WR
28	Romey Kelso	10	RB
29	Kendall Edwards	12	DB
30	Neil Robinson	12	DB
33	Jacob Pate	11	DB
34	Connor Shannon	11	DE
35	Zachary Stewart	11	DE
40	Spencer Staples	11	DT
42	Corbin Crow	12	LB
44	Isaac Gonzales	12	RB
47	Dewayne Clemmons	12	LB
48	Jacob Garner	12	LB
50	Dalton Lunday	12	DT
52	Drake Rowland	11	OL
54	Kody Brabson	12	OL
55	Jude Jeffress	12	DL
56	T.J. Armstrong	12	OL
58	Kevin Quinn	12	OL
59	Ian Medford	12	OL
60	Tyler Voos	12	OL
64	Chase Karnstadt	12	DE
65	Hunter Siddons	12	OL
67	Kelby Radford	12	OL
68	Sam Richardson	12	OL
69	Erick Anton	12	OL
70	Marshall Womack	12	OL
71	Daniel Breedlove	12	DT
72	Brandon Quinterro	11	OL
73	John Breedlove	12	DT
75	Dominic Cassaro	12	DE
76	Ty Anderson	10	OL
81	Tyler Boddorf	12	WR
82	Tyler Payne	12	WR
83	Aubrey Metcalfe	12	WR
84	Ryan Jones	12	WR
85	Cody Claybourn	10	WR

Head coach: Hank Carter
Assistant Coaches: David Collins (OC), Randall Edwards (DC), Ryan Luedecke, Judd Thrash, Kevin Halfmann, George Oakes, Kyle Spano, Robbie Coplin, Jarrett Lambert, Jonathan Coats, Ryan Priem, Robert Rayos, Roy Kinnan
Trainers: Brandy Gothard, Ashley Bernard
Superintendent: Susan Bohn (Interim)
Principal: Kim Brents
Director Extra-Curricular Programs: Gary Briley

Championship Season Game-by-Game Scores

2007

Lake Travis 32, Texas City 31
Westlake 28, Lake Travis 21
Lake Travis 18, Westwood 10
Lake Travis 30, Burnet 14
Lake Travis 33, Vista Ridge 28
Lake Traivs 58, Lampasas 14
Lake Travis 34, Dripping Springs 24
Lake Travis 31, Connally 27
Lake Travis 49, Marble Falls 20
Lake Travis 33, Hendrickson 13
Lake Travis 37, New Braufels Canyon 7*
Lake Travis 45, Kerrville Tivy 29*
Lake Travis 45, Calallen 14*
Lake Travis 57, Beeville Jones 43*
Lake Travis 49, Dayton 13*
Lake Travis 36, Highland Park 34*
Final State Ranking (all-divisions): 9
Final National Ranking: 64

2008

Lake Travis 27, Westwood 20
Lake Travis 38, Westlake 17
Lake Travis 35, Cedar Park 21
Lake Travis 46, Evangel Christian 31
Lake Travis 50, Killeen 9
Lake Travis 55, Hutto 20
Lake Travis 57, Lampasas 0
Lake Travis 57, Hendrickson 0
Lake Travis 42, Dripping Springs 3
Lake Travis 54, Marble Falls 14
Lake Travis 55, LBJ 14*
Lake Travis 38, Cibolo Steele 21*
Lake Travis 55, Alice 32*
Lake Travis 71, Killeen 9*
Lake Travis 56, Friendswood 22*
Lake Travis 48, Longview 23*
Final State Ranking (all-divisions): 2
Final National Ranking: 16

2009

Lake Travis 55, Westwood 31
Lake Travis 42, Westlake 21
Lake Travis 54, Cedar Park 17
Lake Travis 52, Boerne 0
Lake Travis 56, Killeen 31
Lake Travis 57, Hutto 16
Lake Travis 38, Lampasas 7
Lake Travis 58, Hendrickson 15
Lake Travis 52, Dripping Springs 0
Lkae Travis 52, Marble Falls 7
Lake Travis 58, Crockett 7*

Lake Travis 27, Cibolo Steele 20*
Lake Travis 52, C.C. Flour Bluff 13*
Lake Travis 27, Alamo Heights 13*
Lake Travis 57, Pearland Dawson 12*
Lake Travis 24, Longview 17*
Final State Ranking (all-divisions): 2
Final National Ranking: 20

2010

Lake Travis 32, Westlake 21
Lake Travis 34, Hendrickson 24
Aledo 14, Lake Travis 10
Lake Travis 37, Kerrville Tivy 33
Lake Travis 38, Dripping Springs 0
Lake Travis 62, Vandegrift 7
Lake Travis 42, Vista Ridge 0
Lake Travis 62, Rouse 14
Lake Travis 45, Marble Falls 0
Cedar Park 35, Lake Travis 21
Lake Travis 28, McCallum 20*
Lake Travis 48, Kerrville Tivy 42*
Lake Travis 59, Victoria East 28*
Lake Travis 21, Cedar Park 20*
Lake Travis 24, Friendswood 3*
Lake Travis 27, Denton Ryan 7*
Final State Ranking (all-divisions): 10
Final National Ranking: 47

2011

Lake Travis 35, Westlake 7
Lake Travis 43, Hendrickson 14
Lake Travis 62, Aledo 35
Lake Travis 56, Kerrville Tivy 14
Lake Travis 54, Dripping Springs 19
Lake Travis 42, Vandegrift 10
Lake Travis 51, Vista Ridge 20
Lake Travis 62, Rouse 19
Lake Travis 57, Marble Falls 0
Lake Travis 24, Cedar Park 21
Lake Travis 58, McCallum 7*
Lake Travis 42, Smithson Valley 21*
Lake Travis 58, Flour Bluff 15*
Lake Travis 14, Cedar Park 9*
Lake Travis 45, Pearland Dawson 14*
Lake Travis 22, Waco Midway 7*
Final State Ranking (all-divisions): 1
Final National Ranking: 6

* - UIL Playoff Game
Rankings according to MaxPreps

Texas High School Football Championships by school (min.3)

The University Interscholastic League began crowning state champions in football with the 1920 season. Since 1920, through growth and expansion of conferences and divisions, 447 individual championship trophies have been handed out. The state's most decorated championship schools are:

School	Championships	Title Game Appearances	Most Recent Title
Southlake Carroll	8	9	2011
Celina	7	10	2007
Abilene	7	9	1956
Plano	7	9	1994
Brownwood	7	8	1981
Daingerfield	6	8	2010
Converse Judson	6	11	2002
Katy	6	10	2008
Wichita Falls	6	10	1969
Lake Travis	**5**	**5**	**2011**
Sealy	5	6	1997
Odessa Permian	5	11	1991
Waco	5	10	1948
La Marque	5	10	2006
Fort Hancock*	5	6	1991
Richland Springs*	5	6	2011
Mart	4	8	2010
Breckenridge	4	6	1958
Sonora	4	6	2000
Goldthwaite	4	6	2009
Amarillo	4	6	1940
Garland	4	5	1999
Aledo	4	5	2011
Ennis	4	4	2004
Stephenville	4	4	1999
Cuero	3	10	1987
Port Neches-Groves	3	6	1975
Wheeler	3	6	1987
Groveton	3	6	1990
Schulenburg	3	6	1992
Euless Trinity	3	5	2009
Tyler John Tyler	3	5	1994
Stamford	3	5	1958
Borden County*	3	5	2009
Carthage	3	4	2010
Newton	3	4	2005
Panther Creek*	3	4	2000
Midland Lee	3	4	2000
Cherokee*	3	4	1978
Austin Reagan	3	4	1970
Lubbock	3	4	1952
Stratford	3	4	2008
Bartlett	3	3	1999
Thorndale	3	3	1995

* - 6 man

Consecutive Texas High School
State Football Championships (3 min)

Lake Travis (4A)
2007: Lake Travis 36, Highland Park 34
2008: Lake Travis 48, Longview 23
2009: Lake Travis 24, Longview 17
2010: Lake Travis 27, Denton Ryan 7
2011: Lake Travis 22, Waco Midway 7

Celina (2A)
1998: Celina 21, Elysian Fields 0
1999: Celina 38, Elysian Fields 7
2000: Celina 21, Mart 17
2001: Celina 41, Garrison 35

Sealy (3A)
1994: Sealy 36, Atlanta 15
1995: Sealy 21, Commerce 20
1996: Sealy 36, Tatum 27
1997: Sealy 28, Commerce 21

Fort Hancock (6-man)
1988: Fort Hancock 76, Zephyr 30
1989: Fort Hancock 48, Jayton-Girard 24
1990: Fort Hancock 66, Christoval 17
1991: Fort Hancock 64, Christoval 14

Waco
1925: Waco 20, Dallas Forest Avenue 7
1926: Waco 20, Dallas Oak Cliff 7
1927: Waco 21, Abilene 14

La Marque (4A)
1995: La Marque 31, Denison 8
1996: La Marque 34, Denison 3
1997: La Marque 17, Denison 0

Abilene (4A)
1954: Abilene 14, Houstin SF Austin 7
1955: Abilene 33, Tyler 13
1956: Abilene 14, Corpus Christi Ray 0

Southlake Carroll (5A)
2004: Carroll 27, Smithson Valley 24
2005: Carroll 34, Katy 20
2006: Carroll 43, Westlake 29

Daingerfield (2A)
2008: Daingerfield 26, Cisco 0
2009: Daingerfield 62, Bushland 14
2010: Daingerfield 33, Cameron Yoe 27

Amarillo
1934: Amarillo 49, Corpus Christi 0
1935: Amarillo 13, Greenville 6
1936: Amarillo 10, Kerrville 6

Aledo (4A)
2009: Aledo 35, Brenham 21
2010: Aledo 69, La Marque 34
2011: Aledo 49, Manvel 28

Carthage (3A)
2008: Carthage 49, Celina 37
2009: Carthage 13, Graham 12
2010: Carthage 47, Coldspring-Oakhurst 22

Midland Lee (5A)
1998: Lee 54, S.A. MacArthur 0
1999: Lee 42, Aldine Eisenhower 21
2000: Lee 33, Westlake 21

Big Sandy (B)
1973: Big Sandy 25, Rule 0
1974: Big Sandy 0, Celina 0 (co-champions)
1975: Big Sandy 26, Groom 2

Information compiled from Lone Star Gridiron and Texas Football.

Acknowledgements

As the 2011 high school football season began and Lake Travis became odds-on favorite to win its record fifth straight crown, it occurred to us that the achievement, if reached, would be a much larger story than a small, weekly newspaper stretched thin on space and resources could devote to it. It so happens, though, that by the season's mid-point, both of us found ourselves no longer at the *Lake Travis View*. At that point, the story began to take shape and become a reality. By the time the Cavaliers vanquished Waco Midway and huddled around Hank Carter on the field at Cowboys' Stadium, the story had written its own happy ending.

In the weeks leading up to the championship game and the months that followed, many people gave their time and went out of their way to help us get information that proved crucial to telling the whole story of Lake Travis' rise to football power. Without their graciousness, time and willingness to answer every question with tremendous, detailed recall of things that happened years ago, this story could not have come together as it did. We will always be grateful to everyone who met with us, spoke on the phone and welcomed us into their homes to tell the story of Lake Travis football.

We also couldn't have pulled this together without the help of key people at Lake Travis ISD, including communications director Marco Alvarado, athetic department administrative assistant Evelyn Sorrells, and Hank Carter and the football coaching staff. They helped obtain background information and provide on-field access during games as well as interviews with players after the season wrapped up.

Finally, we'd like to acknowledge the support of our families and friends, who provided us not only the time to pursue this story to the fullest but with vital feedback that, we hope, makes this unlikely, incredible story an interesting, pleasant read.

About the Authors

Jay Plotkin and Max Thompson have covered, watched, suffered through and enjoyed Lake Travis football for a combined 20 years.

Plotkin spent 15 years covering and following Lake Travis athletics while at the *Lake Travis View* and Cox Texas Newspapers. He joined the staff in 1996 and served as sports editor, editor and publisher (often at the same time) until leaving the paper in 2011. He covered Lake Travis High School sports full-time from 1996 until 2000 and part-time from 2000 until 2011. He occasionally tweets @jayplot. He lives in Austin with his wife, Karen, and twin daughters Rachel and Lindsey.

Thompson spent nearly five years covering Lake Travis athletics as the sports editor at the *Lake Travis View,* where he worked from 2007-2011. He won multiple Texas Press Association awards for his coverage of Lake Travis football from 2007-2011 and is currently a Sports Editor at Yahoo!. Wyatt Church is still his favorite Cavalier of all-time. Find his commentary on all things, sports or not, @maxthompson.